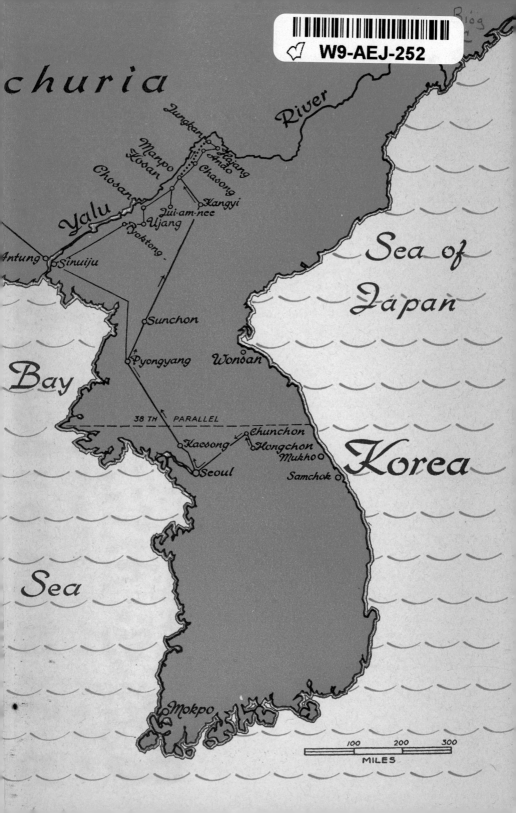

March Till They Die

March Till They Die

by

Philip Crosbie

DUBLIN
BROWNE & NOLAN, LIMITED

March Till They Die

by

Philip Crosbie

DUBLIN

BROWNE & NOLAN, LIMITED

First published 1955

PRINTED IN THE REPUBLIC OF IRELAND AT THE PRESS OF THE PUBLISHERS,
CLONSKEAGH, CO. DUBLIN.

FOREWORD

FROM July of 1950 till May of 1953 I was a prisoner of the People's Democratic Republic of North Korea.

In the winter of 1952–53 I wrote the original manuscript of this story. I wrote it in the hope that some day it might go with me into the free world, to be offered to my friends as a simple record of days in which they were often in my thoughts, days in which I was sustained by the confidence that I was often in theirs.

Several false starts I made, with pencil stubs and scraps of paper contributed unwittingly, and all too rarely, by interviewers and other officials. Then, one happy day, I found myself the proud and excited owner of one whole new pencil, made in Czechoslovakia, and two large sheets of paper. This largess—and more that was to follow, including eventually pen and ink—came through our North Korean hosts from the People's Government of China. Now, indeed, I was a plutocrat who could afford to write my story.

I wrote it during those winter months in our last place of internment near Ujang, working sometimes far into the night by the flickering light of an oil lamp. Then, to double the chance of getting my manuscript past the frontier in the event of our release, I made a duplicate copy and entrusted it to a companion. Both he and I, as it turned out, failed in our separate attempts to take the written story with us to freedom ; but after my release I put on paper yet again a narrative which those two previous writings had impressed clearly on my memory.

I have limited my aim to reproducing my story substantially as it was written in internment. Everything is described as it was experienced then, even events about which I now have definite knowledge but could then only speculate. (One such speculation was the fate of my fellow Columban missionaries in Korea. It was only after my arrival in Europe that I learned that seven had given their lives, among them Chicago-born Monsignor Pat Brennan, Prefect-Apostolic of our southern mission in Mokpo, and Father Tony Collier, my colleague in Chunchon.) The method may perhaps have an interest of its own as showing how our minds groped and guessed after truth in those days when news of any kind was denied us.

CONTENTS

CONTENTS

LIST OF ILLUSTRATIONS

March Till They Die

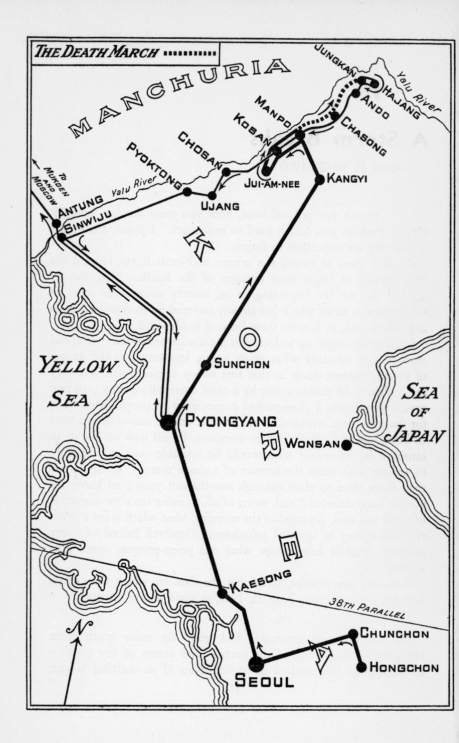

THE DEATH MARCH ··········

MANCHURIA

JUNGKAN

Valu River

HAJANG
ANDO
MANPO
KOSAN
CHASONG
CHOSAN
PYOKTONG
JUI-AM-NEE
KANGYI

To
MUKDEN
AND
MOSCOW
ANTUNG   Valu River
UJANG
SINWIJU

K

YELLOW

SEA

SUNCHON

PYONGYANG

SEA
OF
JAPAN

WONSAN

N

KAESONG

38TH PARALLEL

CHUNCHON

SEOUL

HONGCHON

I

A Storm Breaks

COULD you say, off-hand, how you spent Sunday, June 25, 1950? Perhaps you find it hard to remember. For me, the events of that day are impossible to forget.

On that date, at dawn, the armies of North Korea crossed the 38th Parallel to begin their invasion of the South. That Sunday marked for me the beginning of an acutely memorable series of experiences; a series which has already covered more than two years and whose end, as I write these lines, is hidden still.

I was to be caught up suddenly in the maelstrom of war; to spend anxious days awaiting what might come, knowing that the danger of sudden, violent death in that first sweep of the storm was very real; then to be made captive by a most unfriendly enemy; to find myself thrust into a close-packed community of people who were, for the most part, strangers to one another and to me—a driven herd of bewildered folk with little in common, forced now to live in an intimacy far exceeding what would be tolerable even in a family; to endure with them the horrors of a death march; to be herded then from place to place through months and years; to know the ache of hope deferred; and, worst of all, to suffer the slow starvation of mind and soul, deprived of the morning Mass which is for a priest the well-spring of spiritual refreshment, deprived indeed of every outward spiritual help except what one priest-prisoner could give another.

You will not wonder, then, that the date on which the curtain rose for such a drama, June 25, 1950, is vivid in my memory.

*　　*　　*

On the previous evening I had gone six miles north from Hongchon—chief town of the county, and centre of my parish— to minister to the hundred or so Christians of an outlying village.

As I was offering the Holy Sacrifice of the Mass there with my Christians on the Sunday morning, we were blissfully unaware that soldiers of the Red Army, having overwhelmed the frontier guards just twenty miles to the north in a surprise attack at dawn, were already speeding down the road towards us.

Tired but happy, I walked into the mission residence at Hongchon about midday to be greeted by Father Athanasius Chae, my Korean assistant, with the news that fighting had broken out at several points along the Parallel. I dismissed the news lightly enough. "Incidents" had been occurring along the Parallel for two years now, and I merely concluded that a number of "incidents" were taking place simultaneously.

I had business to transact that day in Chunchon—which meant, as business generally does for a missionary, that funds were low and needed replenishing. I was looking forward to combining pleasure with business, for our procurator, Father Hubert Hayward of New Zealand, was a long-standing friend with whom I had shared many memorable experiences, including a period of internment during World War II.

Chunchon, headquarters of our mission district and residence of the Prefect-Apostolic, Monsignor Thomas Quinlan, was some sixteen miles to the north as the crow flies, but twenty-six by road. I sent a messenger to find out what time a bus would be leaving. They had a schedule, of course, but no one took any heed of that ; it was necessary to make inquiries each time one wanted to travel. The messenger returned to say that all buses had been cancelled, so I betook myself to the Chunchon road, which ran below the church grounds, and waited for a passing vehicle.

By and by, a light South Korean army truck came along. It was packed with telegraph linesmen, but they kindly made room for me. They were a cheerful group to travel with, and I was later to reflect, recalling their laughter and merriment, that they must have been as completely unaware as I was of the gravity of the situation. I fell into conversation with a lad beside me, who proved to be a Christian from a district far to the south. His name was John Pak.

A two-hour journey brought us within sight of Chunchon. As we approached the first buildings of the town we found military police holding up all traffic. Away to the north we could hear the crash of artillery and the angry chatter of machine-guns. The road before us was choken with evacuees, whom the M.P.s were diverting into the fields.

My companions on the truck became silent and tense. An officer went to make inquiries and soon returned. During the consultations that followed John Pak took me aside.

"Father, this is far more serious than we thought. It looks like an invasion from the North, and already the enemy are landing shells at the northern edge of the town. I think you should return to Hongchon immediately."

I thanked him and said I would think it over. Then I stood for a few moments looking down the seething road. My destination was only a mile away. Having come so far, I might as well go on. I shouldered my kitbag, stepped into the crowd, and began threading my way slowly northwards against the tide of humanity pouring south.

It was not a pleasant spectacle, this sudden flight of most of the townspeople from their homes. Young and old, rich and poor, weak and strong : all alike were here. The majority carried some of their belongings with them, the women gracefully upright with huge bundles balanced on their heads and some with babies tied to their backs, the men bowed down under great loads carried on their shoulders. Some few trundled their possessions along in handcarts. A very few walked beside heavily-laden carts drawn by meek-eyed, plodding oxen.

They could be, and usually were, so light-hearted and happy, these patient, genial, careless-of-the-morrow people upon whom the burden of a hard life rested lightly ; but their gaiety had fallen from them now, and their faces were anxious and strained. Some, no doubt, would find refuge in the homes of relatives or friends, but the vast majority knew not where they would sleep tonight, nor what they would eat when the food they carried—enough for a day or two—was gone. Already families were becoming separated. Lost children were wailing piteously and distracted parents anxiously calling.

These thronging thousands had gone to sleep last night, as usual, on the floors of their tiny, crudely-built homes, thinking to wake this morning to just another day like any other in their lives—lives which might seem drab and nearly intolerable to us, but which for them were full of simple joys. Instead, they had woken to find their country torn by war, and the peaceful, if monotonous, routine of their days abruptly shattered. Homeless, bewildered, afraid, they were facing today what was to prove only the beginning of months and years of bitter trial.

As I moved along I attracted some curious stares. Who was this crazy foreigner making his way into town when everyone else was hurrying out ? Now and then I met Christians. Ordinarily they would have stopped to talk with a priest, but today they must hasten on, pausing only to salute the *Siu-bu* with a bow.

From the summit of a small hill the cathedral of Chunchon, now almost completed, looked out over the southern sector of the town. It was a fine sight as the rays of the sinking sun gilded the cut granite of its walls and made of its brass roof a sheet of golden fire. I recalled, as I approached the building, what a monument it was to the zeal and patience and courage of Monsignor Quinlan, who had planned it as far back as 1938. He had seen its very beginnings interrupted by war, had set about his task again when peace was restored in 1945, and had pushed it through to within an ace of completion in the difficult years that followed. Now, in June of 1950, it needed only a little more work on the interior and on the tower to be ready for solemn dedication, and the ceremony was planned for August 15. But, as one war had interrupted its beginnings, so another war, it seemed, was now to prevent its completion, perhaps even to destroy all that had been accomplished.

A hundred yards from the front of the cathedral, and on a lower level, stood Monsignor Quinlan's " palace "—a Korean house with three rooms. Further down the slope was a tiny hall. Lower still, almost at valley level, stood a group of Korean-style buildings forming a quadrangle. An L-shaped chapel occupied two sides of the quadrangle. The rest of the premises consisted of a kitchen, a diningroom, and living quarters for the priests.

In the dining-room I found Monsignor Quinlan and Father Frank Canavan at their evening meal. Greetings over, I immediately asked if I should return to Hongchon that evening ; but the Monsignor, in his optimistic way, was inclined to make light of the situation, and suggested that I should at least stay for the night, and, if the Red advance had not stopped, set out next morning.

We sat on after supper, exchanging news and views. I learned that Father Hayward, the procurator, and Father Paddy Burke (who, like Father Canavan, had only recently arrived in Korea and was still learning the language), had left on a visit to Seoul very early that morning. Rumours of fighting on the Parallel had come in before they left, but they had no notion that anything serious was developing.

As we talked on in the growing darkness the sound of artillery ceased, but rifle and machine-gun firing continued and seemed to be creeping ominously nearer. An American army major from the Korean Military Advisory Group came to tell us that it was doubtful whether the town could hold out, that Headquarters was about to move back, and that it was time for us to move too. Monsignor Quinlan thanked the officer but explained that he and his priests had decided to remain at their posts.

By and by we bade each other good night, and went off to get some sleep if we could. I lay awake for a long time, reviewing the day's events and the evening's talk, and wondering what the future might hold.

Aroused at dawn by artillery fire, I dressed and made my way to the chapel. Monsignor Quinlan and Father Canavan were there before me. Father Anthony Collier, who had charge of a newly-opened parish at the northern end of the town, arrived while I was vesting for Mass. In his usual calm and deliberate way, he told me that shells had been landing near his house since the previous afternoon, and that he had had a narrow escape while taking home a frightened child who had fled to his church for shelter. As they were going down a lane, the whine of a shell warned him to drop to the ground and pull the child down with him. The shell burst a few yards away, and shrapnel buzzed angrily over them. This morning he could see enemy troops just across the river that skirted the northern edge of the town, and bullets were already coming through the walls of his house. His advice to me was that I should leave Chunchon very soon, if I wished to leave at all.

Counsel of that kind from so imperturbable a man as Father Collier was not to be taken lightly, so after Mass and a hurried breakfast I reduced the contents of my kitbag to essentials and took my departure. In the hope of getting transport I made my way to the local headquarters of the South Korean Army, a large school on the southern edge of the town. My luck was out. Some trucks had gone south at dawn, but no one knew of any more heading in that direction.

Evacuees were still streaming out of the town. Military police were still stationed at the point where we had met them the evening before, and were turning the crowds off the main road into nearby valleys. At their challenge I identified myself and explained my purpose, and was allowed to pass on down the road. There were twenty-six miles of this road, and four high mountains, between me and Hongchon. With short cuts, I would be able to reduce the distance by perhaps three or four miles. I stepped out and kept on steadily. The constant booming of guns, still faintly audible when I was two mountains and twelve miles away, was a grim reminder that the peace of these leafy valleys and hillsides would soon be shattered.

Several times I came upon little groups of people, all heading south like myself. Some of them quickened their steps to fall in with me and chat for a mile or two. Some brightened visibly when I told them I was bound for Hongchon. No doubt they were calculating that a foreigner would be making for a safe place, and that therefore at Hongchon they, too, might find refuge. Their faces would fall when I explained that Hongchon was anything but safe, and that my reason for going there was to be at my post, as Catholic priest in charge of the district. They would drop back then, puzzled and disappointed.

I reached Hongchon about four in the afternoon, to be met by a barrage of anxious inquiries from Father Chae and others. Had the Monsignor and the priests left Chunchon ? Where was the fighting now, and in what direction was it moving ? To these and many other questions I gave what answers I could, and then I asked what news had reached Hongchon in my absence. Northern troops, I was told, had crossed the Parallel at a point some twenty miles to the north-east of Hongchon and had advanced some distance down a road that led directly to the town, but their initial drive had now been halted.

I conferred with Father Chae and Francis, our catechist. What should we do with the contents of the church and sacristy ? We decided to send the more valuable things next day by ox-cart to a neighbouring village off the main road, where they could be stored by the Christians. But the frantic evacuation of the town had already begun, and next morning we were told that not even a sack of gold would hire an ox-cart in Hongchon that day.

We fell back on an alternative plan. Our living-quarters here were built on to the church, and a separate building took in the housekeeper's room, the kitchen, and a room leading off it which we called "the workshop." Between the ceiling and roof of our living-room was a storage-space, reached by a ladder, and here we put most of the vestments and sacred vessels, some of the church supplies, and the bulk of our own books and clothes. To conceal everything would be to advertise our distrust of the Reds and invite their hostility, so we left a certain minimum of goods in the church and sacristy. Finally, with the aid of the carpenter who was employed at the mission, we removed the door of the storage-space and replaced it with a partition. This we whitewashed to match the surrounding wall, leaving, we hoped, no evidence that a door had ever been there.

During that day, June 27, many country folk came streaming southwards through the town from homes that lay in the path of the approaching Reds, and a large number of them came by the road that passed our church. Among these were Christians who called in to talk with us, and some took the opportunity of going to Confession.

It was evident now that the rumoured halting of the enemy advance from the north-east had, at best, been temporary. The same day, refugees from Chunchon brought word that the town had fallen in the early morning. Monsignor Quinlan, we learned, had been struck in the face by shrapnel when a shell burst nearby.

With resistance at Chunchon broken, the Reds were now advancing on Hongchon from the north-west as well as the north-east, and it would be only a matter of time till they arrived. Moreover, as our church lay north of the town, between the two converging roads by which the Reds would come, the fighting was likely to pass right through our grounds if the Southern troops made a stand.

Throughout the day loud-speaker vans were touring the streets of Hongchon. With the idea, apparently, of bolstering up morale, they blared out hopeful reports from various battle-fronts. In contrast, I learned that same day from a radio broadcast that the Reds were within a few miles of Seoul, the Southern capital ; that the President had fled south with the members of his government ; that the enemy were advancing on all fronts, and had made landings on the east coast, well south of the Parallel. I learned also that President Truman had ordered units of the Fleet to patrol Formosan waters ; that American planes were assisting the South Korean Army ; that a hurried meeting of the United Nations had been convened and an ultimatum delivered to North Korea.

I have a particular reason for remembering that broadcast. Just after I heard it, the power failed and my receiver fell silent. I have not heard a broadcast since.

Towards evening there was a rumour that the Red column approaching from the north-east was now only a few miles away. Father Chae was to escort a party of young people to a parish further south, and we felt that it was now high time they left. So I said goodbye to my assistant, and the group was soon on its way out of Hongchon.

A couple of hours later I was surprised to see my housekeeper, Susanna, walk in the door. I had sent her to Seoul a few days earlier to consult a doctor-missionary there, hoping that he might diagnose a long-standing illness that had baffled our local physician. She had an interesting story to tell. She had left Seoul by train the previous day. The train was strafed from the air, but arrived safely at its terminus. From there, Susanna had a further thirty miles to travel to Hongchon, but the bus service had been abandoned, so she had set out and walked the thirty miles home. Footsore and weary she was, but still serene and smiling. Her only anxiety was for the welfare of the *Sin-bu*. In fact, she had to be restrained from starting in then and there to cook supper for him.

★   ★   ★

I shall not soon forget the loyalty shown me in those anxious days by Susanna and the four other members of my mission staff—Francis the catechist, Rosa Kim who for some months had assisted him, the carpenter, and an odd-job man who was known as " the outside man."

Susanna was a widow with a small son. On the morning after her return from Seoul, I tried to persuade her to leave Hongchon. Her reply was that if the *Sin-bu* intended to remain and help the people, then she was going to remain to help the *Sin-bu*. Later in the morning I sent for Rosa, who lived in the town with her husband and their young family. I spent some time urging both her and Susanna to leave for the country. They and their children, I said, should be away when the Northern troops arrived. They could return after the town was occupied. At last, reluctantly enough, they agreed. About four o'clock that afternoon they were back again, a little diffident about facing me, but quite determined to stay. " Father, we do not like waiting in the country. We prefer to wait at the mission." Well, there may be men brave or foolhardy enough to resist two determined women, but I am not one of them.

The outside man and the carpenter likewise insisted on bearing me company in those days of anxious waiting. They sent their wives and children out of town, but themselves remained with me at the mission. These two were not, as yet, baptized members of the Church, a fact which makes their loyalty still more memorable.

Francis, the catechist, I strongly urged to leave. As a North Korean who had taken refuge in the South, he would be in special peril when the Reds arrived. I told him he owed it to his family, as well as to himself, to go south while the chance remained. He stayed on, however, till the last possible moment.

*   *   *

On the Wednesday (June 28) it was again rumoured that the enemy advance from the north-east was rapidly nearing us, and we soon had evidence that the rumour was well-founded. We saw truckloads of troops, rushed back from the north-western sector, tearing through the town and out by the north-east road to meet what was obviously an urgent threat.

That night, a trusting old granny arrived to say that she and her daughter-in-law and children, plus their belongings, wanted asylum at the church. She had brought the first instalment in the form of a diminutive grandson and a huge bundle of goods, and she wished to deposit both on my doorstep while she went back for the rest of her household. I told her that she and her relatives, and their belongings too, would be quite welcome at the church, but that I thought they would be much safer at home. The church, I explained, would probably be one of the first places to be searched, and possibly looted, by the Communists. Nothing daunted by my remarks, the old lady went off to get the rest of the family and their belongings, leaving the tiny grandson perched on top of the bundle of clothes and blankets. Whenever I passed that way, two little pagan eyes followed me suspiciously.

The hours dragged by—hours of waiting, for there was nothing else to do. Waiting for Granny. Waiting for the Reds. Waiting for we knew not what.

The carpenter and I were chatting outside the church, our eyes fixed on the northern hills, when suddenly we saw an eerie spectacle that will always come back to me when I see the moon shining on a wooded hill. Ghostly figures, silhouetted against the sky, were darting furtively from tree to tree. For a long time we watched the flitting shadows pass. They were Southern soldiers in retreat.

From the other end of the town came sounds that heralded the evacuation of the army barracks—banging and hammering, the clamour of many voices, the roar of motor engines. It was then that the catechist, Francis, came to me. Till this eleventh hour he had postponed leaving with his family, in the hope that he might induce me, at the last moment, to leave too. Now that it was obvious that the town must fall, he made a final effort to persuade me. Didn't I realize what the noise from the barracks meant? With tears in his eyes, he begged me to go with him and his family. But I could not agree. I gave him what money I had to help him on his way, and the sound of his weeping came back to me as he went off into the night.

It was now long after midnight. What had happened to Granny? Weariness had worn down the suspicion and hostility of the grandson, and eventually he had responded to my friendly overtures and allowed me to take him to the housekeeper's room. There, no doubt, he was now sleeping soundly. Well, I needed some sleep myself, and I decided I could wait up no longer for his relatives.

I was aroused from a deep sleep by loud and peremptory banging on the outside door. Dressing hastily, I went to meet the Reds— and found on my doorstep Granny and the remainder of her household. Relief from tension sometimes has perverse effects, and my feeling of welcome for them at that moment was not, I fear, much warmer than it would have been for the Red visitors I expected. Granny explained that she had hit on a compromise plan : she would leave only her goods and chattels here, and take her family to the country. Resisting the temptation to bid her take the whole lot to the nearest lake, I went to arouse her grandson.

As the little group moved off in the pre-dawn darkness, I wondered what fate lay before them. I wonder still.

2

Under the Red Star

BY SUNRISE on Thursday, June 29, I had offered Mass, taken breakfast, and settled down to await the Reds' arrival. I thought they would come with the daylight, but the morning wore on and they did not appear. Waiting with me were Susanna, Rosa and the carpenter. The outside man had gone off at an early hour to see how his family were faring, intending to return before night.

Around ten o'clock some South Korean vehicles towing artillery came racing down the road from Chunchon. Just below the church they turned off into a field, and presently their guns went into action, hurling shells back along the road. If the enemy got the range, shells would begin falling near the church, so I sent the women to a cellar under the kitchen which had been made ready for such an emergency.

The artillerymen, however, were soon on the move again. Not long afterwards, a thunderous detonation from the southern end of the town suggested that they had crossed the river there and blown up the bridge behind them ; and that suggested that theirs had been the last motorized unit defending the town.

We saw no other troops till after lunch, when a group of Southern soldiers carrying a mortar came down the other road from the northeast. They set up their mortar in a field beside the church, and fired at the enemy for a short time. Then they, too, moved on south through the town.

After that there fell a profound silence, broken only by sporadic rifle fire in the hills. A stillness of death was on the town. A few old and feeble folk remained, but most of the homes were deserted.

The carpenter and I were chatting quietly in the workshop when, about four o'clock, we heard a barked command from the direction of the back gate. Peering through cracks in the wall, we saw a score of soldiers filing in from the lane that ran behind the church.

"They're soldiers from the North," the carpenter whispered. "I've seen prisoners who were captured in some of the border incidents, and I know the uniform."

The uniform was distinctive enough : baggy trousers, shirt-like jackets tucked in at the waist, cylindrical peaked caps adorned with a red star.

"We'd better go and meet them," I said, and began to move.

But the carpenter, wiser than I, laid a restraining hand on my arm. "Not yet," he whispered. "These men will pass on, and we'll meet those who come later."

They filed past within a few feet of where we watched them through the chinks in the wall. Tense and alert, they darted curious glances all around them. As they passed, I saw how the leafy branches they wore for camouflage were held by loose stitches of string sewn into the shoulders of their jackets. The majority carried rifles of Russian type, the bayonets long and fluted. Some had sub-machine-guns.

A large stone came crashing through a window of the workshop. Shattered glass fell near us on the cement floor. We held our breath, but without further incident the whole group passed on. As the sound of their footsteps faded, the carpenter and I exchanged a nod that expressed quite adequately the oneness of our thought. We had just passed, in a matter of seconds, from one world to another—by merely standing still.

Before very long there came the tramp of many feet, and a large body of troops turned into the church grounds. It was some comfort to deduce from the sound of their easy chatter that these men were far less tense than those who had come before.

We heard feet ascending the steps to the kitchen door, then a loud knocking. Leaving the carpenter in the workshop, I passed through to the kitchen and went to unlock the door.

"All right," I called, " I'm opening this door."

Outside stood an officer, flanked by two of his men. Below, at the foot of the steps, more soldiers were crowding.

With the best of intentions, and as pleasantly as I could, I said as I stepped out to meet the officer : " Take it easy. There's no danger here."

Either he was determined not to be friendly, or my manner piqued him. He drew his pistol and levelled it. Down below, half a dozen soldiers fell into line and flung up their rifles.

"Who's talking about danger?" the officer snapped. "Put up your hands!"

I raised my hands. Then the questions came. What place was this? Who was I? What was my name, my nationality? How many people were on the premises? Who were they? Where were they? I gave the replies. Then the officer pointed to the church building.

"Go before me into that house and open all doors!"

"The place is locked," I explained. "I'll have to get the keys."

He nodded permission, and I sighed with relief as I turned back into the kitchen. I felt that one storm had been weathered. I returned with the keys and came down the steps. The throng of soldiers parted to allow me to pass along, with the officer at my heels, to the other building. On his instructions I went from room to room, opening every cupboard for him to peer in.

We returned to the smaller building, and the carpenter, Rosa and Susanna were summoned for questioning. I remember how Susanna, imperturbable as ever, made of her interrogation an opportunity to give the Reds a lesson in religion, explaining calmly and clearly what it was and what it meant to her.

Meanwhile more soldiers were pouring into the grounds, and with them came another officer to whom we were now handed over. He was of higher rank than the other, and also more friendly. He took me on a second tour of the premises. In the church he sat at the harmonium and played snatches of several classical melodies.

The inspection over, he asked if he could quarter soldiers in the main building for the night. I pointed out that this was a church, and that churches were not usually taken over for that purpose.

"I'm sorry," he said, "but all other large buildings have already been taken, and still we're short of room. We'll have to have it."

Then I heard the first of the many promises North Korean officials have made to me: "I noticed the fine polished floor in the church. I'll see that the soldiers take their boots off and that they don't do any looting."

Well, this first promise was fulfilled fifty per cent. better than most of the others I have been given since. The soldiers, as it happened, did take off their boots.

Before leaving, the officer told me : " You'll be all right. Only don't leave the church grounds."

A third officer came to ask if we had drinking-water on the premises. I showed him the pump in the kitchen. He pumped some water and had me taste it.

" Fine," he said. " Pump some and give it to the soldiers."

We collected some large vessels, and for over an hour the carpenter, Susanna and I pumped water, while a procession of soldiers filed past the kitchen door, carrying the filled vessels away and bringing them back for replenishment.

Next morning (Friday, June 30) celebration of Mass was out of the question. When at length the soldiers left the church building, I went to inspect it. Some things had been taken : fountain-pens, clocks, a radio, a portable sewing-machine, a camera, and such-like. To facilitate selection, the looters had thrown the contents of suitcases on the floor and spread them out.

This morning, the dead town of yesterday was alive with soldiers. They seemed to emerge from every house in town, and more came streaming in from every nearby valley where there were houses. A little later, more still came pouring in along the two main roads from the north-east and the north-west.

I watched the procession that came down the north-west road from Chunchon. First came the infantry, in disorderly groups. Then came men riding horses, pedal-cycles, motor-cycles. Vehicles of every conceivable kind rolled into town : carts and wagons drawn by oxen, mules, horses ; old Japanese trucks carrying supplies, new Russian ones towing artillery ; cars, jeeps, tanks, large and small, ancient and modern. It was a motley collection, not very impressive in terms of modern warfare—except for its size. The troops that came on and on in this strange cavalcade were very numerous. They also looked very determined.

*   *   *

For the best part of a week I suffered no serious interference. Except for that first morning when the church was occupied by troops, I was able to say Mass each day. I did so in the sacristy, very early. Evacuees who had not gone far began to creep back into town. Among them were some Christians, and a few of the more courageous came along to Mass.

I had numerous visits, of course, from official interviewers and from search parties. When one set of visitors came on the heels of another, I would point out that their work had already been done, but the answer was always the same : " We belong to a different department and must therefore satisfy ourselves."

Then there was the problem of trying to protect the church property and my own. It was a waste of energy, as later events proved, but it was natural that I should do my best at the time.

On the first morning the sound of frantic cackling took me to the fowl house. I found a pair of young soldiers cheerfully wringing the necks of my pullets. They seemed surprised to see me, and desisted. They explained that they were hungry, and went off with a couple of corpses apiece.

I returned to find two stalwarts emerging from the church with their hands full of candles.

Several times I answered a distress call from Susanna, and found her trying to bar the way to the larder against invaders.

I adopted the policy of keeping all doors locked during the day except the kitchen door, and of spending most of my time seated on the back steps of the church building. From there I could see the kitchen door, and it was as good a station as any for keeping an eye on would-be visitors to either the church building or the kitchen block. Staying outside, I found, had a further advantage. Soldiers who came out of curiosity, and not on authorized business, would usually accept my invitation to sit and chat. Then, after thay had done a little window-peeking, they would often be content to leave. Whereas if they got indoors they would generally see something that took their fancy.

They were mostly simple country lads. Their heads had been filled with propaganda against everything Western and everything religious, but the majority proved friendly enough when they found I was human. A few were openly hostile. One told me vehemently that he would not rest until every foreigner had been killed or driven from the country, and all traces of religion removed.

★   ★   ★

A few days after the Northerners arrived I received a visit from a grief-stricken girl, who told me a story that reflects badly on the Southern police.

In these pages, references to the Northern police will be frequent, and rarely favourable. It should in justice be stated that the standard of police behaviour in the South also—as I saw it in the period between the expulsion of the Japanese and the outbreak of the present North-South struggle—fell far below the demands of the high responsibilities involved. The Japanese, admittedly, had bequeathed a bad police tradition to the whole country. Another major factor of the problem was the gross inadequacy of police salaries. A pittance hardly sufficient to cover the purchase of winter fuel is unlikely to attract many recruits of intelligence and ability, and those who do accept it must be men of exceptional idealism if they are to resist the temptation to supplement their income by misuse of their powers.

The girl's story was this. Her brother had been among a score of men arrested in Hongchon as suspected Communists when the first news of the invasion arrived. Shortly before the Reds reached the town, these men had been taken away by truck. They would be lodged, the police said, in jail further south. The bodies of half of them had now been found in the mountains. Their hands had been tied behind their backs, and there were bullet holes in their heads. The fate of the other half of the party, which included the girl's brother, was unknown.

I had known her brother well : an intelligent, industrious and very likeable boy. His only association with Communism, I believe, had been for a short period soon after the end of Japanese rule in Korea, a period when Communist propagandists were active in the South as well as the North. He had thought for a time that Communism was perhaps the answer to the social evils he saw around him. He was soon disillusioned—but not before his interest in Communism had been noted by the police. Thereafter, whenever disturbances were caused by Communist activity, he was arrested and jailed as a matter of course till the crisis passed. It was a classic instance of "giving a dog a bad name."

He had long since realized that in Christianity, not in Communism, lay the solution to the social problems he deplored. Some months before this last arrest he had completed a course of religious instruction and had been received into the Church. The history of his change of view was common knowledge in the town.

*   *   *

There were, however, many genuine friends of Communism living in the town, who proclaimed their allegiance openly as soon as the Northerners arrived.

Three of these gentry, two men and a women, paid me a visit on July 5. They wore red armbands of authority, and were accompanied by an unprepossessing little man beneath whose coat-tail I could see the muzzle of a large pistol. I was to meet this little man again, and soon. On this occasion, however, he seemed less interested in me than in my furniture, from which he proposed to select items suitable for the police station.

" That," he said, gesturing magnificently towards the ice-box, " will suit our purpose fine."

I suspect he thought it was a filing-cabinet.

3

Guest of the People

BY THIS time most of the troops had moved on, leaving only a few in the town for garrison duty. Consequently there was not the same need to maintain my station on the back steps of the church in the hope of distracting soldier visitors from interest in my property. On Thursday, July 6, I decided to retire for a few hours from the fight with the Reds, and go to do battle with the weeds in my garden ; for this was the rainy season, the season of growth. I donned old clothes and sallied forth.

Shortly after midday Susanna came to say that lunch was almost ready, and I was preparing to move in when our dog began to bark furiously near the back door of the church. Hurrying around, I found the diminutive visitor of yesterday backed into a corner, his large pistol levelled at the dog.

I called off the dog, and told the man his artillery was not needed. He explained then that he was a member of the Internal Security Department of the People's Government, and that my presence was required at the police station for an interview. I told him I must change my clothes, and asked him if I should also have my lunch.

"No need. The interview will take only twenty minutes."

When I emerged again from the house, I was wearing light underclothes, black trousers, a T-shirt, a white shower-proof jacket, light socks and Korean-style rubber shoes. On my head I wore an Australian cricket cap that a friend back home had included in a gift parcel. I had a watch on my wrist, and around my neck was a chain carrying a cross and some religious medals. In my pockets were a rosary, a handkerchief, a pocket-knife, a cigarette-lighter, keys on a ring, and a miniature can-opener.

I have good reason to remember these articles so clearly and to list them so carefully. Before I bade them, one by one, goodbye—

whether because they were taken from me, or were sold, or fell apart from use—I came to know them well, and some I even came to regard as old friends.

In a light drizzle, I walked with my escort to the police station. There he left me in the main office. Curious police and detectives gathered around me and made exhaustive but friendly inquiries about my antecedents, my religious and political beliefs, my hopes and plans for the future. The spokesman in the discussions on religion was an intelligent young fellow who wore a university badge. He may have been a student temporarily employed as a detective. He knew all about the Benedictine monks and nuns of Wonsan in North Korea, who had been taken from their monastery and convent by the Reds in 1949. The lad was friendly in his manner, but definitely not sympathetic.

" How many bishops," he asked me, " do you think are exercising their authority in North Korea now ? "

He answered his own question : " None."

He moved away, and I heard him relaying some of our conversation on religion to others.

" We couldn't possibly work with a fellow who holds these views," he told them. " He'll have to be expelled from the country."

The hours crept by and I was still waiting. It was late in the afternoon when the little man who had brought me from the church reappeared, accompanied by one who proved to be the Chief of Police. Apparently they had spent the intervening hours searching the mission and questioning the staff. I was summoned to the Chief's office to recount my life history and political views. They knew well, the Chief assured me, that this profession of religion was all eye-wash ; that I was really a political agent for my country. His assistant volunteered the opinion that the most potent weapon the West held against its enemies was not the atom bomb, but religion.

The discussion grew a little hot, and they raised their voices and thumped the desk. I raised my voice and thumped the desk still harder in return, wondering where it would all end. Then to my surprise—and I must confess to my relief too—they both leaned back in their chairs and laughed. The small man offered me a cigarette, but I declined.

THE AUTHOR

Left—On his release in May, 1953, after nearly three years' captivity in eight different internment camps in Communist North Korea.

Below—On his arrival in Dublin in June, 1953, in conversation with Mr. W. T. Doig, Chargé d'Affaires at the Australian Embassy, Dublin.

[*Independent Newspapers*

"They ought to be all right," he grinned. "They're your own."

They adopted a friendlier line. Wouldn't I like to go to Chunchon ? I told them I had been instructed by my superior in Chunchon to remain at my post, and couldn't leave voluntarily unless he gave further orders. Then they told me that I was going to Chunchon whether I liked it or not, and that I would be sent out of the country when they had defeated the enemy.

"You'll leave here," said the small man, "in what you stand up in, and all your property will be confiscated by the People's Government of Korea."

After that they disregarded me and began to chat together.

"You know," the small man told his Chief, "I found a couple of cases of excellent wine up there. Plenty of food, too, in cases. We could have a little celebration there tonight." ·

Apparently he had discovered the altar wine and some rations we had received from the American occupation troops. He had also noted the fine drapings behind the altar.

"There's some excellent cloth in the chapel, too. It would make splendid covers for our tables here." That was music for my ears !

They unearthed a policeman who was going to Chunchon, and handed me over to him. He was friendly enough in a distant way, giving the impression that he had nothing against me personally, but considered that fate had played him a dirty trick in landing in his lap a prisoner requiring escort. He didn't know the way, and insinuated that I could pay for my passage by acting as guide. No vehicles seemed to be going that way, so we must walk, he explained.

We left the police station, and I struck a pace that my escort found rather fast. Christians here and there stopped to stare as we passed, and some courageously bowed to me. We passed through the heart of the town, and out along the road that led past the mission.

Just a few weeks before, we had finished the task of renovating and repairing the church. It was a simple building with mud walls, stuccoed and plastered, and a corrugated iron roof. The roof and woodwork had been freshly painted. Inside, there was a new ceiling, a new polished floor, a new sanctuary with green drapings and a new altar of teak. The altar was of simple design, but well polished, and surmounted by a circular dome-topped metal tabernacle. These improvements had made of the chapel a sight that the Christians proudly brought their pagan friends to see. The generosity of good friends at home had made it all possible.

I looked at the little building, and wondered what its fate would be. The fine fittings and furnishings would soon, no doubt, be carried off; the building itself might be destroyed. But it was the Lord's work, and if He allowed men to destroy, He would, in His own good time, find men and means to build it up again.

We passed up the road and out of the town. Off to the left some people were talking in front of a house. A man detached himself from the group and started across the fields in our direction. I recognized him as the building contractor who had worked with us on the church. Just recently he had lost his wife. During her last illness I had been able to help him in various ways. He was a pagan, and had once become involved in Communist activities, but he had given them up and finally managed to clear himself with the police. When the Reds arrived they offered him some minor post. His friends urged him to accept it, saying that if he didn't take it someone far worse would.

He hailed my escort now, and chatted pleasantly for a time. Then he asked : " Where are you taking this man ? "

" To Chunchon," the policeman replied.

"Are you sure it's to Chunchon ? I thought you might be taking him to the mountains," he persisted. I gathered that " taking a man to the mountains " was a technical term, like " taking a man for a ride." " No," the policeman answered, " I'm only taking him to Chunchon."

" That's all right," the other said. " Because if you were taking him to the mountains, I wanted to tell you he's a fine fellow who has minded his own business and helped the poorer folk. You should have nothing against him."

It was a kindly and courageous act, and I tried to thank him with my eyes. In the polite Korean formula, he bade us depart in peace, and we bade him remain in the same.

Resuming our journey, we plodded on up the road towards the first of the four mountains that lay across our path. It occurred to my escort to ask how far it was to Chunchon. I told him the distance was ninety *li*, which meant about twenty-five miles. That staggered him a little.

"Do any other main roads join the Chunchon road?"

"None," I replied.

He slowed to a stop.

"I think it's too late to walk there tonight. We'll return to Hongchon and wait till tomorrow morning, unless we can get a ride."

We retraced our steps. It was approaching supper time when we passed the church again, and I had eaten nothing since morning. I hopefully suggested to the policeman that he allow me to entertain him to a meal in my house, but he declined.

Back in the town we saw a truck that had just come in. Soldiers were climbing aboard, and they told my guard they were bound for Chunchon, so we climbed on with them, and were soon passing out of Hongchon once more.

Darkness was falling as we wound our way up the first mountain. About half-way up we left the main road to detour around a bridge that had been blown up. Rain had fallen during the day, and our truck, a standard commercial vehicle, was unable to make the sticky climb back to the road. The soldiers tumbled out of the vehicle to make tracks of brush and branches, and slowly the truck moved along. I had made a move to get out, but my escort motioned me to remain. Finally, a panting and exasperated young warrior interrupted his labours to ask : "What's that fellow doing up there? He looks young and strong enough. Why doesn't he get down and push too?"

The flustered policeman ordered me down then. I had thoughts of slipping away into the trees. It would have been easy enough amid the darkness and confusion. But the front line, as I had seen it, was moving so fast that it might reach the south coast and vanish, before I could overtake it. So I stayed.

Finally the truck crawled up the last and worst pinch, and was back on the road again. We climbed on board, and were very soon rattling along on our way.

It was after midnight when we halted in the middle of Chunchon. There was no electric lighting in the streets, but as far as I could see there was not a great deal of damage, except for a building here and there battered by shells or gutted by fire.

My escort and I left the truck, and toiled up the steep main street to the provincial government headquarters. Some sort of light

flickered at the main gate, and there my escort produced his creden-
tials and explained his mission to the sentry. Meantime two civilians
in Korean clothes passed out through the dim circle of light, and I
saw the flash of long, wicked-looking knives held against their thighs.
Perhaps they were bent on legitimate business, but the sight sent a
shiver down my spine.

We passed on into the building, and did a lot of tramping around
gloomy corridors without finding any sign of life. As we tramped,
I told my policeman companion I had not eaten since breakfast,
and he assured me he would attend to the matter. Eventually, in a
dingy office near the back of the building, we found an officer
crouched over a desk. The policeman explained his business, received
a receipt for me, and departed—without mentioning the matter of
my day-long fast. The briefest study of my new guardian's face was
enough to decide me, too, against mentioning it.

The policeman and I had never reached the stage of bosom friendship. Still I was sorry to see him go, for it meant the breaking of my
last link with Hongchon.

The surly one at the desk snapped some questions at me, made
entries in a book, then took me out a back door, across a yard, and
into another building. Here I was introduced to my new lodgings,
and the scene was not unfamiliar. Nine years before, as a prisoner
of the Japanese, I had been consigned to similar lodgings—in the
police station just across the road from where I was now. Even the
hour had been about the same : two o'clock in the morning.

Just inside the door of the building a guard sat drowsily at a desk,
facing a grill which ran the full length of the room and extended from
floor to ceiling. Wooden beams, six inches by six, set about four
inches apart, formed the vertical members of the grill ; the hori-
zontals were heavy iron pipes passed through the beams. The space
behind the grill was divided by solid walls into four separate cells,
to which wide low doors, set in the grill and similarly constructed,
gave entry. In the outside wall, high up, were barred windows.

The sleepy guard arose and saluted the officer who had brought
me. Then I was searched, the contents of my pockets were taken,
and I was relieved of belt, cap and shoes. The guard opened the
door of the nearest cell. I passed through, and heard the door clang
shut behind me.

Within the cell there were only two features to add to the description I have given. In one far corner was a tiny basin, and over it a water tap—from which no water flowed, as I was in due course to discover. In the other corner was a trap-door whose primitive purpose I knew from my earlier experience in Korean jails, and would immediately have deduced in any case from the appalling stench that rose through it.

The cell already had eight or nine occupants. As I sought a place on the floor among their prostrate forms, some raised their heads to look at the newcomer—and looked again with greater interest when they saw I was a foreigner. I stretched out between two of my companions in misfortune, and told myself I needed sleep. So I did, but I said a good many decades of the Rosary on my fingers, and pondered long on the past, the present, and the possible future, before I finally dozed off.

The daily routine of the jail began shortly after six in the morning, when a shouting guard aroused us all and made us sit up with our backs to the wall. Some time later the roll of prisoners was called. The guard began at our cell, then moved on to the second, the third, finally the fourth. On that first morning I listened with keen interest to all the names. As the fourth list was being called I recognized, in mutilated form, the names " Quinlan " and " Canavan." Well, it was not good news to learn that the Monsignor and Father Frank were prisoners too ; but since it had to be, I found great comfort in the knowledge that they were so near.

After roll-call came the counting of the prisoners, and it was sometimes a lengthy process, arithmetic not being a strong point with our worthy guard. He would ask at each cell what was the number of the prisoners (usually it was around ten), write down the four answers, finally arrive at a total. Often it was unsatisfactory, so the whole process started again, this time with the aid of an abacus.

When the counting was satisfactorily disposed of, we settled down for the next item on the program, which was breakfast. On that first morning it arrived at ten o'clock. By that time I was very hungry indeed. My thirst was even more acute, as the weather was hot, but I had the misfortune to miss my ration of water that morning through not being conversant with the rules of the game. First the guard passed through the bars to each prisoner a pair of chopsticks and a bowl containing perhaps a cupful of rice. At an order from the guard, everyone started eating. About three minutes later he passed along with a kettle of water, from which he half filled the bowls held out through the bars. Small as the ration of rice was, I was still battling with it after the three minutes, not having acquired the phenomenal speed at which Orientals can wield chopsticks. To my dismay, I found the guard would not return a second time with water. So I thirsted till lunch-time, and was punctual thereafter in all appointments with the water-kettle. Even so, the ration of water, as of rice, was far too small, and we suffered continuously from thirst until, after a few days, the water taps in the cells returned to duty. Their offering was very muddy, but it was very gratefully received.

Meals varied between boiled rice with a piece of pickled turnip, and boiled rice. The prison rules said we must have three meals a day, and reports must show we got them. We did, too, but the meal-times were extraordinarily elastic. One day, for instance, we got breakfast at two o'clock in the afternoon, lunch at four, and supper at six. Nobody ever seemed to know where supplies were to come from, or who was to prepare them when they came.

Prisoners usually remained in these cells for a few days only, then moved on—some few to freedom, the majority to a more permanent prison, some no doubt to worse. Among the prisoners I met were South Korean soldiers who had been picked up or had surrendered after the fighting had passed on, members of the South Korean police force and other government bodies, and civilians who had fallen foul of the new administration. We were forbidden to talk to each other, but we often managed a whispered conversation when the guard moved down to speak to prisoners in another cell. Neither were we supposed to stand up, but this rule we also ignored whenever possible, to ease the aches in cramped limbs.

Prisoners were constantly being called out for interrogation. The calls could come at any time of the day or night, but they were more frequent in the night hours. Monsignor Quinlan was summoned one day for an interview, but Father Canavan and I were spared the ordeal in that place.

★   ★   ★

We were to be interrogated many times in the months that followed, and as often as not in the small hours. The general pattern

of these interrogations was the same, and it may be of interest to
outline it here.

There was always a refresher course in one's life history—name,
nationality, date and place of birth; profession, schools attended, and
dates of entering and leaving each school; religion, political affilia-
tions, wealth and property possessed; names, ages, occupations and
addresses of father, mother, brothers and sisters, and close friends.

In all the interrogations in those first months, special attention was
devoted to finding out who had sent us to Korea, and why. Other
favourite questions were, what weapons we had in the house when
arrested, and where we had hidden them. It was taken for granted
that we were agents for our countries and that our houses were
crammed with weapons to fight their battles.

It was—and in this I am completely serious—quite inconceivable
to our captors that we had left our countries, without expectation
of reward in this world, to spread the good news of a life of happiness
that could be won in a world to come. And yet, strangely enough,
the men who could not understand this had left their homes, and
were burning themselves out, and were prepared to risk their lives,
to spread a doctrine of earthly prosperity. Yes, many of the
Northerners we met really were aflame with zeal for the cause they
served.

*   *   *

Each day more prisoners would be brought in, one or two at a
time, searched, and pushed into the cells. Some were obviously
scared and dazed at finding themselves in such surroundings. We
old hands, by now quite at home, felt a little inward pride and
superiority towards the novices, and took the first opportunity to
inquire into their lives and crimes and to initiate them into prison
life. A strange bond of fellowship and sympathy soon united the
inmates of a cell.

Very late each night, grim-looking civilians carrying rifles with
fixed bayonets would come into the corridor before the cells, and a
number of prisoners would be called out and taken away.

"They're probably taking them to the mountains," a companion
whispered in my ear, the first night it happened. It was easy to
believe it.

On the night of Sunday, July 9, I heard the names of Monsignor

Quinlan and Father Canavan called, and with a heavy heart I saw
them pass in front of our cell. The next morning one of our guards
came to talk to me.

" They took away your friends last night."

" I saw them go," I replied.

" They're dead by this, and *you'll* be taken tonight."

Again I had no difficulty in believing. However, I was not called
out that night nor the next. On the Wednesday (July 12) it was
whispered around the cell that the prisoners taken out each night
were merely being transferred to the regular penitentiary at the
other side of the town. My Korean companions seemed to be
satisfied that this report was well founded, and we all relaxed a little.
Thus, I was not very greatly alarmed, though far from nonchalant,
when the call did come for me late that night.

With half a dozen Korean prisoners I was escorted to the gloomy
office where the grumpy official had accepted delivery of my person
five days before. I was relieved to find in his place, on this occasion,
an officer whose manner was much more agreeable. He returned
the property which had been taken from me on arrival, and had me
sign a receipt. The hands of the other half-dozen prisoners were
bound behind their backs, and they were then tied one to another
in a line. But when it was my turn to join the line, the officer intervened and said I could go unbound.

We shuffled along the dark corridors and out to a waiting truck.
I drew in great lungfuls of fresh air. It was like wine, after the heat
and stench of the cell. The truck rolled down the main street, turned
off to the left, passed along by a huge brick wall and drew up at a
massive arch which I recognized as the entrance to the penitentiary.
Here I was singled out from the rest of the prisoners and escorted
through the gates by two blue-uniformed warders.

I had passed through that grim portal only three weeks before,
and had been glad on that occasion that I held a visitor's pass. I
had come to see a parishioner who had been involved in a serious
accident and was awaiting trial for negligent driving of his truck.
A couple of days after the invasion began, he walked into my house
in Hongchon. All the prisoners, he told me, had been removed
from the Chunchon penitentiary as the Reds approached, and most
of them had been freed.

We entered the dismal building, passed along a corridor lined with cells, turned into another wing where there were more cells, and stopped at the first door. Once again I was searched, my pockets emptied, belt and shoes removed. Then once more I heard a cell-door bang behind me—this time a solid wooden affair with a small peep-door in the centre.

In the darkness I verified that there were no other human occupants of the cell, but I soon discovered that I had other company, and that it was numerous and hostile. The enemy launched a massed attack that was to continue without intermission during my stay. Tonight and every night the aerial assault was to be pressed by zooming, dive-bombing mosquitoes. By day, a host of flies would assume responsibility for the overhead attack. The ground-troops were fleas, and they were on duty all the time.

When daylight came streaking through a barred window, I saw that my new home was built of white-plastered brick. It was some-what smaller than the former cell, being meant for only one or two prisoners. My inventory of the furnishings was soon complete : a removable latrine in one corner, and, under the window, a small shelf on which a former occupant had left a couple of pairs of chop-sticks. Scratched in the plaster were sundry signatures, relics of my predecessors. Today, and in the days to come, I would speculate on the owners of those names, wondering what manner of men they were, what crimes they had been guilty of, and what had been their fate.

At nine o'clock that morning I had my first experience of meals in this new abode, and found a great improvement in the quality and quantity. Meals here consisted of a fair-sized bowl of mixed rice, barley and millet, a soup in which vegetables were abundant (if rather stale in flavour) and as much cool spring water as one desired. How I enjoyed that water ! On a couple of mornings I even got a basinful for washing.

Companionship, comings and goings, occasional chances of con-versation, had in the other prison helped a little to relieve the monotony, yet time had passed very slowly. Here, with none of these diversions, I found that time almost stood still. Not only had I the cell to myself, but I was the only occupant of that whole wing of the building, as I soon knew from the silence, and from the fact that the footsteps of the warders who brought me food never stopped at any other cell in the vicinity.

I was helped, however, by the memory of a lesson learned in my former internment : that the first few days of forced inactivity were the worst, and that one needed only patience to achieve in a short time a partial adjustment to the new conditions. One did what one could to break the monotony—varying one's position, sometimes sitting, sometimes standing ; at other times pacing up and down the cell or doing physical exercises ; now and then reciting the rosary with one's fingers for beads, or making other attempts at prayer. One found too what diversion one could in even the most insignificant little happenings seen or heard—the arrival of warders with meals, the chirping of birds at dawn or dusk, the sound of drill or rifle-practice in the afternoons. Even the pettiest happenings gradually assumed interest and importance, and one's mind found in them a sort of crazy pattern and watched its daily weaving. And time began to march once more.

Occasionally guards came to survey me through the peep-door, and sometimes they stayed to talk a while. Usually they asked what crime I had committed, and seemed surprised when I replied that I was not conscious of having committed any crime and had not been charged with any, but was here solely because I was a foreigner and a missionary. On these occasions I took the opportunity of inquiring about Monsignor Quinlan and Father Canavan, who were, I felt sure, somewhere on the premises ; but such queries always drew a blank.

One day I received a visit from an officer whom I afterwards learned to be the governor of the jail. He half opened the door of my cell and stood there talking. He was dressed in white uniform and had a pistol strapped to his hip. He made the usual inquiries, and then told me that the Reds would soon control the whole country, and that I and all the other foreigners would be sent home. We began to discuss religion, and he laughed when I mentioned my belief in another world.

" Is your mother alive ? " I asked.

" No, she is dead."

" Do you really believe that your mother died as animals do, that now she exists no more and you will never see her again ? "

"Yes, that is what I believe."

That answer, from a man belonging to a people who are devout ancestor-worshippers, staggered me.

We discussed Communism, and I told him I objected to its unjust and ruthless methods.

"We don't kill good people," he said, "only the bad." Then, after a pause : "Have you ever seen a man die ?"

"Yes."

"Have you ever seen a man *shot* ?"

"No."

"*I* have," he said, and his hand touched the pistol at his side.

A few months later I was to have the opportunity of seeing a man shot—and shot by that same hand and that same pistol. When the time came I would forgo my opportunity, forced by horror and revulsion to avert my eyes. An innocent American officer would be murdered in cold blood by the man who stood before me now.

This was the man we were to know later as "The Tiger." In these pages you will meet him soon again—too soon. And when you know him better I think you will remember him a long, long time.

Company in Seoul

JULY 16 TO 19, 1950

THE OFFICER IN WHITE had told me the Communist armies were sweeping rapidly south and would soon have the whole peninsula in their hands. I had no grounds at the time for questioning his statement. I remember speculating on the length of time the South might be expected to hold out and coming to the conclusion that it might be as long as several weeks. So long, therefore, I might have to stay in custody, but afterwards there was a chance—since I had survived thus far under the Red régime—that I would be either released or expelled from the country. So I settled down to wait, with some confidence, for one or other to happen.

I was therefore quite surprised when, on the night of Sunday, July 16, only a few days after my arrival, the cell door opened, and a voice from behind a light bade me get ready quickly and come out: it was easy to obey, as getting ready meant merely changing from a horizontal to a vertical position. Outside were two guards with my shoes and other belongings. They escorted me to the front gate, and there to my delight, were Monsignor Quinlan and Father Canavan. We had got no further than exchanging greetings when a guard warned us sternly not to talk.

The three of us were taken to the railway station in company with a fourth prisoner, an aged Korean. We later learned that he was a man of law, arrested, probably, for having acted as prosecutor in the past when Communists were on trial. At the station the prison guards handed us over to the North Korean Army, in the persons of an officer with a pistol and a private with a tommy-gun. We were put into a freight car and told to sit at one end. Midway along each side of the car was an opening where once a door might have been. Beside one opening the officer took up his station with pistol

4

Company in Seoul

July 16 to 19, 1950

THE OFFICER in white had told me the Communist armies were sweeping rapidly south and would soon have the whole peninsula in their hands. I had no grounds at the time for questioning his statement. I remember speculating on the length of time the South might be expected to hold out, and coming to the conclusion that it might be as long as several weeks. So long, therefore, I might have to stay in custody, but afterwards there was a chance—since I had survived thus far under the Red régime—that I would be either released or expelled from the country. So I settled down to wait, with some confidence, for one or other to happen.

I was therefore quite surprised when, on the night of Sunday, July 16, only a few days after my arrival, the cell door opened, and a voice from behind a light bade me get ready quickly and come out. It was easy to obey, as getting ready meant merely changing from a horizontal to a vertical position. Outside were two guards with my shoes and other belongings. They escorted me to the front gate, and there to my delight, were Monsignor Quinlan and Father Canavan. We had got no further than exchanging greetings when a guard warned us sternly not to talk.

The three of us were taken to the railway station in company with a fourth prisoner, an aged Korean. We later learned that he was a man of law, arrested, probably, for having acted as prosecutor in the past when Communists were on trial. At the station the prison guards handed us over to the North Korean Army, in the persons of an officer with a pistol and a private with a tommy-gun. We were put into a freight car and told to sit at one end. Midway along each side of the car was an opening where once a door might have been. Beside one opening the officer took up his station with pistol

45

drawn ; from the other, the private covered us with his tommy-gun.   Our guards, we realized, were definitely of the nervous type.

The train jerked into motion, and as it gathered speed the lights went out.   At this the officer grew frantic, and began shouting commands to his companion and bellowing to us above the rattle of the train that we would be shot if we moved.   But we simply *had* to move at times to ease cramped limbs, and as often as the officer detected the movement of a light-coloured garment in the darkness he would begin shouting again.   The noise, the dust, and the panic-stricken cries of our escort made it a nightmare journey.

Ever since the first morning in jail, when I had heard the names Quinlan and Canavan at roll-call, one question had been burning in my brain :   What had become of Father Anthony Collier ?   Now, as we rattled along through the night, Monsignor Quinlan brought his lips close to my ear and whispered :   " We think Tony's dead." More conversation he could not risk.

Some time before dawn on the following morning (July 17) we reached a station on the outskirts of Seoul.   We were marched to a nearby police-station, with the officer warning us that we were likely to be challenged by guards and shot, and ordering us at intervals of about twenty yards to halt and then to march again.   Our old Korean fellow-prisoner seemed thoroughly dazed, and once the officer berated him long and angrily for his failure to stop immediately when the order was given.

At the police-station we were given respite from the frantic attentions of our army escort.   The officer and private went off to wash and eat, leaving us in the temporary care of a pair of policemen who took little interest in us.   We found we could talk freely, and I learned for the first time how Monsignor Quinlan and Father Canavan had fared since I parted from them in Chunchon three weeks earlier.   Before I relate the story I heard from them that morning, let me tell you something of the men themselves.

★   ★   ★

Monsignor Thomas Quinlan was at this time close to his fifty-fourth birthday.   At Thurles, in his native Tipperary, he had almost completed his studies for the priesthood when the newly-formed Missionary Society of St. Columban opened its first seminary in 1918.

He was among the first students to enrol, and was one of the pioneer group of Columban priests who left Ireland for China in 1920. After ten years in the mission of Hanyang, he worked for two years in Nancheng, the second mission entrusted to the Society, before returning on furlough to Ireland.

In the rare moments when he can be induced to talk of himself, the Monsignor can tell stories of his twelve years in China which even old hands find enthralling. There were not only the ordinary problems of missionary life, the sorrows and snares of learning first one and then a second Chinese dialect ; such things were taken for granted. Those years were studded with more exciting episodes— with bandits, floods and famine. Of such things he has reminiscences in plenty, and every gleam of sunshine or humour that could be extracted from those crowded years has been specially treasured in his memory.

On his return to the Far East from Ireland in 1934 he was assigned to Korea, where the Society had been entrusted with the mission of Kwangju in the south-west. Here he had a new language to learn. Five years later, when Columban missionaries took over a second Korean district, a mountainside province in the east, he went with the pioneering group as superior. A year later the district was made a prefecture, with Monsignor Quinlan as Prefect.

He had scarcely taken over his new responsibilities when Korea, at that time a colony of Japan, became involved in war. For him and his priests this meant immediate imprisonment. Later this was relaxed to internment, and later still to house arrest. The work of the mission was forcibly suspended for more than three years.

When American troops landed in Korea after the Japanese surrender, the first of them to enter Chunchon found Monsignor Quinlan still smiling, still optimistic, ready to set about his task once more. Now, after less than five years, he was again enveloped in the meshes of war, facing another internment. And he faced it with the same strong faith and buoyant hope that had made him the man we knew, the leader we followed.

I, who faced it with him, found immense comfort, on that early morning in the police-station in Seoul, in the thought that such a man would bear me company in the uncertain days to come. Some of them would be darker days by far than either he or I could then foresee ; but this prince of a man—big in body, big in heart, big in soul—has been a friend and a father, not only to me, but to all of us who have lived through those days in his company. And this he was to those others too who lived with us through only some of them, and whose worn-out bodies, laid to rest, not a few, by his hands, lie here and there along the paths we trod.

Among these last was to be Francis Canavan, the thirty-five-year-old Irish priest who talked with us there that July morning in Seoul.

My acquaintance with Father Frank, a native of County Galway, dated from 1936, when I came from St. Columban's Seminary in Melbourne to continue my studies at St. Columban's in Ireland. He was then in his third year of preparation for the priesthood, I in my fourth. In the four years that we studied together I came to know him well : a quiet, unobtrusive man, not over-strong, a steady worker and a genial companion. He combined a serious attitude to life with a delightful gift of dry but kindly wit.

When we met again in Korea in 1949, after an eight-years' interval, I found him little changed. The burden of chronic illness lay heavier on him now, but the flashing star of his humour twinkled irrepressibly, as of old, through the seriousness that was still his basic mood.

I have described my hurried departure from Chunchon on the morning after war began. Father Canavan had called me aside that morning for a brief consultation. Should he go or stay ? Monsignor Quinlan had made it clear that he was free to leave, and had urged upon him that, as a newcomer to the country and one still unfamiliar with the language, he could not contribute anything to the welfare of the people by remaining ; whereas, if he left now, he might live to help them more another day. He had told the Monsignor he would think it over. Now he was asking my advice. It was a difficult request, and I told him it was hard to advise him either way. He was free to go, and there were excellent reasons why he should go. But the decision must be his own.

He thought this over in his deliberate way. Then came the question : "But what would you do if you were in my place ? " Of the answer I had no doubt ; and there was no alternative with this transparently honest man but to say so. He nodded then, and relief showed in his eyes. He had already decided, he told me, that he should stay to bear Monsignor Quinlan company. His reason for

Life in Korea is hard: or the countless war refugees, of whom these are typical, it became all but intolerable.

consulting me had been to make doubly sure that his decision did
not run counter to any duty.

And so he stayed. As I trudged back to Hongchon that day, the
image had flickered in and out of my mind of a small, sick man,
with a smile in his eyes and peace in his heart, turning his face to a
gathering storm.

★   ★   ★

As we waited now to be reclaimed by our army escort, I heard
the missing details of the story.

Only a few hours after my early-morning departure from Chunchon on Monday, June 26, shells had started landing in the town,
and in the course of the day several fell in the church grounds.
Shrapnel from one of them struck Monsignor Quinlan on the chin,
but the wound, fortunately, was not severe.

The town's last natural line of defence to the north was the river
that skirted it there. Throughout that Monday the Southern troops
maintained command of the river, but at dawn on the Tuesday
(June 27) the Reds launched a fierce attack, and eventually succeeded,
after several hours of stubborn resistance by the Southerners, in
establishing a bridgehead on the southern bank. The Reds were
soon across the river in force, and the Southerners had to fall back.
At eight o'clock in the morning Monsignor Quinlan and Father
Canavan saw troops moving southwards out of the town. Around
nine o'clock a shell crashed through the roof of the new cathedral,
but did not start a fire. A few minutes later another shell fell on
the old chapel lower down the hill and fire broke out immediately.

Soon afterwards all shelling and firing ceased, and the two priests,
with the mission servants and a few Christians who had remained
in the town, formed a fire-fighting team in an effort to save the old
church, and then, when this proved impossible, to save what they
could of the furnishings, and to prevent flames from spreading to
neighbouring houses.

The battle against the fire, which was to last till eleven that night,
had been in progress for an hour and a half when the first representatives of the North Korean Army arrived at the mission. They
were two privates, with rifles at the ready. The improvised fire
brigade was strung out in a line between the water supply—a deep
well—and the burning building. Monsignor Quinlan was hauling

a bucket of water out of the well, with Father Canavan waiting beside him to pass the bucket down the line.

The two Red soldiers covered them with their rifles.

" How do you do ? " said the Monsignor in Korean. " Can we offer you a drink of water ? "

" Comrade, who are you ? "

" I'm a Catholic priest."

"Are you an American ? "

When they learned that the Monsignor was not American, but Irish, their hostility diminished.

" You speak Korean well. When did you come to Korea ?"

" I've been here for twenty years."

"And who," they asked Father Canavan, " are you ? "

" I'm Irish too."

They wanted to know what was going on, and were told that the idea was to stop the fire from spreading to neighbouring houses.

" That is a good work. Carry on, comrades ! " And the two soldiers departed.

Meanwhile there was no news of Father Collier. The Monsignor had sent word to him early that morning that it was unnecessary and unwise to remain alone in his house at the northern end of the town ; that he ought to come and join Father Canavan and himself. Father Collier had sent back word that he would come during the day. But Tuesday wore on and the occupation of the town was accomplished, and still he had not shown up.

On Wednesday morning he was still missing, and the Monsignor, by now extremely worried, began to make inquiries. Eventually a pagan lad who lived near Father Collier and was a frequent visitor at his house brought a story that was not reassuring. This boy had been at Father Collier's mission the previous afternoon, and when the priest started out with his catechist, Gabriel Kim, to make his way to Monsignor Quinlan's church, he had gone with them. But when they were passing by the lad's house, Father Collier said to him : " There's no sense in your running risks by coming with us. You run along home now and we'll see you tomorrow." The priest and the catechist had then continued on down the road, and this was the last the boy had seen or heard of them.

Monsignor Quinlan obtained permission to visit the local commandant, to whom he explained that the missing man was a missionary and belonged to a nation that was not involved in any way in this war. The commandant was not very helpful. This was war and people were likely to get killed, and he had more urgent affairs to engage his attention.

Next, the Monsignor got in touch with the people who had been told off to bury the dead, but he could find no one who had seen the body of a foreigner.

All efforts to trace Father Collier and Gabriel proved unsuccessful. Certain it was that they had not left the town of their own free will, and it seemed unlikely that they had left it at all. The Monsignor and Father Canavan could only presume the worst, and when they told me the story I had to agree that my feeling was the same.

*   *   *

My friendship with Father Collier, as with Father Canavan, goes back to college days.

I think every American soldier who was in the Chunchon area after 1945 will remember him. In the first few months of the occupation he acted as interpreter, and men of all ranks came to have a great respect for this cool-headed, quiet-mannered Irishman who was so calm and cheerful in any crisis ; a man who could speak as naturally of his ministrations to the sick in a typhoid epidemic when every second house had a corpse outside awaiting burial, as he would of a stroll through the village or a visit to a neighbouring pastor.

It surprised more than one army man to find that this backwoods missionary was also an expert technician. In mechanical problems he could hold his own with specialists. They found he could operate any kind of machinery and drive anything on wheels.

Among the people committed to his care his name was loved and honoured. Pagans, equally with Christians, brought their troubles to him with confidence, sure of a sympathetic hearing and of all the help he could give.

If I am ever released, one of the first questions I shall ask of the first confrère I meet will be : " Is there any news of Tony ? "

*   *   *

After the visit of the two Red soldiers, Monsignor Quinlan and Father Canavan suffered no interference till the following Sunday. The old church was completely burnt out, but the adjacent buildings had escaped, and they were able to offer Mass in one of the priests' rooms each morning.

On the Sunday morning (July 2) Father Frank had already said Mass, and the Monsignor, succeeding him at the improvised altar, had got as far as the *Gloria* in his Mass, when boots thumped into the compound. Shots were fired and soldiers burst into the room.

Monsignor Quinlan was forced to interrupt the Mass. The few Christians present fled in terror, but were forced to return. The soldiers were truculent and abusive. They demanded watches and fountain-pens, hurled articles off the altar onto the floor, smashed the glass in doors of cabinets. Finally the two priests were led away, with hands held up, to army headquarters.

The first officer who interviewed them was surprised that they were there at all, explained that there must be a mistake, and said he would send them home. On second thoughts, he sent them to a higher-ranking officer, who wasn't so sure that they shouldn't be there. He interrogated them at length, and at last had them escorted to the police-station. Father Canavan was suspect because he spoke very little Korean.

At the police-station the interrogation went on all through the hot afternoon, ending with a demand that the Monsignor give a brief outline of the history of the Catholic Church. He pointed out that they had neither eaten nor drunk that day, whereupon the interviewers desisted and provided a meal. The two missionaries spent the night in chairs in the office, and next day the interrogations continued. That evening they were placed in the cells. Since then their experiences had been similar to mine.

* * *

When traffic began moving some time after daylight, our guards showed up and put us on a city-bound tram. North Korean and Russian flags hung everywhere, and pictures of Stalin and Kim Il Soong, Premier of North Korea, were very much in evidence. Red sentries were posted at many points. Red soldiers, on foot and in vehicles, patrolled the streets. Occasionally shots rang out. Our escort had no idea where to deliver us, and we wandered from building to building in the city. We came at last to a large building in the main street where police abounded ; and there, apparently, they agreed to accept us.

A policeman escorted us to a room in the basement—and introduced us to bedlam. The room was about twenty feet square, and it was crammed with people. How many were there when we arrived I cannot say, and during our stay the number was constantly changing ; but once, when the crush was at its worst, I estimated the population of that room at three hundred persons.

It took us some moments to take in the whole of the extraordinary scene. Just inside the door a guard sat at a desk, with some scores of male Korean prisoners squatting before him. Overhead, flies swarmed in countless cohorts. The atmosphere of the ill-ventilated room was stifling. The guard was shouting and gesticulating at the dazed and scared Korean prisoners squatting there, motionless, in the overpowering heat. The significance of this did not immediately strike us, but we were not long in the room before we realized that this was Communist " indoctrination " in action. Hour after hour, day and night, we were to witness the whole ghastly cycle endlessly repeated—interrogation, badgering, bullying, lecturing, and again and again the cry : " Confess ! Confess ! " Then the writing by the stupefied prisoners of their life-histories and " confessions " ; and, if the " confessions " showed insufficient contrition for the writers' non-Communist past, more bullying, more shouting, more lecturing, and the order to write again.

All this we had ample opportunity to observe later, but for the moment our attention was caught by a little group of foreigners pressed into a far corner, and to them we made our way.

The first person I recognized was His Excellency the Apostolic Delegate to Korea, Bishop Patrick Byrne of the Maryknoll Missionary Society, who was smiling and beckoning to us through the crush. We joined the group in a flurry of welcomes, handshakes, excited introductions. With Bishop Byrne was his secretary, Father William Booth, also of Maryknoll. They introduced us to the rest of the party : three priests of the Paris Foreign Mission Society, five nuns from the Carmelite convent in Seoul, and three lay-women. The French priests were Fathers Antoine and Julien Gombert (brothers) and Father Celestine Coyos. The Carmelite nuns were Mother Thérèse Bastin (Prioress), Mother Henriette de Lobit (sub-Prioress), Mother Mechtilde Devriese, Sister Marie-Madeleine (who was blind) and Sister Bernadette Descayaux. Mother Thérèse and Mother Mechtilde were Belgian, the others French. The lay-women were Frau Charlotte Gliese, a German ; Maisara Daulatsch, a Turkish girl born in Korea ; and Helena, a Polish-Korean, whose surname I never learned.

★   ★   ★

Bishop Byrne, a slight, rather tall man, was at this time approaching his sixty-second birthday. His hair was grey, almost white. If his pale, strong-featured face suggested the ascetic, one knew from his merry grey-blue eyes, which twinkled upon all the world, that his asceticism could never be morose or repressive.

In 1922 the Maryknoll Society was asked to staff a mission territory which was then part of the vicariate of Seoul, but later became the prefecture of Pyongyang. Among the first Maryknollers to reach the Korean mission was Father Pat Byrne. He had joined the newly-formed Society soon after his ordination, and had already been entrusted with major tasks of administration. In 1927 he became the first Prefect-Apostolic of Pyongyang, but that same year he was elected as an Assistant in the central administration of the Maryknoll Society, and the Holy See allowed him to resign his office to take up this appointment in the United States.

Five years later Father Byrne led a pioneer group of Maryknollers to Kyoto in Japan. When the area was made a prefecture in 1937 he became its first Prefect-Apostolic. Again he resigned his office, this time as a tactful gesture to enable the Holy See to appoint a Japanese. This was in anticipation of the hostility soon to be shown by the government towards any religious activity which could be shown to be under the direction of a foreigner.

It is a signal proof of the respect Father Byrne commanded among the Japanese, as a man devoted only to his work and beyond all suspicion of self-interest, that in spite of his nationality he was not arrested after Pearl Harbour. When other American nationals, after a period of internment, were repatriated in exchange for Japanese nationals held by Japan's enemies, Father Byrne was allowed, at his own request, to remain on in the Maryknoll house in Kyoto, and was still there when American troops arrived in 1945. After a holiday visit to the United States, he returned as superior of Maryknoll's personnel in Japan.

In 1948 he was sent as Visitor-Apostolic to Korea, to study the problems which had been created for the Church by the change in civil administration, and to advise on any necessary adjustments to the new situation. In this delicate task he was eminently successful, and in April 1949 he was made Apostolic Delegate to Korea, with headquarters in Seoul. In June of that year he was consecrated a bishop in Seoul cathedral.

When the invasion from the North was approaching Seoul a year later, Bishop Byrne had to choose between staying to meet the Reds and moving south. His only concern was with the question of where he could serve the Church best, whether north or south of the battle-line. He decided that a Church overrun by Communists would have more need of such aid as he could offer, and, in the hope that he might be allowed to give it, he remained at his headquarters in Seoul.

As events turned out, his hope of giving any direct help to the Church under the Reds was not fulfilled. On the contrary, his decision had cost him his freedom, and was soon to cost him his life. But in the wider and longer view, the choice he made will not be baulked of its noble purpose : the greater good of his beloved Korean people. No one who knew this Christ-like man can have any doubt that the sacrifice he made of himself in the interests of Christ's Church will bring grace upon grace, in the years to come, to countless souls in this land where his earthly relics are laid to |rest.

Still among us, as I am writing this, is Father William Booth, whom Bishop Byrne chose as his secretary when he became Apostolic Delegate.

Father Booth, like Bishop Byrne, was one of Maryknoll's pioneer missionaries in Korea. Repatriated when the civilian internees were exchanged in 1942, he worked as a missionary in Chile till re-entry to Korea was made possible by the surrender of Japan. Maryknoll's mission territory, however, was now behind the Iron Curtain, so Father Booth offered his services in the vicariate of Seoul, and was engaged in pastoral work there till he joined Bishop Byrne.

When you have lived for more than two years in bondage with

a man, you know his quality. To me, the revelation in this grey-haired Brooklyner has been both inspiring and humbling. Whatever the future holds for me, it has been worth living through these long months of internment to know this patient, kindly, modest, saintly man.

*　　*　　*

We newcomers were still exchanging news with the other foreigners an hour after our arrival, when three more joined our company. They were Father Paul Villemot, Mother Béatrix Edouard, and Mother Eugénie Demeusy. All three were French, and they came from the St. Paul of Chartres Sisters' orphanage beside Seoul cathedral. Father Villemot, veteran Paris Foreign Missionary, was chaplain to the Sisters there, and Mother Eugénie had been mistress of novices for the past eighteen years. Mother Béatrix was provincial superior of the St. Paul of Chartres congregation in Korea.

Father Villemot was eighty-two, and very feeble. Mother Béatrix was a frail woman of seventy-six. We shared the grave anxiety felt for them by their faithful guardian angel, Mother Eugénie, and we were greatly relieved next day when some compassionate official sent the three back to the orphanage. But unfortunately their exemption from our lot was to be only temporary.

Consulting my memory recently as to how long we spent in that basement room, I was surprised to find, after careful thought, that we stayed there only two nights and not much more than two full days. So bad were the conditions under which we spent those fifty hours or so, that I had carried with me for two years and more the vague impression that our stay had lasted many days, perhaps even a couple of weeks.

We were allowed out of the room for essential functions only twice a day, and at fixed hours. We got two meals each day, consisting of a ball of cold boiled barley wrapped in newspaper, and a cupful of water dipped from a bucket. If one wished to eat all the barley, one had perforce to eat some of the newsprint too ; and the ration of water was miserable in that stifling heat.

Bishop Byrne, who had suffered for years from a digestive ailment, found it extremely difficult to take even a little of the cold barley. We were delighted when Father John Yu, from Seoul cathedral, got permission from a friendly guard to bring in a bottle of wine and some sandwiches. Everyone agreed that Bishop Byrne must have them—and so did he ; but we found to our dismay that he had accepted the gifts only to ensure that he would have the sharing of them, and he gave himself the smallest share. We were to find in the months to come that Bishop Byrne never claimed his fair share of anything, except of work ; and of that he always claimed more than was his due.

We will long remember the Korean priest, Father Yu, for this and other courageous visits he paid us. On these occasions he brought us such comforts as he could, and gave us what news he had. The sympathy he showed towards us foreign internees could have cost him his liberty or his life ; and maybe it did, for all we know at this date.

He managed to bring in a couple of blankets. We used these, together with a few quilts and blankets the Sisters had brought, in an effort to give the old and sick some rest.

Real or prolonged rest, however, was impossible for any of us. The rules required that we should sit up all the time, by night as well as by day. When the room was completely crowded, our group would be pressed so tightly in the corner that some had to stand. At other times, when the crush diminished, there was room for some of the older folk to lie down. We remember with gratitude some kindly guards who ignored such breaches of the law, but others were not so generous. Several times we had just got the older people settled down to rest when a new guard came on duty, bellowed at the old folk for not sitting up, and lectured them for seeking special privileges and giving bad example to the Korean prisoners. Once a thoughtful guard went to the length of procuring some arm-chairs for the old and weak, but it was not long till another guard angrily ordered them to be taken away again.

Day and night the work of " conversion " went on among the unfortunate Korean prisoners. I watched the sickening spectacle of hungry, thirsty, dog-tired men being threatened and scolded and shouted into a state of desperation, their minds battered till their thoughts were drowned in the relentless waves of Communist jargon loosed upon them hour by hour.

Were they knaves or fools, I wondered, these Reds who appeared

quite serious in attaching importance to " confessions " so obtained ?
Knaves or fools, they brought to their task a zeal that amounted to
fanaticism : a fact which gives food for thought.   The "indoc-
trinators " who worked in that room were very few for the number
of the prisoners, and they worked almost round the clock.   Every
few hours one would vanish for the time it would take to have a
hurried meal, and then return to the attack.   They had no regular
breaks for sleep.   When one or another became utterly exhausted
he would lay his head on his desk and sleep for half an hour or so,
then rouse up and resume his questioning, his lecturing, and his cries
of " Confess !   Confess ! "

To have seen this devilish process in operation is to know that
people of a free world should not easily assume that every " collabora-
tor " of a Communist régime deservedly bears that name and its
reproach.

Say, if you like, that those unfortunate Koreans whom we watched
were traitors to their principles.   We saw them reduced, group after
group, to a state of mental and physical prostration in which mind
and will at last groped desperately toward the one goal visible in the
haze of weariness and pain : to find, if they could, what their yelling
torturers wanted, to give it to them, and be relieved of this intolerable
ordeal of heat and thirst and hunger, this stupefying barrage of noise.

Few of these men, probably, had ever been very clear about what
they stood for, and even those few would be hopelessly confused
after a few hours of such treatment.   I did see one exception—a small,
slight young fellow who was a captured South Korean Air Force
pilot.   After the usual preliminary questioning and torturing and
badgering, he was presented with pen and paper.   He said he had
nothing to write.   He was interrogated and lectured some more,
but still enlightenment would not come.   He was taken from the
room.   When he came back his face was pale and battered, but the
determined line of his jaw had not changed. They tied his hands
behind his back, and his ankles to his hands.   He was dumped on the
floor and left trussed like that all night.   At intervals he was beaten
and kicked.   In the morning he was untied and placed on his feet,
but the numbed limbs had no power, and he fell to the ground like
a paralytic.   When some use of his limbs at length returned, he was
set at a desk with pen and paper.   Again he stated that he had nothing

to write. He was taken out once more and did not come back. The rumour went round that he was shot. Whether this was his fate I do not know, but I do know that he was a hero.

We foreigners were all called out in turn for interrogation in another room. The formula was of the pattern I have described elsewhere, and the only point of interest that comes back to me is the fact that my interviewer, when we came to the usual part about having had weapons hidden in my house, added in for good measure the accusation that I had a Morse transmitter hidden too.

"You had a cellar in your house?" (Apparently this detail had been passed on from Hongchon.)

"I did. There was a cellar under the kitchen."

"And of course you had a *da-di-da-dit, da-di-da* down there, didn't you?"

There was bright confidence in his tone as he pounced with that question. It seemed almost a pity to have to disappoint him.

During Tuesday, July 18, the day on which Father Villemot and the two St. Paul of Chartres Sisters were sent away, we realized that some or all of the rest of us would soon be leaving these barracks. One of the three lay women was allowed to go with a guard that afternoon to the French Legation, where she had been sheltering with the other two when arrested, to bring a few articles of clothing. Then, next morning, word came that all the foreigners would be taken away at two o'clock that afternoon, with the exception of Monsignor Quinlan, Father Canavan and myself. At a quarter to two we three were told we were going too.

We assumed that we would be marched off to other quarters in Seoul, and there was great excitement and jubilation as we lined up in the barracks yard. Anything would be better than existence in the crowded, stifling room we had just left. Even the air of the yard, tainted though it was from the garbage that littered the ground, was already a welcome change.

As we stood awaiting the signal to move off, a group of fussing little guards passed in through the yard, escorting a tall, lone American soldier. I do not know who he was and I never saw him again, but my memory holds the picture of a tousled head held high, an unshaven chin thrust out, a bronzed face strikingly calm.

The word to move was given, and we marched out, only to find a truck waiting. Our jubilation at being released from the atmo-sphere of the basement room was considerably dampened as we began to wonder whither, and how far, the truck would take us.

We had been rather optimistic about the chances of early release. Some of the party had been arrested only a few days before we three arrived from Chunchon, and they had brought us up to date with the news. The United Nations, they told us, had declared North Korea an aggressor and had undertaken to liberate the South. Already American troops were fighting with the South Koreans, and other United Nations forces were hastening to join them. It seemed that soon the Northerners must be pushed back over the 38th Parallel, and that South Korea—and we, who were still in it—must be free.

There had, however, been a disquieting rumour that the staff of the French consulate had been taken north from Seoul. We had speculated on the possibility that they were taken across the 38th Parallel. Now, as we saw the truck, and realized that something more than a local change of residence was before us, we began to have forebodings that we, too, might be going north. If so, the day of release might be far away.

As we climbed aboard the truck we all had questions, but nobody knew the answers. The truck moved off, and we noted and discussed every turn it made. Some who knew the city said we seemed to be heading for an outer railway station on the line that led from Seoul to the Northern capital, Pyongyang. They were soon proved right. We were not a cheerful party as we alighted from the truck at the station and were marched along to a freight-car.

The car already contained a large number of Korean prisoners, and was grossly overcrowded by the time our party of sixteen had squeezed in.

Our depression was slightly relieved by the purchase of some buns and fruit. Those who had a little money pooled it to buy these delicacies from vendors on the platform—delicacies indeed after our diet of barley and newsprint. If only there were more !

5

Mustering in Pyongyang

JULY 19 TO SEPTEMBER 4, 1950

THE first night's journey in the heat and dust and general misery of that crowded freight-car is mostly a blur in my memory, but one thing I recall vividly : the kindness shown to Bishop Byrne, who was wretchedly ill that night, by the three lay women, Frau Gliese, Maisara Daulatsch, and Helena. The Sisters were unable to help much, as most of them were sick themselves, but those three ladies rose to the occasion magnificently. It was an unusual and touching version of " United Nations "—the American bishop nursed by a German, a Turk and a Polish-Korean, while representatives of France, Belgium, Ireland, America and Australia looked on.

If the atmosphere of the car was stifling during the night, it became overpowering when the train halted next morning at a station and was left to bake in the summer sun. By midday we were in such a state of prostration that the guards allowed us to leave the car and sit outside in its shade. A meal was served, the first since our scant repast of fruit and buns the evening before, but we found ourselves too thirsty to be hungry. We finally persuaded the guards to let us go in small groups to a nearby well, where we drank great draughts of cool water, and took the opportunity of washing some of the grime from our bodies.

(Just the other night I overheard Monsignor Quinlan and Father Booth recalling the experiences of that day, after more than two years.)

" Do you remember the afternoon we drank at that well, and poured water over ourselves ? "

" Do I remember it ? " came Father Booth's reply. " I'll just never forget it, it was such a relief."

When the journey was resumed that evening we graduated to a battered passenger car, and we rolled through the night in comparative comfort, to arrive by daylight in Pyongyang. It was now Friday, July 21.

We were lined up, foreigners first, then the Korean prisoners, and marched through the streets of the Northern capital to the courthouse. I wondered what thoughts were in the minds of the passers-by, as they turned to view this strange parade. Was it with pride or shame that they saw, among the spoils of war, eight foreign women, of whom one was blind and only three were young, and eight foreign men, two of them septuagenarians and two others chronically ill ?

We arrived at the abode of Justice and took our seats in a court-room. From huge portraits hung to left and right of the judge's bench, the eyes of Joseph Vissarionvich Dzugashvili, *alias* Stalin, and Kim Il Soong, Premier of North Korea, smiled down on us.

The bench was empty now, but my imagination gave it an occu-pant and conjured up the spectacle of a Red " trial " in progress. Was it here in this room, I wondered, that the Vicar-Apostolic of Pyongyang, Bishop Francis Hong, knelt more than a year before to hear the verdict of The People ? He might well have made his own the wistful plaint from the liturgy of Good Friday : " O People mine, how have I treated thee ? Or in what have I caused thee grief ? Answer me . . . What else should I have done for thee, and did not do ? "

We were provided with pens and paper and told to write the history of our lives. We were in the midst of this now familiar task when a plane zoomed down and a bomb crashed nearby. The building shook and the blast through open windows sent our papers flying as we dived under tables.

Another notable interruption was the arrival of a meal—a good one, consisting of rice, and soup that was really soup. It was served by a remarkable two-legged mobile food unit : a man arrived with a great load of buckets and crates—the former full of rice and soup, the latter of bowls and spoons and chopsticks—and had set them all down and served half the party before we recovered from our amaze-ment at his capacity as a carrier.

Towards evening we were told we would have to spend the night in the courthouse. We were taken across a yard to a small room and were given another meal. Some of the party who went to collect trays got a glimpse of some foreigners being served a meal in a room beside ours, but who they were we do not know to this day.

We had just settled down for the night on chairs and benches when a truck drove into the yard. We heard excited talk, and then a guard flung open our door and announced that we must leave immediately. Those who had little bundles of belongings hastily collected them. The rest of us had no impedimenta and had only to get on our feet to be ready for the journey. The guards produced bundles of blankets and tossed them on the truck. A pompous little police colonel had appeared, and we found he was to accompany us.

We pushed and pulled one another aboard and away we rattled for some three or four miles out of the city. Then the truck turned off the road and bounced along for a further mile across fields. Finally we were unloaded from the truck, loaded with the blankets, and told to walk.

We stumbled along in the dark over rough ground and loose stones, and then found ourselves splashing through muddy water. To help some of the older folk cross on stepping-stones, Frau Gliese and I went barefoot through the slush beside them. This was to have a sequel.

Eventually there loomed through the darkness the outlines of two large buildings—abandoned schoolhouses, as daylight would show us. We were taken into one of the buildings and assembled in a big room which evidently served as an office. From the deference of the guards, it now became obvious that the rotund little colonel who had come with us was their commanding officer, and was therefore the head man as far as we were concerned too.

He soon let us know it. We asked for water—for our journey had left us, as Monsignor Quinlan put it, " dry enough to spit cotton "—but the colonel chose to give us spiritual refreshment first, in the form of a long sermon on the evils of capitalism. When his lecture ended at last, we renewed our entreaties, and this time a bucket of water was produced.

There was enough for drinking, but not for washing, and now two muddy-footed pilgrims were in disgrace for the state they had got themselves into. Frau Gliese, as she told me later, was sent off to bed with a scolding. I, too, got a scolding, a long and angry one, from the guard to whom I put my case, but I persuaded him that it would be a pity to have me clutter up our new palace with mud, and eventually I got some more water.

By now it was long after midnight. Each of us was given a

blanket—very rough, very thin, and very ancient—and some got an unbleached sheet as well. Then we were divided into three groups and taken across to the other building. The women formed the first group, Bishop Byrne and Father Booth the second. The rest of us were brought to a room which already had three occupants. We saw their prostrate forms when the guard switched on the electric light for a brief instant to enable us to find places on the floor.

As Monsignor Quinlan and I lay down near one of the recumbent figures, it stirred, and a voice said : " I'm Lord, of the Salvation Army." We introduced ourselves and settled down to rest. It was the first opportunity we had enjoyed for some time of stretching out at full length, and the Monsignor murmured something which I heard our new companion recalling later : " Thanks be to God ! This is heavenly ! " Comfort is, after all, a relative thing.

When morning came, we learned that there were four other rooms in the building besides ours, with a group of civilian internees in each. Regulations, we found, forbade any communication between occupants of different rooms. Nevertheless we soon knew the names of all our fellow-prisoners, and, in one way or another, made the personal acquaintance of most of them even before we left this camp.

Taking the five rooms in order, the occupants in residence when we arrived were :

Room One

Captain Vyvyan Holt, Minister ⎫
Mr. George Blake, Vice-Consul ⎬ of the British Legation in Seoul.
Mr. Norman Owen, Secretary ⎭

Room Two

Herbert A. Lord, O.B.E., Lieutenant-Commissioner in the Salvation Army, and head of that organization in Korea. (English.)
The Reverend Charles Hunt, an Anglican missionary of Seoul. (English.)
M. Alfred Matti, manager of the Chosen Hotel in Seoul. (Swiss.)

To this room the three Paris Foreign Missionaries and we three Columban missionaries were now assigned.

Room Three

M. Georges Perruche, Consul-General ⎫
M. Jean Meadmore, Vice-Consul   ⎬ of the French Legation
M. Charles Martel, Chancellor   ⎭ in Seoul.
M. Maurice Chanteloup, correspondent of the French Press Agency.

Room Four

Miss Bertha Smith ⎫
Miss Helen Rosser ⎬ of the Methodist Mission in Kaesong.
Miss Nell Dyer   ⎭   (Americans.)

With these ladies were now accommodated the five Carmelite
Sisters and the three lay women who had come with us.

Room Five.

The Reverend A. Kris Jensen, D.D., of the Methodist Mission in
    Seoul. (American.)
Reverend Lawrence Zellers, of the Methodist Mission in Kaesong.
    (American.)
Ernst Kisch, M.D., of the Methodist Hospital in Kaesong. (Austrian.)
Mr. Walter Eltringham, of the American ECA (Economic Co-
    operation Administration) staff in Seoul. (American.)
Mr. Louis Dans, assistant manager of the Traders' Exchange in Seoul.
    (American.)
Mr. William Evans, a mining engineer. (American.)

With these were placed Bishop Byrne and Father Booth.

For ready reference, we in Room Two called the first room " the
British room," the third " the French room," the fourth " the
Women's room," and the fifth " the American room."

*   *   *

We found excellent friends in the men who welcomed us to their
company in Room Two.

Commissioner Lord had begun his work in Korea as an officer
of the Salvation Army at the age of twenty-one, some years before
the country passed from Chinese to Japanese control. He married a
fellow Salvationist who was, like himself, English. Five sons were
born to them in Korea.

In 1936 the Commissioner was sent to organize the work of the Salvation Army in Singapore. There he was captured by the Japanese in 1942 and interned for three and a half years. After his release in 1945, he was called to England to receive the award of O.B.E. in recognition of his work for social welfare. Subsequently he returned to Korea to take charge of Salvation Army work, with headquarters in Seoul, and on the outbreak of war he remained to meet the Reds, hoping he might be allowed to continue his work. He was arrested at the British legation on July 2, with the Reverend Charles Hunt and the three members of the legation staff.

Commissioner Lord is an authority on the customs and the language of Korea. As the best Korean speaker among us, he has been in constant demand as official and unofficial interpreter. All of us owe much to him for his services in that sphere, as also for his unfailing readiness to work in any capacity for the good of his companions.

Finally, the Commissioner is an exceptionally brave man, as will become evident in the course of my story.

Of the Anglican missionary Charles Hunt, and the Swiss hotelier, Alfred Matti, I must, to my deep regret, speak in the past tense. As I write these lines, it is two years since they left us for a better world.

On a day in 1947, I was in the Seoul office of the Chief Chaplain of the U.S. Forces when a tall, heavily-built man came in, wearing the uniform of a British Navy chaplain. He introduced himself as Charles Hunt, and told me he had just resigned from the Navy and was returning to his former post at the Anglican cathedral.

The missionary career of Charles Hunt began during the First World War, under the late Dr. Trollope, first Anglican bishop in Korea.

The bishop and his young assistant shared a taste for exploration and archaeology, and made long walking tours together through the Diamond Mountains in eastern Korea, visiting the ancient Buddhist monasteries scattered there. Both were members of the Royal Geographic Society of Asia. Articles on Korea under Charles Hunt's name were published by the Society, and he became in due course president of its Korean branch, an office which he still held at the date of his arrest.

Another keen interest of his was the stage, and he had directed amateur dramatic societies in Seoul. We found him a fascinating

entertainer, with a prodigious memory and a genius for story-
telling.

The genial companionship of this cultured and gifted man helped
greatly to relieve the depressing monotony of our prison life. A
few months later we were to see his powerful body worn out by
privation and exhaustion and sickness, till he gave back his generous
soul to the God he had served so sincerely.

Alfred Matti, tall and debonair, scarcely looked his forty-eight
years. As hotel manager or tourist guide, he had sojourned in many
countries, including my own. When I met him he was wearing a
souvenir of his Australian visit : a wrist-watch, guaranteed waterproof, made in Switzerland and bought in Sydney.

He was in Shanghai when it fell to the Japanese, but they respected
his neutral status as a Swiss and allowed him to manage the affairs
of the International Red Cross until the war ended. He then sailed
for home with his wife and two sons, but their ship went down in a
storm off the Philippine Islands. One of his sons was drowned, and
he and his wife and the other son reached safety only after a battle
of several hours through mountainous seas. Recounting this tragic
story one day, he recalled a minor detail : the Swiss watch he had
bought in Sydney accompanied him through that nightmare experience and, as he added with a touch of national pride, it did not
stop. " It really is waterproof," he explained.

M. Matti, at the time of his arrest—an event which greatly surprised and disappointed him, after his favourable experience under
the Japanese—was manager of the Chosen Hotel in Seoul. President
Syngman Rhee, whose government owned the hotel and feared the
enterprise was failing, had asked the Swiss Hotel Association to
recommend a man capable of improving the situation. Alfred Matti
had been the answer.

In those early days of our internment, when we thought release
was near, M. Matti was already planning a sumptuous banquet he
would give at the Chosen Hotel to all those who had been prisoners
with him. It was a delight to hear him working out the details of
the menu ; it was also a torture, for in those days we were near to
starvation. However, this amiable and accomplished man was not
to see the Chosen Hotel again, nor to know any banquet this side
of the grave. His bones rest today among the Korean hills whose

beauty he so much admired, and to whose scenic wonders he dreamed of bringing tourists from all over the world.

*   *   *

I said we were near to starvation in those days. This is literally true. Who was responsible, our guards or higher authorities, I do not know ; but despite two hunger-strikes in " the American room " and repeated complaints from all of us, we never saw any real improvement while in that camp. The fare was gravely inadequate, both in quantity and quality. A meal usually consisted of a little rice—enough, perhaps, to fill a small cup—and a bowl of hot water barely flavoured with leek or cabbage. Occasionally we got a little sugar, and a few times we were given unripe apples or plums. Once our camp cook tried to improve the watery soup by adding green plums. The word " once " should be underlined. We saw with interest and high hopes the arrival one day of some bags of flour. But the only results were the appearance of some dumplings in the soup, or the issuing of a little steamed bread ; and on such occasions the rice was withheld.

For washing, some buckets of water and some basins were placed in a corridor, and the members of each room in turn were allowed to avail of these amenities in the mornings. A cake of toilet soap had been issued to each prisoner, and also a toothbrush and tooth-powder. Those who came earlier than us had received, in addition, a comb apiece and a mirror to every three or four persons, but the supply of these had apparently run out before we arrived.

Cigarettes were supplied at intervals, but the intervals grew longer and longer. When other goods were lacking, our guards attributed it regularly to the bombing of transport vehicles, but when tobacco ran short they invariably referred the catastrophe to the very source of supply. According to them a phenomenal amount of pin-point bombing must have been directed by the U.N.O. at tobacco factories. This anti-tobacco complex of the U.N. powers will undoubtedly be the subject of investigation by a number of disgruntled smokers if ever they reach freedom. During one period of shortage, our guards' explanation went one better than usual. The tobacco factory bombed on this occasion had, they told us, been destroyed before, and had just been rebuilt and re-equipped when it was again laid low.

In this camp we seemed to be under the joint custody of the army and the police force. Our immediate custodians were policemen who did not carry arms. They lived in the other building, but there was always one of them on duty in our building, sitting at a desk in the corridor outside our room. (The desk, incidentally, over-looked the windows of the room where the Sisters and other women were quartered, so they lacked all privacy during the day.) The perimeter of the camp was patrolled by armed soldiers, but they never came inside the boundaries. They lived in barracks at some little distance from the camp. Apparently they were rookies in training, and the solemn changing of the guard provided us with diversion three times a day. The fat little colonel who had come with us from Pyongyang had his headquarters in the city, but came to inspect us from time to time. He had been christened " The Pan-jandrum " by the prisoners before we arrived, and we never knew him by any other name.

We had passed a week in this camp before any more prisoners arrived. On the morning of July 29 we heard a truck approaching. We crowded to the windows, as we always did at the sound of a vehicle. Usually it meant the arrival of officials, who might or might not have business with us. But on this occasion we saw, with excitement, that some Europeans were alighting from the truck.

As they approached, we recognized, with mixed feelings, three people who had parted from us in the police barracks at Seoul, and who we had hoped were to be spared the ordeal of internment. Father Paul Villemot, the eighty-two-year-old Paris Foreign Mis-sionary, was being helped along by Mother Eugénie ; and beside them walked the other St. Paul of Chartres nun, seventy-six-year-old Mother Béatrix.

There were two other prisoners. One of them was identified by Charles Hunt as his bishop, the Right Reverend Cecil Cooper, who was head of the Anglican Church in Korea and resided in Seoul. The Paris Foreign Missionaries recognized the other as Father Joseph Bulteau, a member of their Society.

The newcomers were taken first, as we had been, to the other building, where our guards had their office.

★   ★   ★

As we watched at our windows for their reappearance, I talked with Father Celestine Coyos, the youngest of the Paris Foreign Missionaries who have shared our internment, and the only one who is still with us as I write.

He had first come to Korea in 1933, shortly after his ordination to the priesthood, and had been only three years in the country when illness forced him to return to France. After a period in a sanatorium, he was sufficiently well to take up an appointment as history professor in a college, but his ambition was to regain the health needed to resume his missionary career. After more than ten years of determined effort he won the uphill battle, and was allowed to return to Korea as professor of philosophy and ecclesiastical history in the major seminary at Seoul. He had scarcely settled down in his new post when the Red invaders came.

Father Coyos belongs to the Basque race, a dogged people who know how to take the rough with the smooth. At forty-two, he had already found plenty of need for his hardy Basque endurance in adversity. He was to need it even more in the months to follow. As one after another of his confrères passed from us through the gates of death, this frail, sensitive man held on to life by sheer will-power, as it seemed to us. " One of us," he was to say in the worst days of all, " must live to tell the story." And he has lived thus far, and is growing stronger. Please God he will live to see liberty yet.

Meantime, an outstanding professor is lost to the world, as we can testify who have enjoyed his company in the past two years. His knowledge of history, both secular and ecclesiastical, is wide and deep, and his power of exposition would grip any audience. For my own part, it has been an interesting experience to watch the unfolding of history's pageant when the lighting and perspective have not necessarily been those of the texts one conned at school.

*   *   *

Presently the new arrivals were escorted over to our building. The two Sisters were put with the other women, and Bishop Cooper and the two priests were brought to our room.

Poor old Father Villemot ! We welcomed him with smiles and cheery words, but our hearts were heavy within. He looked all of his eighty-two years. Father Antoine Gombert was seventy-six, but

his back was still straight and his shoulders square, his step firm, his
eyes bright, his voice strong, his laugh hearty, and his appetite good ;
while the sprightly Father Julien, a mere youngster of seventy-four,
was still addressed as *Mineur* by Father Antoine. But Father Villemot
was really old. He was stooped, he tottered a little as he walked,
his voice was cracked, he had no appetite. Long ago he had retired
from active missionary life, and for years had been little better than
an invalid. As chaplain to the St. Paul of Chartres Sisters in Seoul,
he had received the care he needed. Now he must live in a cold and
draughty room, with the hard floor for bed, and his food would be
neither palatable nor nourishing.

Father Bulteau, whom I had not met before, was fifty years old,
very stout, very cheerful, and possessed of a beard of magnificent
proportions. Comparing notes with him, Monsignor Quinlan and
Father Canavan and I learned that his experiences when the Reds
reached his mission, far south of Seoul, hed been similar to ours in
Chunchon and Hongchon. He was arrested a few days after the
Northern troops arrived, and his house and church were ransacked,
religious objects and pictures thrown about, missals despoiled of their
covers. He was taken to Seoul, and there he met the other four
missionaries who had now been brought with him to Pyongyang.

At the time of his arrest he had in his pocket the current volume
of the Breviary (the official prayer-book of priests, comprising four
volumes, one for each season of the year) and he had managed to
retain it since. Father Bulteau's " Summer Quarter " did duty hence-
forward for all the priests in camp, passing from hand to hand
through the day. We have had only two other books among us all
this time : the New Testament of one of the Methodist missionaries,
and a French prayer-book belonging to one of the Sisters.

Bishop Cooper, third of the newcomers to our room, was clad in a
purple cassock and little else. He had, he told us, been on a journey in
the country when the war broke out, and Seoul had already fallen
when he returned to his residence there. Red soldiers came to arrest
him during the night, and refused him time to dress. The cassock
was hanging near his bed, and they told him to put it on and come
at once.

He told us of his journey with the priests and nuns from
Seoul to Pyongyang. Their train, like ours, had travelled only by

night, and even more slowly than ours. We had remained in the vicinity of our train during the day-time stops, but they had twice been lodged in jails while awaiting resumption of the rail journey. This had happened in Kaesong, and again in Maltong. In both jails they were subjected to interrogation, and on their passage through the streets of the two towns they attracted a good deal of unpleasant attention which must have been particularly trying to the Sisters.

★　　★　　★

Bishop Cooper, an Englishman and a graduate of Cambridge University, came to Korea more than forty years ago. He therefore, like Commissioner Lord, had memories of the country as it was before the Japanese came in 1910. He had worked ever since in Korea, except for the two World War periods. His missionary field had lain mainly in the north, and he could tell of extensive travels through that part of the country.

When Bishop Trollope died in 1930, Cecil Cooper succeeded him in Seoul. His predecessor had given a strongly High Church character to Anglicanism in Korea, and Bishop Cooper, who shared his views, maintained the same tradition.

The bishop, a man slight of build, is now about seventy, but hardy and active still. In our various camps he has shared the work with an energy that younger men have envied. I have seen him in vigorous action as a hewer of wood and drawer of water, and he has carried on with the hauling of rations and firewood when all but a few had lost their strength.

As a hobby he had kept bees, and he has drawn on the fruits of his lifelong study of their habits to lighten many an hour for us. He has been the scholar of our company, and has revealed himself as a delightful poet. To brighten our days he has composed verses, and read them to us ; and many have asked for copies of his work.

I do not remember that I ever saw Bishop Cooper angry or even excited, and whenever there has been a crisis in camp we have been able to depend on him for calm and impartial advice.

★　　★　　★

Air raids over Pyongyang were common by this time, and from our camp five miles out of town we had, as someone put it, a grand-stand view. We were supposed to keep away from the windows at

such times, but we often risked the anger of the guards to watch
the raids. There was a slit trench which we were told we could use
for shelter, but as this was the rainy season and the trench was half
full of water, the invitation was declined.

Apart from what we saw from our windows, our only knowledge
of the progress of the war was derived, through Commissioner Lord
as translator, from North Korean newspapers. These we " borrowed," as opportunity offered, from our guards.

The fixed determination of our captors to deprive us of all news,
even such as was current in their own newspapers, is hard to understand, but such has been the policy. It is a commonplace of war-
prisoner psychology that two great preoccupations tend to occupy
the mind : a desperate interest in food, and a desperate craving for
news. Sometimes the craving for news can outweigh even the
instinct of self-preservation, as was proved during World War II
by the many instances of prisoners risking their lives to obtain or
retain wireless sets, to contact outsiders, to get even the smallest
snippets of news from any possible source. And it seems that there
was hardly a camp which did not succeed in finding some channel
of information. But we in North Korea have, on the whole, failed—
so opaque is the Iron Curtain and so carefully is it patrolled.

Even at the time of writing this, when, after more than two years
of internment, some relaxation of conditions allows us to talk occasionally with North Korean civilians, we find that they usually know
less about outside affairs than we do ourselves. The ignorance even
of our guards is sometimes startling. One of them told Nell Dyer,
with considerable pride, that North Korea now had some tractors,
and asked her if there were any in the United States. Miss Dyer
is reported to have replied that the one they had in the States was
out of repair ; but possibly this part of the story is apocryphal.

Our information derived surreptitiously from the guards' newspapers in this Pyongyang camp had to be subjected, of course, to a
good deal of interpretation. Only by reading between the lines did
we gather that the North Korean armies had been halted in their
southward drive, that they were making desperate efforts to smash
the resistance, and that the tide would probably turn against them if
only the U.N. forces could hold out a little longer till reinforcements
arrived.

Excitement ran through the news-hungry camp when Commissioner Lord came back from the guards' building one day with the information that a professional newsman had arrived. It was the last evening in July. We had seen a jeep drive in from the main road, and watched the passengers alighting. All were Korean officials, except for one khaki-clad, bare-headed foreigner. One of his arms was in a sling, and he limped as he was escorted to the other building. Commissioner Lord had been summoned to act as interpreter. Now, on his return, he told us the newcomer was Philip Deane, a war correspondent for the London *Observer*.

In due course Philip Deane was brought over, and was assigned to our room. (Soon after he came, Bishop Cooper and Commissioner Lord were transferred to the room occupied by the British diplomats, as ours was now becoming overtaxed.) We found he had been captured on July 23 at Pyongdong, in the central sector of what was then the battle line. Pyongdong is some sixty miles south of Chunchon, and the Reds were still sweeping south at that time. Deane, therefore, was not as up to date with the present situation as we were, but such news as he had, he dispensed to us with the clarity and graphic style of the trained journalist, and we heard with intense interest the account of his own experiences. We did not press him for the full story then, for he was tired and a sick man, but we heard it in detail in the days that followed.

He is a native of Greece, and was in his middle twenties when we made his acquaintance. During the second World War he served in the British Navy. When peace was restored, he went back to Greece to act as correspondent for the *Observer*. On the outbreak of war in Korea, he hastened there by plane to report the fighting for his paper.

Arriving on July 10, he went at once in search of copy to the central front, which was then just north of Taejon. Having left Taejon shortly before it fell to the Reds he reached the front line again some twenty-five miles to the south-east, just north of Yongdong, on the morning of July 23. American forces were already withdrawing southwards from Yongdong as he moved northwards out of the town by jeep. After a few miles' travel the vehicle was immobilized by sniper fire, and he found his retreat cut off. He took shelter in a farmhouse with some American soldiers, but the

thin mud walls offered little protection. Some of his companions
were hit, and enemy troops were moving closer. He crawled out
to some jeeps standing near, but as he tried to get one of them moving
he was wounded in the hand and thigh, and next thing the vehicle
itself was hopelessly crippled by bullets. Nothing to do but crawl
back to the farmhouse and await the Reds. They arrived at three in
the afternoon, ordered Deane and the rest to their feet, shot those
who were too badly wounded to rise, and marched the others out
to the road.

The prisoners were deprived of their footwear, and their hands
were tied behind them. Then began for them a nightmare journey.
Barefoot and bleeding, they travelled over mountain paths and
country roads for five days, to Communist Army Headquarters near
Suwon. This is a journey of nearly ninety miles as the crow flies,
but a good deal longer by the route they took.

The discovery by an interpreter that Deane was a journalist meant
the beginning of long interrogations, which were renewed when he
was brought north by jeep to Seoul, and again when a truck took
him to the Northern capital. Eventually he convinced his captors
that he was a non-combatant, and so was sent out to our civilian
internees' camp. When he arrived he was wearing shower-slippers.
These he found lying, of all places, on top of a disabled American
tank which he passed during his five-day march.

Early in August, a few days after Philip Deane joined us, we
watched from our windows the arrival by truck of a group of
people numbering about a score. They were taken to the guards'
building, and as they straggled along we saw that there were men,
women—and, to our surprise—children. Two of the latter were
young babies, and some others were mere toddlers. Three of the
women were identified by members of our party as Sister Mary
Clare, an Irish-born Anglican nun from Seoul, and Madame Amelia
Martel and Mademoiselle Marguerite Martel, mother and sister of
Charles Martel who was already with us. The rest were strangers
to us all, but we found later that they included Turks, White
Russians, and a French-Korean woman and her son.

The three Europeans—Madame and Mademoiselle Martel, and
Sister Mary Clare—were presently brought to our building and
lodged with the other women. The rest of the new arrivals stayed

in the other building, and we did not meet them till a month later, when we all left Pyongyang together.

*　　*　　*

The Martel family was well known among the foreign residents in Korea. Madame Martel, who was seventy-six when her internment began, had been widowed only a year before. Her French husband had won an honoured name for himself during his several decades of residence in the country, and was a professor in Seoul University at the time of his death. Madame herself was German. Her father was Professor Eckart, musician and composer. He had been invited by the Mikado to write songs for Japan at a time when that country was awaking to an interest in Western ways and culture, and among his compositions was the national anthem that is used in Japan today. Later he was invited on a similar mission to Korea, whose gaze was likewise turned admiringly at that time on the Western world.

Besides Charles and Marguerite, with whom she was now sharing internment, Madame Martel had other sons and daughters. One of the daughters, if she was still alive at this time, was probably a prisoner in North Korea too. She had joined the Benedictine Sisters in Wonsan many years before. All the Benedictines of Wonsan, both monks and nuns, were known to have been arrested in May of 1949, but since then there has been no definite news of them.

Charles Martel, who had been chancellor at the French legation in Seoul, will be long remembered by his fellow-internees for his unfailing courtesy and kindly solicitude.

With his French diplomatic colleagues and the journalist Maurice Chanteloup, Charles Martel was transferred, after six months in our company, to a separate camp. With them went also the British diplomats and Philip Deane. These eight men, even while they were still attached to our party, were frequently quartered not so much with us as near us. I never had the opportunity to know them very well, but such contacts as I had with them have left me many pleasant memories.

Georges Perruche, the French consul-general, impressed us equally by the courage he displayed towards our captors in defence of our interests, and by his gracious kindliness towards ourselves. He had

been allowed to bring with him some extra clothing and a small
stock of medicines, but he freely gave all away. I remember a personal experience of his generosity. One day when I was washing
my shirt he noticed that I had no other to wear, so he waylaid me
later and pressed me to accept one of his. He took every possible
opportunity of denouncing the conditions in camp and fighting for
improvements, and was especially solicitous for the welfare of the
women. I recall with particular relish the dramatic protest he made
about the food : storming out of his room with his rice bowl in one
hand and his soup bowl in the other, he thrust them both under the
guard's nose and demanded from that astonished man what sort of
a meal *this* was.

Jean Meadmore, the vice-consul, was the handsome man of the
party, but he had more than exterior qualities to make him likeable.
We found him, like his superior officer, ever courteous and kindly
and ready to be helpful. Incidentally, both M. Perruche and he had
served in China before coming to Korea, and both were experts on
Chinese language and culture.

Maurice Chanteloup had also been in the diplomatic service
originally, but had resigned to become a press correspondent. He
was in Japan when the Reds invaded South Korea, and was one of
the first foreign correspondents to reach the new battle scene. He
was captured in Seoul, after sending out to the free world some of
the earliest accounts of the situation. I remember him chiefly as a
fiery little fighter who was regularly dismissed by disgusted interviewers as an incorrigible reactionary.

The gaiety of the four Frenchmen, which they maintained in spite
of all adversity, often penetrated to our room next door. Once I
heard a dancing lesson in progress, and, taking the opportunity of
passing by their door, I saw that master and pupil were dancing
together, while a third member of the quartet, humming *Put Your
Little Foot*, was the orchestra, with the fourth presumably for
audience. The monotony of our days was relieved, too, by their
foresight in bringing in a pack of playing cards, which passed back
and forth from time to time between their room and ours.

My first sight of the British diplomats was on the morning after
our arrival, when, shortly after daylight, Captain Vyvyan Holt, who
had been minister of the legation in Seoul, led the vice-consul,

George Blake, and the secretary, Norman Owen, through our room (which was the only way of exit from theirs) out to the wash-place.

Captain Holt, who was lean and tall, with a slight stoop, some of us had met before. We remembered the kindly hospitality we had enjoyed at his residence in Seoul, and knew how friendly and generous a nature lay behind his reserved and rather taciturn manner. His sterling qualities we were to appreciate more and more in the days we spent together. George Blake, a well-built and athletic young man, had been in Holland when the second World War broke out ; had escaped from the Germans and made his way south ; and had finally reached England, where he joined the Navy. He spoke several European languages fluently. Norman Owen was a hearty, genial soul who cheered us all with his motto : " Home for Christmas ! "

That these men, British or French, should be detained at all was of course contrary to all diplomatic tradition ; and it was more preposterous that they should be detained under such conditions. However, they will probably think of their North Korean captors more in sorrow than in anger, recalling incidents such as this :

The diplomats were being interrogated after their arrest in Seoul.

" What is your work ? " the presiding officer demanded of Captain Holt.

He patiently explained that he was the accredited representative of the British Government to the Government of South Korea.

" Yes, yes," said the officer, dismissing irrelevancies, " but what do you do for a living ? "

*   *   *

As I hinted in an earlier chapter, North Korean officialdom is a " promising " institution. After more than two years' experience of this, I am still unable to fathom the reason for it. Countless promises have been made to us by guards and higher officials, and always, apparently, with sincerity. Very few of these promises have been fulfilled ; but why were they made at all ? Did our captors take delight in tantalizing us ? By and large, I do not think so. Very few of those with whom we have had dealings would have had either the cruelty or the subtlety for that. They were, on the average, ordinary run-of-the-mill folk, neither specially vicious nor specially virtuous, and usually simple rather than subtle. I prefer to believe that this habit of making promises which they either could not or would not fulfil is to be attributed to the Oriental's distaste for direct refusal, to his traditional tendency to let people down lightly if they are going to be let down at all. Sometimes, too, our immediate custodians may have said " Yes " to our requests simply because they had no idea at the time what their superiors would say, and preferred not to admit the state of ignorance and confusion in which they themselves were kept.

As I say, I cannot explain the phenomenon, but some examples of it that occurred in the Pyongyang camp may be of interest.

Dr. Kisch asked for medical supplies to treat the sick. A guard had him write out a long list of what he required. A month later that same guard was going through his pockets in search of something else, and out came that same list.

Again, we had visits from time to time from a Korean doctor and his assistants, who took notes of the medical condition of the prisoners and promised to send remedies next day. The remedies regularly failed to arrive.

Another time, we protested about the many panes of glass missing from windows and doors, for the summer was now waning and the nights were getting cold. Our guards sent for a carpenter. He measured all the spaces needing glass, and noted also other desirable repairs in the way of broken window-frames, rotting beams, woodwork needing paint, etc. Everything was painstakingly written down in the carpenter's notebook, and he went his way. We were assured that the work would be completed in a short time. It never began.

On the night of August 22, as I remember very clearly, the temperature suddenly dropped considerably. Before that, the nights, though gradually getting colder, had been bearable ; but during that night we were quite unable to sleep as we shivered on the floor. Most of us were clad only in light summer clothing, and few had any more covering than the one threadbare blanket issued to each of us on arrival. Next morning we renewed our demands for warm clothes and more blankets. " Soon," we were told, " very soon." And there the matter ended.

*   *   *

We filled in the dreary days as best we could. We were confined
to our respective rooms day and night, except for the procession,
room by room, to the wash-place every morning. To go out to the
toilet during the day, individual permission was required, and the
guard was supposed to see that no two people from different rooms
went out together.

This determination of our custodians to prevent communication
between the five groups is hard to understand, seeing that there was
complete freedom of conversation inside each room. Some strange
consequences followed from the rule. M. Martel, for instance, could
talk all day with his diplomatic confrères and with M. Chanteloup,
but not with his own mother and sister in the next room ; while the
French priests had free converse with one another, and with Englishmen, Irishmen, a Swiss and an Australian in our room, but could not
pass the time of day with the French Sisters or with the French
diplomats.

Needless to say, we often got around the rule. It was not hard,
we found, to get the guards confused about which rooms we belonged
to, and it became a matter of routine to bamboozle them in this way
whenever one or other group had a bit of news to communicate to
the rest.

Another puzzling feature was the denial of any opportunity for
exercise out of doors. Relaxation of this kind would have kept us
more healthy and more contented with our lot, and surely that
would have helped our custodians as well as ourselves. We were
surprised, in fact, that open-air exercise was not compulsory.

We continued to watch with interest the comings and goings of
visitors to the camp, but no more prisoners joined us. The arrival
of officials sometimes meant interviews and interrogations for us.
On one occasion we were all taken, group by group, to the office
in the other building in the dead of night, and were each asked to
write on a special form the name and address of a near relative at
home. There was also a query on the form about the state of our
health. A good many answered that question with one word :
" Hungry." The whole incident gave us matter for excited speculation all through the following day, but nothing came of it.

We were always apprehensive when a tommy-gunner accompanied
visiting officials, for by now we all knew the story of Andrea, the

In 1949, after many years' missionary work in Korea and Japan, Bishop Patrick Byrne of the Maryknoll Fathers (*left*) was appointed Apostolic Delegate to Korea. Taken prisoner by the Communists in July, 1950, he died in captivity four months later.

With Bishop Byrne in captivity was his friend, Monsignor Thomas Quinlan of St. Columban's Society, who was Prefect-Apostolic of Chunchon. He survived the rigours of captivity and in April, 1954, just a year after his release, he returned to Korea as Regent of the Apostolic Delegation.

[*Irish Press*

White Russian, who had been employed as an engineer by ECA in Seoul, and had been brought to this camp with the five Englishmen, Lord, Hunt, Holt, Blake and Owen, and the two Americans, Dans and Eltringham. (Theirs had been the first party to arrive.) Andrea, it appears, was a cheerful giant of a man who spent most of his time sleeping in a corner from meal to meal. His chief activity had been on behalf of Charles Hunt, who at that time was crippled with gout. Whenever the missionary needed to move about the building, the White Russian carried him pick-a-back, heavy load though he was, with the greatest ease. A day came, some time before our group arrived, when an official party appeared, and with them a tommy-gunner. Andrea was taken away, and never returned.

Some time after our arrival, Helena, the Polish-Korean girl who had come with us from Seoul, was taken away in like manner. She spoke several languages fluently, and possibly they wanted her services as an interpreter ; or, since she had been employed by the Americans in Seoul, they may have thought some information could be got from her. We never saw her again.

On August 4 Philip Deane was taken away. He and the French journalist, Chanteloup, had often been called out for special interviews in the other building, but to see him taken from the camp altogether aroused in us great anxiety for his well-being. Nearly a month passed. Then, on the last evening of August, we were delighted to see him brought back safe and sound, and his delight at his return to the fold equalled ours.

He had been taken to a large house in Pyongyang and made to sit in a stuffy room, with a bright light close to his face, before a team of interrogators who questioned him and argued with him ceaselessly for three days and nights, till he finally lapsed into unconsciousness.

The object of his interviewers was to get him to write articles or make broadcasts favourable to the North Koreans. Previous interviewers had tried unsuccessfully to interest him in the idea, and this seemed like a desperate all-out attempt to break his resistance. He gathered that he had been taken from the camp to deprive him of the moral support of the British diplomats. If the North Koreans had learned that Deane was not British by birth but Greek, and if they discovered in addition that he was the son of a Greek general who had commanded anti-Red partisan forces, there is little doubt what his fate would have been.

After his collapse he was given good treatment and good food. Moreover, he was not very closely guarded in the room to which he was confined. Air raids were common over the city of Pyongyang during this period (as we had seen from a distance ourselves) and Deane was often left alone in the house while its occupants, including his guards, took shelter. During such periods he explored the rooms, and discovered several radio sets. None of them was functioning, but by exchanging parts he succeeded in getting one to work, and enjoyed himself picking up various news broadcasts from the United States, Britain and Australia.

It was remarkable how much he was able to remember without notes. He had brought back detailed war news for us all ; he had memorized baseball scores for the Americans, and had items of interest from Australia for me. His news of the fighting in the South was very encouraging. The Northern armies had definitely been halted, United Nations reinforcements were arriving, and the battered South Korean armies were being formed again into a strong force.

Throughout August Monsignor Quinlan had been taking wagers on the chances of our liberation before the end of the month. To-morrow would be September 1, but after hearing Philip Deane's news the Monsignor developed scruples about running a book on the coming month. We agreed with him that it seemed like betting about a certainty.

Five days later we had reason to change our views.

6

Whither the Droving?

SEPTEMBER 5 TO 11, 1950

SEPTEMBER 5 dawned. The sun climbed slowly, wearily, in the sky, looked down upon our camp to find it as dull as yesterday and so many days before, and passed drearily on, beginning his long decline. Grasping at straws in the sea of monotony, we found mild diversion in the arrival of a truck carrying supplies. Idly we watched the driver and his mate unloading rice and firewood.

A guard emerged from the other building, came in our direction. We watched him pass our windows, heard his steps in the corridor. Then, suddenly, monotony was shattered.

"All blankets and food bowls to be handed in at once!"

As we brought out our bowls and blankets we pestered the guards to know what the order meant, but could get no enlightenment. Soon another order came.

"Pack up and be ready to leave in half an hour."

So we were moving! But why? And whither? Again we besieged the guards, but if they knew the answers they kept them to themselves.

Those who had personal belongings gathered them up, and in a flurry of excited speculation the whole party was eventually assembled outside. The guards, on this and similar occasions to come, tried to have order and discipline. We were supposed to line up at a specified place in a specified time, then number off, form in column, and march away in military fashion. But we were a difficult platoon to organize. Some didn't want to be organized, some didn't know how to be organized, and a few would always be late. And what did nuns know, anyway, about "dressing by the right"?

The Panjandrum, who had lectured us the night we arrived, now came to make another speech. Boiled down to essentials, it amounted

83

to this : " Life for you here is becoming too difficult and dangerous,
with these rascally Americans raining bombs on women and children,
and especially on schools. So we are sending you to a nice place in
the mountains where you will have peace and comfort." I think
more than one of us rounded off the tubby little colonel's speech,
sotto voce, with the ending it demanded : " . . . And you'll all live
happily ever after."

Next, the prisoners who had been in the other building were
brought to join us, and we saw among them seven Korean men—
Southern politicians, as we learned later. The rest were the people
we had seen arriving a month before with Sister Mary Clare and the
Martel ladies.

The truck which had brought the supplies to the camp was still
standing by, and now a second truck arrived. We were divided
into two groups and told to board the vehicles. The one I was on
did not leave till the other was already out of sight. Then ours
was driven into Pyongyang. As we rattled through the streets we
noticed that buildings here and there, and sometimes half a block of
buildings, had been destroyed. The bombing, however, had evidently been aimed at specific targets, and the city in general did not
seem to be too badly damaged.

We stopped at massive gates set in a high brick wall, and had no
difficulty in knowing even before we passed inside that this was the
city jail. We were assembled in a large room, from which we got
glimpses of wretched-looking convicts and grim-faced warders. A
couple of hours passed, and still we were not consigned to cells—a
point which the more optimistic of us used in our efforts to lighten
the anxiety of our comrades.

Late in the afternoon we were glad to find our optimism justified.
A truck came to take us to the railway station. As we drove into
the station yard in a light drizzle of rain, we saw the folk who had
left camp on the first truck sitting about in small groups. They had
been taken direct to the station.

For the first time in our internment the atmosphere was somewhat
free and easy, and we were able to talk without restriction. The
arbitrary barriers of the schoolhouse camp were gone, and people
who had been together earlier were able to compare notes again.
We priests sought out Bishop Byrne and Father Booth and the

Sisters. The Apostolic Delegate, to our joy, seemed much better than he had been in Seoul and on the journey to Pyongyang.

★　　★　　★

One whom I got to know for the first time here was the Reverend Lawrence Zellers. The long conversation we held that evening was the first of many, and the beginning of a warm friendship that has meant a great deal to me in the ups and downs of the more than two years we have since spent together.

"Larry," as the young Methodist missionary soon became to us all, is a Texan. Tall, handsome, slim-waisted, broad-shouldered, he might in an earlier and more romantic era have been one of those cowboys whose lore and whose lilting songs he knew so well.

He was fresh from college, and planning his future, when the Pearl Harbour catastrophe decided it for him. He trained as a radio operator, and was soon in action in the trans-Atlantic place-ferrying service. His missions took him to France, to Germany, to Italy, to Africa, and he has a rich fund of reminiscences, grave and gay, of people he met and places he visited during those crowded years.

Sobering experiences, including some near brushes with death, set the young airman pondering about life and its ultimate goal, and when peace came he entered the Southern Methodist University to study for the ministry. He decided to go further, and enrolled as a " K.3." This was the popular designation among the Methodists for young missionaries who volunteered for three years' service in Korea during their theological studies. Larry was assigned to teach English at the Methodist Mission in Kaesong, which is only a couple of miles south of the 38th Parallel. The town was overrun in the first hours of the Red invasion, on Sunday morning, June 25. Larry's wife —another " K.3," whom he had married just seven months before— was fortunately spending that week-end in Seoul, forty miles further south, and presumably was evacuated.

I have found Larry Zellers a mine of information on all things technical and mechanical, with an unusual talent for explaining such things to the uninitiated. In the field of radio, his war-time speciality and his peace-time hobby, he has the knowledge of an expert.

The presence among us of this cheerful, unaffected and wholly unselfish man has done a lot to lighten the burden of internment.

Perhaps the best tribute I can pay him is this : If you want to find him at any time, the last place to look is amid any scene of friction or disturbance ; the first, wherever there is a hard job of work to be done.

* * *

In making the acquaintance of the people who had not been quartered in our building at the schoolhouse, we met some language difficulties ; but we discovered that these people were all of either Turkish or Russian racial origin, except for the seven Korean political prisoners and a French-Korean woman and her son.

Madame Simone Hoang, the French-Korean, was born and reared in Paris. As a young girl she had been betrothed by her parents to a Korean scholar many years older than herself, and had come out to Korea to marry him. Their son, Man Seng, was at this time nine or ten years old. The Reds found and arrested the wife and son while searching for the husband, who was a marked man for his "reactionary" views. Madame Hoang still does not know what his fate has been.

The men in the Turkish or Russian groups were either traders in Seoul or employees of the American Mission in Korea, known as AMIK. Each of the two groups includes a married couple with their families. The Turkish people are all with us as I write, but four elderly members of the Russian group have not survived.

The full list of names is as follows. *White Russians:* Madame Funderat, a widow ; Ivan Kilin, with his wife, Marusya, their daughter Olga (eight years old at this point of my story), and their sons Nicolai (six) and Gorgi (two) ; Ivan Nicolai Tihinoff ; Dimitri Verosiff ; Ilian Kijikoff ; . . . ? Leonoff ; . . . ? Smirnoff. *Turks:* Salim Salahudtin, with his wife, Faiza, their daughter Sagida (seventeen), and their sons Sagid (eighteen), Farid (thirteen), Shaucat (nine), Morat (six) and Hamid (one) ; Sultan Ahmet and Sophia Ahmet, who were brother and sister to Mrs. Faiza Salahudtin. I have already mentioned Maisara Daulatsch, who was also Turkish, but had been with our party since Seoul. She usually went by the English name of " Mary."

* * *

About dusk we were rounded up and put aboard a train. The diplomats and the two journalists were taken to a carriage by themselves. The rest of us were crowded into two compartments of another carriage, women and children in one section, men in the other.

Of our carriage, Virgil might have just said : "*Fuit.*" And he would have been right. A "has-been" it certainly was. To mention only two major defects, it had been stripped of all seating, and its windows were gaping, glassless holes. These latter we sealed up as best we could with some plywood the guards found for us.

The blankets we had turned in at the schoolhouse were now handed into the carriage for redistribution, a procedure of which at least one member took a dim view. Only a few days before, by special permission of the guard, he had laundered his blanket in the water-logged air-raid trench with expense of energy, patience, and precious soap. Now he got back an unknown, unwashed blanket.

Next we were fed. Baskets of rice-balls were brought along, warm, clean balls of white rice, and plenty of them too. They tasted like manna from heaven. Then came a bucket of gravy-like liquid in which potatoes swam. One had to make a quick decision on the proper etiquette for this course. No utensils were provided. One could dip into the mixture one's rice-ball of the moment, or use one's cupped hand as a ladle, or let the bucket pass by. Most of us adopted plan one or plan two, and found the anonymous mixture delicious.

Presently we heard the tramp, tramp, tramp of many feet. It was now nearly dark, but we could make out a long column of marching figures approaching. As the first of them came abreast of our carriage and were recognized as American prisoners of war, the end of the column was still out of sight in the gloom. On and on they came. We were touched with sadness, even with anguish, at the sight of these young men filing wearily along, some bare-footed, most bare-headed, all in light summer uniforms still. We watched the last of them pass along the platform to carriages ahead.

Soon afterwards came a jolt as a locomotive was attached to the train. The mustering of our flock was complete. Now it was time for the droving. But whither ?

That question had been haunting us ever since word came to leave the schoolhouse. It was almost certain that we would be taken north, but a faint hope remained that there might be a pleasant surprise in store for us. As our train pulled away from the station, the faint hope died. We were travelling north. The only question left now was which of the northward lines we would follow. We waited for the first fork, which was two or three miles out of the town. There, one line went north-west, to arrive ultimately at Sinwiju at the mouth of the Yalu River, where a bridge carries the railway across to Antung in Manchuria. The other branch went north-east and forked again some thirty miles further on at Sunchon.

As we clattered through the first junction, we knew that we were not bound north-west for Sinwiju, but north-east for Sunchon. Speculation moved a step further. Where would we go from Sunchon? From there one line continued north-east, to meet the Yalu River eventually at the frontier town of Manpo-jin. Another went east, and branched later to several places, of which the most important was the east coast city of Wonsan. We thought it more likely that we would take the northward Manpo line rather than turn east, since our captors' idea in moving us from Pyongyang must be to put us well out of reach of any United Nations advance from the south.

Not many miles from Pyongyang, Monsignor Byrne and Father Booth pointed out the silhouette of a large building which had formerly been Maryknoll's Korean headquarters. Their tones were wistful as they talked. They had once lived there.

Soon the train came to a halt, and the engine was uncoupled and driven away. It was needed elsewhere, we were told, and our train would not be moving again till tomorrow.

When we attempted to settle down for the night we found it was impossible for all to lie down in the crowded compartment. Commissioner Lord, as our interpreter and spokesman, pressed the guard to find accommodation for some of us elsewhere on the train. The guard thought the request unreasonable, and when Commissioner Lord persisted he sent for an officer to deal with the rebel. The officer replied to the Commissioner's renewed protest by threatening him with a pistol. The Commissioner would not be quelled, and the situation now looked grim.

This was one of two occasions on which I saw Commissioner Lord defy the threat of a levelled pistol. It takes a very brave man to do that. Theoretically, I suppose, there is about one chance in a hundred

that an unarmed and helpless person will be shot down by another
when there is no important issue at stake. But a man has only one
life to gamble with, and theoretical considerations are no great comfort when he faces another who may, for all he knows, be just that
hundredth individual who will answer defiance with cold-blooded
murder. As a matter of fact, we *were* to meet such a man in due
course. Not even Commissioner Lord would be able to defy " The
Tiger," and live ; and fortunately he would realize it.

On this occasion, however, both his courage and his judgement
were vindicated. With a little face-saving all round, the officer
abandoned his threatening attitude and even promised to see what he
could do to meet the Commissioner's demand. We were so greatly
relieved for out spokesman's sake that we regarded it as a very minor
matter when the officer's promise went unfulfilled.

Once again we tried to get settled for the night. We found that
most of the group could lie down if a few stayed sitting up. Thus
we passed the uneasy night, our attempts at sleep hampered by the
stifling conditions and by the periodic din of trains roaring south on
the other track. On each night of our northward journey we heard
this evidence of large-scale traffic moving towards the battlefront.
The trains passing in the night were always long, and often had two
engines to haul them. They were composed chiefly of freight cars,
but often included some open trucks or flat cars carrying motor
lorries, tanks and artillery. On some nights they must have passed
us hourly.

At daylight the guards told us there would be no travel till evening,
and we must leave the train because of the danger of air attacks
during the day. If some of us were inclined to ridicule the suggestion, we found before the end of the day that the guards' fears were
justified.

The civilian prisoners were conducted from the train into a nearby
valley. We trudged along the hollow for some distance, till we were
told to climb the slope to one side and take shelter among the trees.
There we sat in free and easy groups, and received for a meal the
surplus of rice-balls left over from the previous evening. Later in
the day we were given another good meal.

This and similar daytime stops were afterwards referred to as
" the picnic days." After the life we had led in the schoolhouse

camp, where we were confined to our rooms and restricted in so many other ways, we found it a glorious relief to breathe the fresh country air, to feast our eyes on green wooded slopes and fertile valleys, to talk freely to any of our companions and to enjoy much better fare than we had known for many a day. It was rehabilitation into something like normal living.

The full enjoyment of our " picnic days " was marred, however, by the grim signs we got from time to time that the lot of the unfortunate POWs was very different from our own. Soon after we settled down that day upon the pleasant hillside, a long line of captive soldiers followed our path along the valley. We saw with misgivings how they moved with the slow deliberation of men trying to save a precious reserve of energy. Laboriously they climbed the opposite slope of the valley to find welcome rest among the trees.

We had seen them only dimly last night. Now we saw only too clearly how inadequate their clothing was for September in Korea. Some had acquired Korean quilted blankets, and wore them like shawls. It reminds me how intently we must have studied every detail, when I find I can still see in my mind's eye even the bulges at the lower edges of those quilts, where the cotton stuffing gathered as the wearers moved along. I can still picture, too, the unwashed, unshaven faces, so many of them emaciated and strained.

Last night, in the gloom, we could only guess at their numbers. Now we estimated that nearly seven hundred had filed into the valley below us. More had been left in the train : sick men and their orderlies. The whole party, as I found when I inquired at the first opportunity, numbered seven hundred and twenty-six when it left Pyongyang in September of 1950. Another thirty or so joined them towards the end of that year. Twelve months after that, when we had our latest contact with them, only two hundred and ninety-two were still living.

It is tragic enough that young lives should have to be sacrificed in actual war. It is even more tragic that others should afterwards be lost when they could have been saved. Some, it must in fairness be said, died because they lost the will to live, or because they lacked the character or the training needed for survival under the conditions they encountered as prisoners. They were the exceptions. Others, not a few, owed their deaths directly or indirectly to the brutality or stupidity of individual guards. The majority died because of the general callousness of a régime that was loth to forgo as much as one truckload of weapons of death to provide the minimum of food and the few simple drugs that would have saved them.

That same morning, while we were still watching the main body settling down on the slope opposite ours, we saw for the first time a sight that was to become all too familiar in the days to come. Another procession was entering the valley in the wake of the one we had just observed, a slower and much smaller procession. Four POWs were carrying in a blanket the dead body of a comrade. We watched them lay the body down and dig a grave. Then a tall, fair-haired sergeant came across the valley and up the slope to where we were gathered.

"This lad we are burying was a Catholic," he told us, "and we heard there were some Catholic priests among you. Maybe one would come and recite the funeral service."

It was agreed that Monsignor Quinlan should go, but then the guard refused permission.

"We don't believe in such things," he said contemptuously. "It's not necessary for anyone to go."

The Monsignor and the American sergeant insisted on being allowed to speak to the Korean colonel who was in command of the entire group of prisoners. To the credit of this officer, who was a fluent Russian speaker and presumably a confirmed Red, I put it on record that he gave a sympathetic hearing to the Monsignor's appeal, and granted him permission to go with the sergeant and perform the last rites for the dead soldier.

Late in the afternoon the roar of approaching planes came to us over the mountains, then the crackle of their guns. The next thing we knew, half a dozen planes came screaming into our valley, so low that we caught glimpses of the pilots. They swept on in the direction of our train, and again we heard their fire. It was a startling incident to us sitting there on the hillside, and some moments passed before we began to talk again.

In the evening we went back to the train, and saw bullet holes in some of the carriages, including those occupied by the sick POWs. Fortunately the bullets had entered the carriages too high to cause any casualties among the men lying on the floor.

We travelled a short distance during that night on September 6–7, and at daylight were again evacuated from the train. We were taken as before into a nearby valley, but in this one there was a number of houses, and we were billeted with their occupants for the day. We found our hosts very kind, and as friendly as they dare to show themselves towards people who were in disfavour with their Red masters.

The rest of our northward progress followed much the same pattern as in those first two days. Each night our train moved on another stage. Each day we sheltered on wooded hills or in the cabins of the country folk, except for one day when we stopped at a town and were accommodated in a school building.

On a couple of occasions pigs were purchased from local people by the colonel, and were slaughtered and cooked there and then. For us civilians this was the first meat we had tasted in weeks. The POWs, as we learned in the course of our occasional contacts with them then and later, had received during their time in Pyongyang better fare than we did at the schoolhouse.

Their reports of earlier experiences were not so pleasant. Most of them had grim memories of their capture and of the period immediately following it. Many had seen helpless men mowed down, and not a few had faced the threat of a firing squad themselves. Moreover, not everything about their imprisonment in Pyongyang was as good as the food. They told us, for instance, that the officers were given the alternative of signing and broadcasting statements that suited the Reds, or being shot. The position was not put to them like that in so many words, but it was made abundantly clear that it amounted to that.

The officers took counsel together, and decided that by limited acquiescence with the Red demands they would save not merely their own lives but probably many others as well. By broadcasting messages they would also be able to publish the names of some prisoners. They trusted America to realize that their statements had been made under threat of death to themselves and their men, and to interpret the messages accordingly. It was a reasonable confidence to place in their country, and I hope to learn, if I am ever released, that it did not prove ill-founded.

Our route, as we had anticipated, was northwards by the Manpo line. From the night that we passed through Sunchon without branching on to the eastern line, the only speculation left to us was whether we would be taken all or only part of the way to Manpo. Rumour had it that if we did not go to Manpo, the frontier town, we would go at least to Kangyi, sixty miles from the border.

During the night of September 10–11 we travelled farther and faster than usual. This must have been a bad night for the POWs, whose carriages had by this time been replaced by flat cars. As I thought of them being rushed through the bitter night air, huddled in their thin summer clothing on cars that gave no shelter, our dilapidated carriage, comfortless and draughty as it was, gave me a sense of undue privilege. In the early hours of the morning we pulled into Kangyi. The train halted, and we wondered if our long rail journey was over at last. But soon we were under way again. At last we knew that Manpo was our goal.

Korea is slightly smaller in area than Great Britain. It has been said, however, that if Korea were rolled out flat it would cover the globe, and my journey from Pyongyang to Manpo made me ready to believe it. Nowhere in Korea will you find a plain that extends to the horizon on every side ; always there are mountains to be seen, near or far, on a clear day. But from Pyongyang north to the Yalu, there seemed to be no plains at all ; nothing but mountains and valleys succeeding each other like the waves and troughs of a heavy sea.

Our train squirmed and panted through the early morning on the last stage of its journey, snaking around and between the tumbled hills, seeking an approach to Manpo, and finding at last a valley that gave entrance from the east.

It was daylight when we got our first glimpse of the frontier town and the broad stripe of silver just beyond, where the Yalu River sweeps swiftly by on its long journey towards the Yellow Sea, goaded and hustled by countless streams that rain and springs and melted snow send streaking down to join it from the hills on either side. Away north, as far as the eye could see, stretched the rippling, rolling sea of Manchuria's mountains.

History has made Manpo a double town. Half of it nestles on the very bank of the Yalu, and dates back to ancient times. Most of the houses and buildings in that part of the town are Korean-style. A

little downstream and back some little distance from the river, the
new Manpo stands on a higher level, built in stucco and brick by the
Japanese.   Here were administrative buildings, residential quarters
for officials, a penitentiary, and the railway station to which our
train now made its way.

We all left the train, and the POWs formed up and marched away
in the direction of the old town.   Two trucks came to collect the
civilians, and we soon overtook and passed the slowly-moving
column. After half a mile we branched left off the main road to enter
the old town.   At the junction stood a tall monument commemorat-
ing the liberation of Korea from Japanese domination.   The effect
was rather spoiled by the large red star that crowned this memorial
to freedom.

We drew up at a large building, but guards came out to say that
only POWs were to be accommodated here.   Civilians were to go
to a different place.   Back we went, passing the weary POWs once
more, to our starting point by the railway station, and from there
took a road that ran westward along the river.   Two miles down
this road a group of buildings showed up on the left.   Here at last
were our quarters.   Our journey from Pyongyang had occupied
five days.

7

Autumn by the Yalu

OUR new quarters were a relic from the days when Japan controlled Korea but had not yet extended her empire to Manchuria. They had served as quarantine station for immigrants arriving from Manchuria at the frontier town of Manpo.

Four buildings were disposed around a large yard. Two of them—long, low structures built parallel and close together—stood out to the left as one entered the compound from the road. Straight ahead was a small building which had been the quarantine hospital. To the right stood the fourth building, which we took to have been the residence of the officials. It was now to serve a similar purpose, for our guards would live there. In the same building were quartered also the six diplomats, the two journalists, and the seven Korean politicians.

The rest of us were taken to the two long buildings on the left, which seemed to have been designed for the accommodation of detained immigrants. Each was partitioned into a number of rooms, all opening on to the narrow lane that separated the two structures. The women and children and elderly men were assigned to one of the buildings, the rest of the men to the other.

In our building the accommodation was eight to a room, and each room had four beds—solid wooden affairs set in the corners—so we slept in pairs. Thus, in the room to which I was assigned, Monsignor Quinlan and I shared one of the beds; Father Canavan and Sagid Salahudtin shared another; Walter Eltringham and Louis Dans the third; and William Evans and Alfred Matti the fourth. Later M. Matti became ill and was moved to another room.

Some of these room-mates I have already introduced. Of the others, Sagid and Dans are with us still, but to Eltringham and Evans we have bid the long farewell.

Sagid is a pleasant, helpful sort of lad. He has solemn brown eyes and a dark, longish face, a goodly nose and wide, generous mouth. He was born and reared in Korea, and was eighteen years old when he joined us in 1950. At that time he spoke English fairly well. He has been an industrious student, making use of his captivity during the past two years to improve his English, and to find among his fellow-prisoners instructors in science and mathematics.

Louis Dans—" Danny " to his friends—is a short, stocky, muscular American. It did not surprise me to learn, when I met him in 1950, that he had once been a professional acrobat. It did surprise me, however, to learn that he was then as old as thirty-seven.

His youthful appearance was even more remarkable when one heard the story of his career, which had taken him all over his home-land, then to Japan and finally to Korea, and had left him with first-hand knowledge of a wide variety of occupations. " Danny " is indeed a rolling stone that has gathered no moss. He went to Japan as lieutenant in the United States Army, and ran hotels for the Special Service section ; then he transferred to ECA, which sent him to manage a hotel in Seoul ; finally he resigned from ECA to work in the Traders' Exchange in Seoul, and was a sub-manager there when the invasion began. He was arrested with Walter Eltringham at a hotel in Seoul, and both were brutally beaten up by their captors.

" Danny " has revealed himself in camp as an accomplished enter-tainer with a good singing voice and an extensive repertoire, and can always be relied upon to keep a concert alive.

Bill Evans was fifty years old when I made his acquaintance, but he did not look his age until, in the ensuing months, he grew a beard. He inherited a tall figure from his father, who was an American doctor, and slightly Oriental features from his Eurasian mother. He was born and reared in Japan, and spoke Japanese fluently in addition to English and French. By profession he was a mining engineer, but he had a wide experience of other occupations, as you learned when he reminisced in his slow, hesitant way.

As a young man he was keenly interested in aviation, and he told us how he had helped Clyde Pangborn and Hough Herndon make preparations for their historic Pacific flight. Herndon, discarding superfluous gear as he sat in the cockpit before take-off, handed Bill Evans a belt. Bill was still wearing it when we met him in intern-ment.

In October, 1951, the mortal remains of Fathers Collier and Reilly, two Irish Columban missionaries who were killed in the early weeks of the war, were re-interred in the grounds of Chunchon cathedral.

This was his second internment in Korea. The first was under the
Japanese in World War II, and Bill kept us entertained for the best
part of three days with his slow-spoken account of that former
captivity.

Walter Eltringham was a native of Pennsylvania, and, like Bill
Evans, was a mining engineer. He was a specialist in safety measures
in coal-mines, and possessed not only a thorough knowledge of his
job, but the ability also to give a most interesting account of it. ECA
had brought him to Korea to help in the rehabilitation of the coal-
mining industry. His headquarters were in Seoul, but his work took
him to every part of South Korea where there were coal-mines, and
he was on the east coast when war broke out. He drove back to
Seoul, to find that the destruction of the bridge over the Han River
had cut off the possibility of escape to the south. At his hotel he met
Louis Dans, and the two remained together till the Reds arrested
them.

Walter's big and burly appearance was in accord with his direct-
ness and force of his personality. He was a classic example of the
" rough diamond." The surface roughness was apparent, but to
some of us who had a better opportunity of knowing Walter
intimately, the diamond core shone through. We discovered that
he sent his precious sugar ration to the sick Sisters, and, when he knew
we had found him out, he gruffly protested that he couldn't eat it.
Put in charge of water-carrying, he would rather overwork himself
than press others to do their share.

We were cheered with many a turn of Walter's laconic wit. He
could put the most unusual situation in a nutshell with one cryptic
comment. It is now two years since he left us, and we are still using
phrases he coined.

★   ★   ★

The Panjandrum had told us that quarters were being prepared
for us in the mountain country. They had proved to be in mountain
country indeed, but we could see no sign that any effort had been
made to prepare them for our coming. Our building, and the other
to which the women and children and older men were assigned,
were dilapidated and dirty. However, when we got settled in and
arranged ourselves, we found the accommodation was not too bad.

The other building had at one end a Korean-style kitchen. This meant that the occupants of the remaining rooms in that building had the benefit of a primitive form of central heating which is common in Korean houses. The principle of it is that the earthen floor of the kitchen is sunk a foot or more below ground level, so that the flue from the fire can be led beneath the stone-and-clay floors of the other rooms to a chimney at the far end of the building. In this way the bedrooms pick up some heat from the smoke and gases passing beneath them. The effect is quite good in the room next to the kitchen, but diminishes of course for each succeeding room. In the allotment of rooms, the short straw was drawn by the seven nuns and the two Martel ladies ; but even in their end room they got some comfort from the fire.

This *ondol* heating system was in full blast quite soon after we arrived, for one of our first steps was to draw up a roster of cooking teams and send the first of them into action right away to get a fire going in the kitchen. We had been told we must do our own cooking from now on, and the raw material for our first meal came by cart from the town shortly after our arrival at the camp.

The Manpo prison was responsible for our food supplies, and we had no cause to complain about either the quantity or quality. This first consignment consisted of rice, Chinese cabbages, turnips, leeks, dried fish, salt, red pepper, soya bean paste and a drum of oil. Thereafter we were kept well supplied with these commodities, and Monsignor Quinlan, who was appointed quartermaster, was always able to distribute a generous daily allowance. Rice in plenty, dried fish reconstituted in water, and vegetable soup rich with oil may not seem an exciting menu to people used to Western fare, but to us it was luxury after our six weeks of semi-starvation in the schoolhouse near Pyongyang. In addition, we got occasional issues of meat and sugar, and sometimes even soap and tobacco.

If we were grateful for the supplies that came from the Manpo prison, we were not at all so happy about an attempt some of its personnel made to give us prison discipline as well. Our guards at this time were army men, but some penitentiary officers and warders came to inspect the camp, and seemed anxious either to take over from our army guards altogether, or at least to tell them how we should be guarded. They announced a whole set of absurd regulations, including a ban on communication between the men and women internees. This was too much for Commissioner Lord, who got himself threatened once more with a pistol for insisting that our party included members of families, and fellow-members of religious organizations, who had a perfect right to associate together, and stating flatly that we were not prepared to obey any regulations to the contrary. His judgement that there was a bluff to be called proved sound. Our visitors' threats evaporated in mutterings to the effect that they would see about this. They departed on that note, and never returned. We heard no more about their regulations.

I am reminded by this incident to mention that we have often been puzzled, at different stages of our internment, to know which service—the Army, the Police Force, or the Penal Department— was the arbiter for the time being of our fortunes. It would appear that these three services are not really distinct in North Korea, but are merely different departments of " the People's Army." At least that is the view taken by the men themselves. Policemen and prison warders, as well as soldiers, speak of themselves as members of the People's Army, and I have learnt from conversation with our guards that conscripts can be assigned to any of these three spheres of duty. Moreover, it seems that they can be transferred at any time from one to another as occasion requires, and we have observed for ourselves that men are often switched from regular police duties to the work of guarding prisoners, and vice versa.

All three services use military ranking and insignia, but with some variety in colours. Red seems to be characteristic of the military forces, green of the police, blue of penitentiary personnel. But then I have occasionally seen military officers with green or blue epaulettes, and police officers with red. And I have spoken with guards who had never associated a particular colour with a particular service at all.

At this point in my story I had already experienced the attentions of each of the three services more than once. From the time of my arrest I had been in the hands of policemen till I was lodged in the Chunchon jail. There I saw for the first time the blue epaulettes of the penitentiary service. Military guards escorted Monsignor Quinlan, Father Canavan and myself to Seoul, where policemen again took charge. In Pyongyang, our warders were still policemen, but the outside sentries were army men. On the journey to Manpo we were in sole charge of the military. Now, in our camp outside

Manpo, we still had army guards, with penitentiary men trying to exercise authority over us.

The officer who had become responsible for us from the time of our arrival in Manpo wore the red epaulettes of the army. He was, I think, a colonel ; but for some reason he was dubbed " The Major " early in our acquaintance, and the title was never revised. He remained in charge of both us and the POW for seven weeks. During those weeks we made several changes of residence, but The Major kept in touch with us wherever we were, and made personal visits from time to time.

If the penitentiary personnel whose unpleasantness I have mentioned took their case higher, it was probably The Major who saved us from their further attentions. That would have been in accord with the justice and humanity which we were to find characteristic of all his dealings with us.

No doubt The Major was also responsible for the fine food supplies that continued to arrive from the Manpo prison. Unfortunately our facilities for turning these excellent raw materials into meals were not nearly so fine.

Picture a room with rough mud walls, earthen floor a foot below ground level, ill-fitting doors and no window, a ceiling black with the soot of decades. Your " range " is a low platform of stone and clay, on which you set your cooking pots of thin cast iron. A cavity beneath is your doorless, grateless firebox. The firewood burns reluctantly and smokily because it is half green. You fan and puff and bully it into flame. If the wind is favourable the smoke goes its appointed way beneath the bedroom floors, to escape by the distant chimney ; if not, your kitchen is blue with acrid fumes that sting your eyes and sear your lungs.

To prepare food for the pot you have two or three large, shallow wooden bowls, a couple of smaller ones of earthenware, and a crude knife. To supplement these utensils you can improvise others yourself : wooden paddles for stirring, ladles for soup, cutting boards, pot scrapers, extra knives, and so on. There is a bucket for carrying water from a well outside the compound, and a large vessel in the kitchen is the storage tank.

It was in the autumn that we came to Manpo, so it was only in later camps we were to know the sorrows of winter and summer cooking. In summer the Korean kitchen is oppressively hot, and swarms with flies. In winter it is almost unbearably cold. Your hands quickly become numbed, and for culinary tasks you cannot wear gloves. In the coldest spells a dense vapour forms whenever you bring a pot to the boil, and you stumble about with visibility reduced to a couple of feet. In the morning vegetables are frozen hard, and chopping them is like breaking stones. The water supply has turned to solid ice, from which you must carve out some chunks with an axe, and melt them in a pot. If you have been foolish enough to leave washed rice standing overnight, you are confronted with a congealed mass which may take an hour's heating to thaw out. All the chores take longer, and usually you must begin and end them in the dark, for daylight is shortened, and often there is no artificial light. And woe betide you if any water is spilt on the floor or steps : it soon becomes a sheet of ice and a menace to limbs.

Perhaps I should explain my reference to " washed rice." Korean rice must always be washed before it is ready for the pot, for in the rough bags in which it comes there is also no small amount of sand and stones and straw. I had my washing lessons from an expert. As a miner, Bill Evans was versed in the art of " panning " the specks of gold from their enveloping clay and gravel. He showed me how to pan sand and stone and straw from rice. You need two large shallow vessels. Put the rice in one, and then add water to it. Break down the lumps to form a fluid mixture, and sluice it thoroughly around in the vessel. Then let the mixture settle. Stones and sand will sink to the bottom, and so, given time, will the rice. The lighter straw will be left floating on top, and you carefully decant it. Add water again, and stir up the mixture as before. This time pour off into your second vessel as much of the rice as you can before it has time to settle, leaving behind as much as you can of the heavier sand and gravel. Empty the residue from vessel number one. Add water to vessel number two and repeat the process. Keep at it, back and forth, until you hope there is only rice left. If you are wrong, you will hear about it at meal-time.

I may never have the opportunity of sharing my knowledge of this subject with an Association of Housewives, or even contributing it to a ladies' journal. But it will be a pity ; for, say what you like about " panning " rice, the Koreans know something about cooking it. Here is the recipe. First add water till a hand laid flat on the rice is just submerged. Cover the pot. Now some fire, quickly! Bring the pot rapidly to the boil and keep it boiling vigorously till the water is nearly gone. If you have put in too much water your rice will be damp and mushy ; if too little, it won't be sufficiently cooked. If the fire was poor, and the pot came too slowly to the boil, or went off the boil again, then the rice will be badly cooked. If the fire was too hot, the rice will be burnt. If you have avoided all the pit-falls you have produced a dish that is not to be despised.

But, even with rice abounding, Western palates hunger after bread. We almost got that, too, in this camp. We did not receive the supplies of flour that were promised, but we heard that the POWs were building ovens and that they would supply us with bread. As events turned out, we all got orders to leave Manpo on the very next day after they produced their first batch of bread. We were able, however, to sample their product while we waited for transport by the river.

We had news of the POWs' fortunes from time to time. We failed when we tried to get permission to visit them as chaplains, but sometimes a couple of them helped to deliver our supplies. There was a Korean doctor, too, who attended to their sick, and came twice a week to visit ours. He impressed us as a kindly man, devoted to his work of mercy, and we believed him when he told us they were faring well. It was by his efforts that we received a stock of common drugs, the first and last issue of medical supplies our captors gave us.

We had among our own ranks an accomplished medical man in Dr. Kisch, and two trained nurses in Mother Eugénie and Miss Helen Rosser ; but hitherto their efforts to help our sick had been gravely hampered by the lack of even the simplest medical supplies. Now Dr. Kisch could hold a regular daily clinic, with Miss Rosser for assistant. Our second nurse, Mother Eugénie, had her hands full caring for the other nuns and the old French priests. Three of the nuns had become seriously ill : Mother Béatrix, Mother Mechtilde and Mother Thérèse. The first two recovered to some extent before we left this camp, but Mother Thérèse remained chronically ill.

*   *   *

Every afternoon about four o'clock a bald, bespectacled little man

appeared at the door of an unoccupied room, and called in a high-
pitched voice: "Clinic time!" Ernst Kisch, M.D., late of Vienna,
was ready to see patients.

The children in our camp had precious few distractions, but this
daily announcement was one of them. They took up the cry "Clinic
time!" and soon became so perfect in their mimicry that the doctor
seemed to be repeating himself.

Dr. Kisch was Jewish by race and Austrian by birth. It was Walter
Eltringham, of all people, who told him very early in their acquaintance: "You have no bedside manner." The doctor, for his part,
had no word for Walter but one: "Terrible!"

In a way, their mutual impressions were mostly right. If you did
not know Walter, his giant form and his gruffness would scare you.
Dr. Kisch was a peppery little man, and a bedside manner would
have choked him. And each, in his way, was a great man.

Ernst Kisch might have been a world-famous figure, were it not
for the extraordinary series of adversities that dogged his career. He
passed brilliantly through the medical schools of his native Vienna
in the days when those schools drew students from all over the world.
While still a young interne, he made the first identification of a
disease which makes war on the corpuscles of the blood, and which
had till then remained mysterious. The scepticism of one of his
professors towards youthful learning delayed the publication of his
thesis. Meanwhile a German professor made and announced the same
discovery, and the disease was called by his name. The name of
Ernst Kisch remained unknown in the world of medicine.

He passed on to private practice and acquired a large clientele.
His success brought wealth and comfort, and leisure to enjoy them.
He had a select circle of friends, a fine home, a car, a grand piano.
This last was perhaps his most treasured possession. A true Viennese,
he loved music, and was himself an accomplished pianist. For years
he would not let a week pass without visiting the Vienna Opera
House, and he was familiar with every opera worth knowing. He
could tell the story, recite the German words, and hum the melodies.
He often entertained a group of us with recitals of this kind as we lay
in the dark on long winter evenings. On these occasions he was
transported back in memory to the old Vienna he loved so well, the
Vienna that was then still basking in the sunshine of royal patronage.

But those excursions left him sad and wistful, reminding him not merely of his happiness, but also of the bitterness of its shattering.

Hitler launched his campaign against the Jews. Dr. Kisch was herded into a concentration camp. His near relations and many of his friends perished. At length, from imprisonment he went into exile, carrying in a suitcase all that was left of his possessions. He found a post in a Methodist Mission hospital in Shanghai, and stayed there for ten years. Forced to leave then, he went to the United States and worked for a few months in a New York hospital, but found he could not remain in the country. He was offered work in the American Methodist Mission hospital in Kaesong, and had been there only a few weeks when the Red invasion began. Kaesong fell in the first hours of the attack.

This genius of a man, exiled from his homeland as a Jew, forced to leave China by the Communist invasion, denied permanent asylum in America, arrested with his American associates in Korea, was to end his life of disappointed hopes not many weeks after he called " Clinic time ! " for the last time in Manpo. We knew at least some of the bitterness he had tasted in life, and there was fervour in our prayer when the time came to lay his tired, worn body down : " Eternal rest grant unto him, O Lord, and let perpetual light shine upon him."

*   *   *

Dr. Kisch's clinical assistant, Helen Rosser, was an American from the State of Georgia. She had begun her work as a Methodist missionary in Korea some thirty years before. Impressed with the importance of supplementing the work of her organization with a medical service, she went back to America to study nursing, and returned to Korea as a qualified nurse and a specialist in public health. Her great ambition was to have a mobile dispensary. The equipment did arrive at her mission station in Kaesong, but the Reds came before she could put it on the road.

Miss Rosser has been prodigal of her services on behalf of her fellow-internees, both as a nurse and in the work of the kitchen. In both spheres she has supplemented her skill with a gift for improvisation. In the medical field, I remember with gratitude how she operated expertly with a pocket-knife on a troublesome swelling

that developed on my neck. I remember, too, an effective salve
she made with resin from the pines.

*   *   *

I have described the season we spent in this camp as autumn—and,
according to the calendar, so it was ; but it would give a better notion
of it to say that we had summer days and winter nights. Walter
Eltringham made a pronouncement one morning at daylight :
" When I get out of here I'm going to write a book about the place."
After a pause, he added : "And the title will be *The Summer that
We Wintered on the Yalu.*" In a wakeful moment during that night,
I had seen him—as I saw him on many another night—sitting huddled
on his bed with his blanket around his shoulders, smoking a cigarette,
too chilled to sleep. Walter felt the cold more than most of us, but
all the occupants of our unheated building found it severe. From
our first night in this camp we began appealing for warm clothes and
more blankets. We were assured, for a good many days, that they
would arrive on the morrow. At last some bundles of cotton-padded
jackets and trousers did arrive. There were not enough trousers to
go round, but everyone got a jacket. The clothes were very dirty,
rather old, and in need of repairs ; but we beggars could not be
choosers, and were glad of what we got.

The bitter cold would set in soon after sunset, but the days were
usually sunny and warm, often warm enough for swimming and
sunbathing. And these delights were not denied us. Nearly every
day there was an excursion to the nearby Yalu River. All who
wished to go would assemble, and a guard would escort us half a
mile down the road, and then through fields and gardens to the
water's edge. There we could launder our clothes, bathe, and bask
in the sunshine. Those hours by the river were among the most
pleasant we had during our time at this camp.

The enjoyment we got from these excursions was used to black-
mail me into parting with my wristlet watch. The villain of the
piece was a guard we christened " Willie the Watch." Some of the
party had been deprived of all valuables at the time of arrest, but
others had been allowed to retain what they carried on their persons.
Hence a few of us still had watches. This seemed to Willie an over-
sight that called for remedy, so he set about buying up the internees'

watches—but at his price. One day he noticed mine. How much did I want for it? I named a stiff amount, for I had no desire to sell. He expected a bargaining session, and fired the first shot by halving my price ; but I declined to return his fire. Suddenly our excursions to the river stopped, allegedly because of the bad conduct of the prisoners. In due course Willie dropped a hint that our misdemeanours could be overlooked if my watch were for sale at a reasonable price. I let him have it. Next day we basked on the banks of the Yalu once again.

Twice during our stay in this camp the guards organized concerts. The first was well attended, and a good number of the internees obliged with items. The second did not go so well, owing to the fact that one of the guards had imbibed a little too freely, and, after rendering an alcoholic ditty or two, began to act as M.C. When it became apparent that this was to be a command performance, a spirit of non-co-operation developed. In the tense atmosphere some remark was made by Dr. Jensen, who at this particular period had a strange facility for getting into scrapes, though habitually he was a patient man and a peacemaker. The M.C. was annoyed at the remark, and forthwith reverted to his role as guard. Dr. Jensen was marched off, with a tommy-gun poked into his ribs, to receive a severe if bibulous scolding.

*   *   *

The Reverend A. Kris Jensen, D.D., who by now was " Kris " to most of us, had come a long way since he landed, nearly thirty-seven years before, in New York as an immigrant from his native Denmark. He was a penniless lad then, of seventeen years, with little knowledge of English, no job in prospect, and no home to go to. His only resources were his enterprise and industry, his grit and perseverance : and these he had in plenty. Soon he had made and saved enough money to give himself a college education. Then he decided he would become a Methodist preacher, and proceeded to qualify himself for this office. His next ambition was to be a missionary, and he attained it in 1927 with an appointment to Korea.

In June of 1950, having spent the intervening years at mission stations in various parts of the country, he was living with his wife

at the Methodist Mission in Seoul. Their two children were attending college in the United States. On June 24 Dr. Jensen decided to
pay a visit to the Methodist Mission in Kaesong. Some of the
Kaesong staff were going back that day after attending a wedding of
fellow-missionaries in Seoul, and Dr. Jensen went with them. None
of them had any notion that invasion was imminent. The following
morning the war closed around them in Kaesong.

Kris is a big, hearty man, hard-headed but soft-hearted, ready to
help anyone at any time. The longer I have known him, the deeper
has grown my appreciation of the rare nobility of his character. His
greatest qualities might, on casual acquaintance, pass unnoticed : a
great generosity that is never ostentatious, a well-nigh inexhaustible
fund of patience, an unfailing capacity to forgive.

*   *   *

On a day towards the end of September, sounds of excitement
in the yard brought me out, to find that another prisoner had arrived
—the seventy-year-old, grey-bearded Paris Foreign Missionary,
Father Joseph Cadars. He had been arrested in the latter half of
July when the Reds entered Taejon, ninety miles south of Seoul.
On the long journey up from Taejon, through Seoul and Pyongyang,
to Manpo, he had been given little food, little rest, and no comfort.
When his French confrères and the rest of us came tumbling out of
our rooms to welcome him, tears streamed down his tanned old
cheeks. Someone hastened to bring him a tray of food, and he
soon recovered the sturdy cheeriness that we were to know in the
days to come as his characteristic mood. Even when he first walked
into the camp, weary and worn after his journey, one could not fail
to be struck by the soldierly bearing of his short stocky figure, and
we were not surprised when we learned that he had in fact been a
soldier. An eye injury had disfigured his face, but could not destroy
his kindly and fatherly expression.

Joseph Cadars was born in 1879 in the department of Tarn-et-
Garonne in south-west France, and was a novice with the Franciscans
when the religious orders were expelled from France at the beginning
of the century. He declined to leave France, and entered the University of Clermont. After his ordination for his native diocese
Father Cadars became a professor in a college. He resigned to join

the Paris Foreign Missions, and was sent to Taikou, Korea. Called to the colours when the first World War broke out, he became a lieutenant in the French Army in Indo-China. Near the end of the war, when French troops were being sent to Siberia, some of the soldiers asked Father Cadars to go along as their chaplain. He went, and when released returned to Korea. There he built up several parishes and erected churches in them during the years that followed. At the time war broke out, he was taking care of the monastery at Taejon in the absence of its French-Canadian community.

The tall guard who had come with Father Cadars as escort was an old acquaintance from our days in the schoolhouse near Pyongyang. The sight of him brought an unregenerate chuckle from Father Canavan. He was remembering a day when "Lofty" had come to our room to borrow Alfred Matti's safety razor, and had decided that he might as well take his shave in our room, too. Wasn't that bowl of warm water on the window-sill the very thing for his purpose? He borrowed soap and mirror, and set to.

Meantime Father Canavan was engrossed in a bridge hand he was playing. The bowl of hot water he had received with his dinner was cooling nicely by the window. It would be a pleasant refresher later in the afternoon. The business of the moment was to decide how best he could use his unsatisfactory ration of trumps. It was only by chance that he looked up and saw what was happening to his ration of water. The next thing Lofty knew, an empty bowl was planked down under his astonished nose, while a cascade of soapy water was still on its way to the ground outside, and an indignant little man went stamping back to his cards. For perhaps ten seconds Lofty was speechless. Then for fifteen minutes he was extremely speechful. The full effect of his rhetoric was dampened down before it reached the culprit (who was not well versed in Korean) in the slow, measured translation provided by Monsignor Quinlan. But even in the Monsignor's version it was an impressive piece of work.

★　　★　　★

By this time we were a miniature United Nations Organization. Father Cadars was to be the last addition to our company. His arrival brought our number to seventy-four. Soon, the hand of

Death was striking names from off that roll, but at this time we
represented more than a dozen different countries.

The U.N.O. itself, unless it has changed a lot since I had contact
with the world of freedom, does not enjoy the perfect unity its name
would promise. Neither have we been always a perfectly united
family, but considering the complex nature of our group, the un-
naturally close association forced upon us, the unnerving conditions
we have all endured, I think we have not done too badly.

Even under normal living conditions we would have had abundant
material for disagreements. We have no common language, no
common bond of religion or profession or education, no common
habits of life or even of thought. And our ages have covered all the
range from one to eighty-two. All these predisposing causes for
disharmony have been magnified by the abnormal living conditions
to which we have been subjected. Often we have been desperately
hungry, and hunger can play havoc with one's normal disposition.
Often, again, we have been desperately cold—sleepless with cold at
night, stupid with cold by day ; and hunger for warmth can be as
torturing as hunger for food. For many months, too, conditions
left us at the mercy of vermin ; and the unequal battle weakened us,
not merely in body, but even more seriously in morale. And, if it
ever happened that there was neither hunger nor cold nor heat nor
illness nor fatigue nor squalor to wear our nerves, we have then
had for irritants the dreary monotony, and the too close confinement
for too long with the same too familiar people, every one of whom
yearned as passionately as oneself for just one hour of solitude and
privacy, and was denied it.

Looking back over more than two years of this, it is a wonder to
me that nerves and tempers have not far more frequently been frayed.

If lack of seclusion tried us all, those who suffered most in this
respect must undoubtedly have been the seven nuns. Yet they set
us an outstanding example in adjustment to the new conditions, and
in making the best of them. In this they were following the wise
advice they had received from Bishop Byrne in the barracks at Seoul :
to face the fact that a difficult and uncertain future lay before them,
and to adjust themselves to their new life as best they could. They
had, he explained, no obligation to maintain their convent discipline
in circumstances for which it was never intended ; rather was it

their duty to take all possible means to prevent their physical and mental health from deteriorating under the unnatural strain they would now have to suffer. As one evident result of the Bishop's advice, they chattered away among themselves all day long. People began to ask us whether the Sisters, and particularly the Carmelites, were making up for lost time !

It was not so easy for our non-Catholic companions—even for some of the missionaries among them—to appreciate fully what it meant to the Sisters to have left the quiet, calm regularity of convent life for the mêlée of an internment camp where nobody knew what the next hour would bring ; to live under conditions that were sordid and disgusting even to those accustomed to rough and crude living ; to be interrogated time and again by officials for whom the most sacred ideals of the religious life were a target for ignorant mockery. Even those who tried hard to understand the Sisters' feelings could not always overcome a vague impression that they must have experienced some sense of release when they were dragged from their convents. These people did not easily realize that the emergence had meant for the nuns the shattering of a way of life which, for the love of God, they had freely chosen—which they had embraced with a deep sense of privilege, and in which they were supremely happy. Within their convent walls the long, quiet hours of prayer, the seclusion from the outside world and its often meaningless hustle and bustle, the calmly-planned concentration of their energies upon essential things, had given to their daily routine an abiding unity of purpose, and to their souls a sense of fulfilment and an ineffable peace. How painful, how frightening, how bewildering they must have found their present life ! If they adjusted themselves to it so well, it was because they had learnt during disciplined, prayerful years in the cloister to make the Will of God their only guide. Bishop Byrne had shown them what that Will was for them now, and their training had prepared them to accept it.

But if the kind of life the Sisters had formerly led has not been understood by all their fellow-internees, there has been general appreciation for the example they have given of patient, gracious, unselfish living in internment.

Sister Marie-Madeleine, the blind Carmelite, was already winning special admiration for the interest she took in the activities of the camp and in her fellow-prisoners, despite a disability that must have made this strange new life doubly bewildering for her. As she moved about the camp, leaning on the strong arm of her constant companion, Sister Bernadette, she was gradually becoming better known, and people marvelled at her ability to identify individuals by their voices, and to remember details about everyone with whom she spoke.

Another source of wonderment in the camp was the ability of the Sisters to conjure up a variety of useful articles: some, such as precious sewing materials, from their capacious pockets; others, like a couple of wash-bowls that appeared in their room about this time, from the thin air—so far as anybody but they and the good Lord knew.

The seven Sisters were, as I have mentioned, quartered at this time with Madame and Mademoiselle Martel. On Sunday mornings their room became a meeting place for the Catholic members of the camp, while the other Christians gathered for religious service in one of the men's rooms. Catholics constituted a third of the whole group. We used to recite the Rosary and sing hymns, using Latin as a common language.

At no time during our internment have we priests been allowed any facilities for celebrating Mass. In this the Reds have been less kind than the Japanese who interned us during World War II.

*   *   *

September passed into October. We were very hopeful of early release, for in this camp we managed to get news of the progress of the war, and the news was encouraging. We had two regular sources of information at this time, and the contrast between their offerings was interesting. One source was a notice-board outside the main gate where official North Korean bulletins were posted for the local people. The information we received from a second source, which must remain unnamed, was derived from a radio station in Japan, and represented the United Nations' version of events. Comparison of both releases made it clear that the U.N. forces were coming steadily northwards, though each advance was reported on the bulletin board several days after we heard of it from the other source, and was reported in quite different terms. Thus, a couple of days after we received the U.N. news of a landing at Inchon, the bulletin-board told us for the first time of the action, and described it as an attempted landing repulsed with heavy losses. Nevertheless, " strategic withdrawals" from Inchon by the North Korean forces were admitted in due course.

The United Nations news continued to reach us, and the North Korean news, duly interpreted, continued to give belated confirmation. After the Inchon landing came news of the capture of Seoul, of landings at Wonsan and at Chinnampo, of the fall of Pyongyang. Fascinated and overjoyed, we began excitedly to calculate how soon the U.N. advance would reach us at Manpo. We were confident that it could not be more than a matter of a few weeks at most. We took it for granted that our captors would keep us at Manpo till the United Nations troops arrived, for it seemed that the only way they could prevent our early liberation would be to take us across the Yalu to Chinese territory, and we reasoned that the Chinese would not want us on their hands.

But it was the Chinese who doomed our high hopes—and that in a manner that had never come into our speculations.

8

Down the River to Kosan

OCTOBER 6 TO 21, 1950

LATE on Friday, October 6, the guards came to tell us that we must be up early next morning. There would be news, they said.

We were dismayed. It looked as if we must be moving. If so, what of our rosy dreams of early rescue by United Nations troops ? It was inconceivable that we would be taken to meet them, and if we were not to be left here, as we had hoped, to await their arrival, then a move could only be for the purpose of taking us out of their reach. Were we then going across the Yalu after all ? We passed a restless night, wondering what the day would bring.

We were right about the imminence of a move, but not about the immediate reason for it. This was, as we deduced later, that the old quarantine station was needed for the accommodation of more important guests. When we passed it again a few weeks later, we saw that repairs had been made, chimneys added, woodwork painted. An expensive car was standing by the gate, and we saw two Europeans take cover behind it as we approached. One of them was recognized by the French consul, M. Perruche, as a former member of the Soviet embassy staff in Peking.

The POWs, too, were about to move from their quarters in Manpo town, though we did not know this yet. Later events led us to the conclusion that they, too, were evacuated to make room for more important guests, the Chinese troops arriving from Manchuria.

None of this we knew on the morning of Saturday, October 7, but we did learn definitely, after breakfast, that we were to move. We were ordered to betake ourselves, with our blankets and our food supplies and cooking utensils, to a point on the river bank a couple of miles upstream, not far short of Manpo itself. We made our

113

preparations in no cheerful mood, for it seemed now that we must be going across the river. If so, even the complete liberation of Korea by U.N. forces would not bring freedom to us. To add to our depression we found that no transport was to be provided for the journey to the assembly point upstream. We went through the routine of protesting and arguing with the guards, but, as usual, they won. Words are no match for guns.

Several of our party were in poor shape for walking, but they all managed the two-mile journey on foot, except Mother Thérèse, who was gravely ill and had to be carried on a stretcher. The supplies and cooking pots were transported by the able-bodied men, working usually in pairs with a load slung on a pole between them. It was necessary for some of us to make more than one trip.

At last we were all assembled on the river-bank with our goods and chattels piled up about us. By this time news had leaked out that our destination was not the other bank. We were to go downstream in boats. The boats, however, had not yet appeared. We waited miserably in rain and icy wind, and eventually took shelter under a bridge which spanned a creek nearby.

Mother Thérèse was as cheerful as ever as we laid her down under the bridge, but she was suffering intensely from the cold. We covered her with extra blankets lent by various members of the party, but could not bring her much relief.

*   *   *

This brave nun whose blue lips kept smiling as we waited hour by hour for the boats was formerly known as Irène Bastin. She was a native of Virton, in Belgium. When the Germans invaded her homeland in 1914 she was only thirteen years old, but she worked during the four years of the war as a member of " La Dame Blanche," a secret group formed by the people of Virton to co-operate with the Allies. Some of her friends were executed and her own parents were imprisoned. In 1918 she was arrested herself, but was eventually released for lack of evidence. The strain and hardship she suffered during adolescent years impaired her health, and later in life she was to be affected with tuberculosis.

When peace came she entered the Carmel at Virton, and remained there till 1938, when she went to Korea as one of the foundation members of a new Carmel in Seoul. Ten years later she was elected prioress of the community, which included now Korean Carmelites as well as Belgian and French.

When the Red invasion started, Mother Thérèse and her four European companions decided to stay with their Korean Sisters. Three weeks later the Reds arrived to take them from their convent to the basement room in the Seoul barracks. They had been there for two days when Monsignor Quinlan and Father Canavan and I arrived.

The health of Mother Thérèse, which had been poor for many years, declined steadily in internment. At this point in my story she was already affected with a mortal illness, and its progress would be hastened by events that lay ahead. Before December came she was to pass to her reward.

We shall remember her as a patient sufferer who never complained of her affliction, except to regret that her weakness at times put a burden on others. She was always apologetic when she had to be helped or carried, and was embarrassingly grateful for the smallest service.

*   *   *

The day wore on, but no boats appeared. Towards evening an officer came to say that they would not arrive till tomorrow, and that we must go back for the night to the quarters we had left. The organizing abilities of our captors were the subject of much bitter criticism as we plodded back with our loads to our old home. The shabby, silent buildings seemed positively funereal as we straggled, weary and dispirited, through the gate. We set up the cooking-pots temporarily and prepared a meal, and then tried to get some sleep.

Next morning was Sunday. We set off again for our rendezvous with the boats. They were not in sight when we arrived, but we settled down to wait in a cheerier mood than yesterday, for the sun was shining, bright and warm. On such a day one could look forward with pleasure to a boat trip down the Yalu.

By and by we saw the POWs marching along the road from Manpo. I remember the painful shock the first sight of them gave me, for I felt that many of these lads were in no condition for walking. I hoped that they had not too far to go. The guards seemed to be

having trouble in getting some of the men to keep up with the rest ;
it must have been an hour before the last stragglers passed.

A little later we were glad to see boats coming down the river,
filled with POWs. So the weakest of the men were not being forced
to walk. We waved to them, and they waved back as the boats went
on downstream.

The next event of the day I have mentioned already. Some sacks
of bread arrived from the first and only batch the POWs had baked
in their newly-built ovens in Manpo. The bread was shared out
and eaten. Still no boats appeared. The afternoon passed, and still
we waited.

Towards evening we were told that no boats could be got, and
that we must return once more to the quarters to which we had twice
already said goodbye. We reacted to this news with open rebellion
and scathing comment. Our guards, to do them justice, were probably as disgusted with the situation as we were, and the repeated
failure of their arrangements was no doubt due to errors at a higher
level. Anyway, they agreed to commandeer ox-carts to spare us
some of the carrying, and in due course we arrived back once more
at our old quarters.

The idea of boats had now been finally abandoned, and we were
told that a truck would come that evening to take the children, the
elderly and sick, and the baggage. The rest of us would follow
on foot tomorrow. The promised truck did arrive, and we saw it
off with its passengers and luggage. We who remained were about
to settle down for the night when a shout went round that another
truck had arrived, and was ready to take us aboard. We collected
such baggage as we had retained, piled it on the truck, then clambered
up ourselves. The last few of us had to cling on precariously, for the
vehicle was too small for its load.

The truck tore along through the darkness, following a road that
at times ran level over flats beside the river, and at times wound
tortuously over steep mountains. A journey of something less than
twenty miles brought us to our destination, which proved to be a
small town called Kosan-jin.

Accommodation was provided in a school building for all of our
civilian party except the Korean politicians. Next day we found that
they had been given a room in a house behind the school. There

were three classrooms in the school, one of which was given to the
women, another to the diplomats and journalists, and the third to
the remaining men.

In all our various camps a complete lack of preparation for our
coming has been the rule. At this camp alone did we find the pro-
verbial exception. The walls of the schoolrooms had been fitted with
two lines of wide wooden shelving, one above the other, to serve as
upper and lower sleeping berths. But this had exhausted our captors'
efforts to make the place habitable. There was a battered bath-house,
in unusable condition. For cooking there was no provision at all.

We were told that meals would be cooked for us by the occupants
of a nearby house for the time being, till we had set up cooking
facilities for ourselves. Attached to the school was a two-roomed
shed, and this we would have to make serve as kitchen and storeroom.

On the morning after our arrival we turned our attention to the
shed, and set about the first task of building from stone and clay a
fireplace and a " range " for our cooking pots. For this project we
selected as chief engineer the little, white-whiskered old Russian,
Ivan Nicolai Tihinoff, whom we had discovered to be an expert on
the subject of stoves and heating appliances of every kind. Whenever we have had to fit out a kitchen, or repair *ondol* floors, or set up
stoves to warm our rooms, Tihinoff has always been willing to place
at our disposal not only his wide experience, but also the skilful
labour of his small and shapely hands.

*   *   *

At the time of his arrest, Tihinoff was a cosmetics manufacturer in
Seoul. I have spoken of him as white-whiskered, and so he is ; but
the description was only partly true when we first made his acquaintance. At that time his beard was white at the roots, but lower down
it was of a rich golden hue that bore witness to his faith in one of his
own products. Possibly he had also drawn on his professional stock
for a hair-restorer. If so, he had used it too enthusiastically. So
luxuriant was the growth on head and face and neck, as well as chin,
that we could easily follow Walter Eltringham's train of thought
when, after one look at Tihinoff, he christened him " Rover." But
this was softened to " Father Christmas " when the gold of his beard
turned to silver, and " Father Christmas " he remained.

With his smooth rosy cheeks, and his twinkling eyes and ready laughter, the old man is well cast for the part. Unlike his prototype, however, he hibernates in winter, scarcely forsaking the cocoon of his blanket except when the cry of " Bowls ! " announces a meal, or when a whisper reaches him that a ration of tobacco has arrived, or that a friendly guard has some to give. But when the longer, warmer days arrive, he comes to life again, and goes trotting about the hills as lively as a mountain goat, for all his weak heart and his heavy load of years. He was sixty-eight when he joined us in 1950.

Besides his native Russian, Tihinoff has a smattering of several other languages. He seems never to have sorted out his non-Russian fellow-prisoners into their respective nationalities, so in conversation with them his policy appears to be to cover all possibilities by stringing together bits of the various languages he knows. A choice example of his polyglot style was memorized by Larry Zellers : " *Pika-wasi* river *ippai* "—Korean-English-Japanese for " Rain having come, the river is full."

If Tihinoff's speech has some interesting aspects, so has his hearing. I have seen him gossiping with a guard who was talking in a normal tone, and the conversation went smoothly on till the guard changed the subject to politics. Then the old man's hand went at once to his ear, and he began shouting : " What did you say ? You know I'm deaf." He always looks as simple as a dove, and as late as the latter half of 1951 he replied to an official interviewer's request for his opinion on the war by saying, with a look of bland surprise : " Is there a war on ? "

★   ★   ★

Our conversion of the shed to kitchen and storeroom was at last completed. The storeroom was stocked with supplies that had come down the river from Manpo, and Monsignor Quinlan was on the job again as quartermaster, rationing out the daily allowance. A new roster of cooking teams had been drawn up, and was working smoothly. We who had worked on the shed turned our attention to other jobs. Heating stoves had arrived for the rooms, and we set them up and gave them a casing of mud and stones. This would serve to smooth out the flow of heat, absorbing whatever the stove had to offer, and passing it on at a fairly steady rate to the room. Next we turned our attention to the bath-house, and found that it would take some time to make it serviceable. We made our plans, and set about the task.

Now that our fear of being taken across the Yalu had vanished, our confidence returned. Rescue, we felt, was only a matter of waiting a little longer, and meantime we were contented enough with our lot. The POWs, too, appeared to be doing pretty well. They had been quartered in a large building in the town, and it seemed that both food supplies and cooking facilities were satisfactory. They even made doughnuts, and sent some along as a gift for us.

Life, on the whole, ran smoothly on, with only occasional incidents to ruffle it. Two such incidents concerned Commissioner Lord and Sister Mary Clare.

Commissioner Lord, who was our camp-leader at this time, intervened one day on behalf of Dr. Jensen, who, for some reason I have forgotten, was being threatened by one of the guards with a tommy-gun. The guard promptly transferred his anger to the Commissioner, and marched him off for denunciation to The Major, who was over at the POW camp at the time. On the way, the Commissioner was knocked down and kicked. When they arrived before The Major, the guard told his tale. The Major, however, with characteristic fairness, asked for the Commissioner's version of the case as well. The guard was reprimanded and ordered to bring the Commissioner back.

I have mentioned the two lines of wooden bunks which were provided in our rooms. Sister Mary Clare, who had been given an upper berth, had the misfortune one night to fall out of it. Happily, she broke no bones, but she was severely shaken. She was still suffering from the after-effects a few weeks later, when she was made to take part in a forced march which I shall soon have to describe. In her injured condition that was to prove fatal to her. Her death was to take from us a gentle, refined, and most unselfish soul.

Though her religion and training led most people to assume that she was English, Sister Mary Clare was of Irish birth. She had abandoned her profession as a schoolteacher to join an Anglican Sisterhood, and had begun her missionary career in Korea during the first World War. There her major work had been the foundation of a native Sisterhood. She trained the first novices and became the first Superior of the congregation. She was an expert in handicrafts, and had made instruction in these a part of the practical training she gave to her spiritual children. In spare moments over the years she had devoted herself to the translation of prayers and spiritual books into Korean. During the second World War she was forced to leave Korea, but the congregation she had founded survived under a Korean Superior of its own, and it was to act as adviser to her that Sister Mary Clare returned after the peace.

*　　*　　*

Towards the end of our stay at Kosan we had a visit from The Major. He delivered a very peculiar speech, which we have referred to ever since as "The Major's Swan Song." It had its puzzling elements, but we gathered from its general tenor that he shared our belief that we would soon be free.

He began by saying that one day we would return to our home-lands, and that he hoped we would take with us happy memories of our stay in North Korea. After dwelling on this happy memory theme for quite some time, he passed to his second point. We ought, he said, to take with us also some knowledge of the regime under which we had lived, and he would therefore arrange for us to be given some lectures on Communism. But his third point was his bombshell. He told us he would like to see the camp reorganized, and for this purpose he was appointing a new camp-leader, Mr. Moon.

To understand our amazement you would need to have known Mr. Moon. He was one of the seven South Korean politicians who had been with us from the time we left the schoolhouse camp near Pyongyang, and who, for reasons we never fathomed, were to remain attached to our group for twelve months. All seven had been candi-dates in the parliamentary elections held in South Korea shortly before the invasion started. Six had been successful. The one who failed to make the grade was Mr. Moon.

Physically, there was a lot of Mr. Moon. He looked as if he had been poured into his ample clothes till his head and hands and feet burst forth. He was, however, active and energetic despite his bulk, and began his day with early morning exercises and a brisk walk.

We always found Mr. Moon friendly, but we never knew him intimately. One gathered that some at least of his fellow-politicians regarded him as an opportunist, though it would be naïve to expect objectivity in one politician's views of another. The fact remained that Mr. Moon was simply an unknown quantity to most of the people in the camp, and we could see no reason at all for his sudden promotion to the position of camp-leader in place of Commissioner Lord.

The Major, however, had presented us with a *fait accompli*. The next thing we knew, Mr. Moon had procured a table and chair and set up an office for himself in a room of the Korean house where he and his companions were quartered. There he sat in state, and issued his directions for the reorganization of the camp. They were as drastic as his own appointment. Commissioner Lord was by-passed as interpreter ; Dr. Jensen was made liaison officer between Mr. Moon and the non-Korean members of the camp. Monsignor Quinlan, too, was informed that his services as quartermaster were no longer required, as that office would now be performed by Mr. Kijikoff.

★   ★   ★

Ilian Kijikoff is no longer with us as I write, but he is well remembered. In our company of seventy-four he was in his way as colourful a character as any.

At this point in my story he was fifty-eight years old. He was of medium height and athletic in build, and one could well believe the report that he had been a Cossack, and no mean horseman. Another theory was that he came of Mongol stock, and this his swarthy complexion and somewhat fierce expression tended to confirm. It was also held that he had been crossed in love, and this again was easy to credit, for, with him, smiling was more rare than laughter, and his laughter tended to be harsh and grim.

He was definitely an individualist. One manifestation of it was his practice in each successive camp of making at the first opportunity a small table for himself, at which he would eat alone in state, wielding a great wooden spoon of his own manufacture. He was fastidious about etiquette, and even gave a lecture on the subject to some of the ladies, who thereafter named him " Emily Post."

If I must record that he had a violent temper (and to describe his kaleidoscopic character I must) I should also record that it was vented with impartiality on inanimate objects as well as humans. In one of

our later camps, he built, behind the house we occupied, a leafy
bower to accommodate himself and his little table, and I well
remember a visit I paid to him there. I had come to collect his food
bowl, which he kept in a tin. The lid was jammed, and he tugged
at it gently, talking to it the while in coaxing tones. It did not
budge, so he tugged a little harder, increasing at the same time the
tempo of his exhortations. It was still obstinate. He gave a snort,
tore off the lid with a jerk that bent it badly, and hurled it from him.
Then he gave the lid a piece of his mind. It was a large and rich
piece, but I knew from experience that it came from a well-stocked
store. I have never met anyone with so wide a vocabulary as Kijikoff
to meet situations like these. Anyway, after the incident, I never again
felt so badly if I happened to fall foul of his tongue. For if a piece
of tin could take it lying down, why not I?

But I will say this for Kijikoff: he was strong in one virtue that
ranks very high in the internee's scale. He was honest and fair. He
wanted his due share of whatever was available, but never more; and
if he happened to be the distributer, he was no respecter of persons.
This was a valuable attribute in a quartermaster. He brought other
fine qualities to his new task as well. He was on the job all day; he
kept his store clean and tidy; and he was conscientious about keeping
a careful check on his stock.

Kijikoff was to survive two winters in internment, but the third
one (in the middle of which I am writing this part of my story) has
taken him from us. He left us but a short time ago, December 17,
1952. We will remember him—tantrums and all—with affection.

*   *   *

On the evening of Friday, October 20, we put the finishing touches
to our work on the bath-house. Water was fetched, and the bath
was filled. First thing next morning the fire was lit, and we proudly
announced at breakfast that the bath-house was now a going concern
and the ladies could begin using it that day.

They never used it. After breakfast the guards gave us the news
that we must pack up at once and make ready to move.

Our stay in Kosan, where we had been so sure that freedom would
overtake us, ended after thirteen days.

9

Prelude to Tragedy

OCTOBER 21 TO 31, 1950

AS USUAL we had been given no hint of our destination, and we wondered, as we hurriedly piled up baggage, whether we would go further down the Yalu or return upstream towards Manpo. The old people were left sitting on the baggage to await transport. The rest of us were lined up by the guards and marched off. To our surprise we went neither upstream nor downstream, but left the river road behind us and took a mountain trail that led towards the south.

After a while the POWs came up behind us, and we were shunted off the path to let them pass. For some reason their guards were hurrying them along, and many were finding it hard to keep up. As we followed behind them I was shocked to see some rice-straw mats lying on the path. Men who discarded burdens as light as these must be weak indeed. Occasionally, too, we came up with weary men who had fallen out to rest by the wayside.

The trail led over a mountain and then along a valley dotted with mining installations. Heavy cables swung high overhead as we plodded on. We passed through a village of identical huts, then another. Evening was falling as we entered a larger valley and came upon a ghost town which proved to be our destination. Our journey had covered about twelve miles.

This broken-down town, now but a hamlet in population, bore the name of Jui-am-nee. It was a relic of some sizeable mining enterprise long since abandoned ; a place of ruined buildings, piled-up debris, and derelict, rusting gear. As I took in the scene, my mind dwelt vaguely on depressing thoughts of sick, impoverished and doddering old age.

To the left, as one entered the town, stood row after row of large huts, and among these we were invited to find accommodation. It was growing dark, and there were no lights. Deep trenches ran between the buildings, and we had to pick our way carefully as we stumbled from one to another seeking habitable rooms. Each hut had four mud-walled rooms at either end, but many of them were in ruins. At last the whole party was distributed among the best rooms that could be found. The selection had to include some with cracked walls or fallen-in floors. The one in which I found accommodation with Bishop Byrne, Monsignor Quinlan and Father Booth had no window, and when we shut the door it became pitch dark. But at least it was something to have a door to shut. Some of the rooms had not even that. In the days that followed, we made improvements by transferring fittings from other huts and patching walls and floors with mud from the trenches.

Some of our kitchen equipment had failed to arrive, and when it did there was a shortage of supplies. For a day or so the local people provided us with food. I have vague recollections of millet. The cooking was done by the Turkish family, the Salahudtins, who occupied, with Mr. Moon, one of the few presentable houses, and had access to a kitchen.

The Salahudtins are usually referred to in camp more briefly as " Sala." Of Sagid, the eldest child, I have already spoken. The second child is Sagida, a sturdy, vivacious, handsome girl with long black flowing tresses. When we first met her in 1950 she was seventeen years old. At that time, in addition to her own Turkish language, she could speak English and some Russian, and she has since learnt French and Korean. The most interesting linguist of the family, however, is the youngest, Hamid, now a hardy, independent young man of nearly four years, and quite a personality. It is fascinating to hear him prattling away in half a dozen languages, in all of which he is able to make himself understood. Between Sagida and Hamid there are three other children, all boys : Farid, Shaucat and Morat.

The father of the family, Salim Salahudtin, is a quiet, industrious man in his fifties. His wife, Faiza, a dark, energetic woman, is much younger. Her brother and sister, Ahmet and Sophia Sultan, round off the family. Ahmet, a broad-shouldered man about thirty, was once a boxer, and is endowed with amazing strength. Poor Sophia

is mentally defective, and spends the greater part of the day com-
muning with herself, alternating between gaiety and grief. Often
I have heard her merrily laughing and singing, only to find her a
few minutes later weeping bitterly and bemoaning her lot.

★   ★   ★

Here at Jui-am-nee we were supplied for the first time with a
grain which I have become accustomed to call "corn," as my
American companions do, but which in my native Australia would
be described more specifically as "maize." In Jui-am-nee and in
later camps it has often formed part of our diet, and sometimes
was our only diet for days on end. It was always supplied "whole,"
and we had not always the means of grinding it. Here at Jui-am-nee
we did have the use of a Korean-style stone mill, and I had my first
experience of such mills when, early one morning, I sallied forth
with Monsignor Quinlan and Walter Eltringham to grind corn for
breakfast.

Korean grinding mills come in three sizes, but they all work alike.
There are two flat circles of stone. The upper stone rotates about a
peg set in the lower one, which remains stationary. The inner sur-
faces of both stones have grooves radiating from their centres. The
grain is fed in through a hole near the centre of the upper stone, and
moves outward along the grooves as the grinding proceeds.

The smallest, or "portable," model is placed either on the floor
or in a large bowl. It has a wooden handle set in the upper stone,
and the operator squats on the ground and turns the mill by hand.
The medium-sized, or "walk-around" model, is set up out of
doors on a stand. The operator circles about the mill, pushing a
pole attached to the upper stone. In the largest model, which is
usually built in a special shed, the turning-pole is pulled around by
an ox.

A new chore of this camp was hunting firewood, which we now
had to find for ourselves. We were forbidden to cut trees, and
when the guards took parties once or twice to the hills to gather fuel,
we came back with a motley collection of dead branches, stumps, and
other bits and scraps. We had not yet learnt, as necessity taught us
later, how to cut brush and scrub with the Korean "nat" (a short,

heavy-bladed sickle) and drag it back to camp in bundles tied with tendril.

On a rise near our houses there stood in solitary dignity a large and venerable oak tree. We pestered the guards for permission to slay it, but they refused, probably because it was reverenced as a " spirit tree " by the local people, as its loneliness, age and position suggested. Meanwhile, despite warnings from our guards, some of the buildings advanced a stage further towards destruction. But at last we were let loose on the old oak tree. Perhaps the authorities decided that they could better bear the indignation of the few remaining inhabitants than our ceaseless importunities. We went to work with tiny axes and saws, and eventually laid the monster low. When the great corpse was hacked to pieces we would have fuel, we estimated, for many days. However, we were not to be left here for many days so the old oak died its slow death in vain.

First news of our next move came from the POWs, who were living further along the road from us, in a large school building. We had been able to keep in touch with them, as we had to fetch water from the well they used. They were having a hard time. Some had been unable to complete the march to Jui-am-nee and had to be brought in on carts, and one or two had died after arrival. The sick list was constantly growing, and the sick had to sleep, like the rest, on the floor in unheated rooms. For food there was nothing but whole corn. In an attempt to make it fit for human consumption, they boiled it endlessly in Japanese bath-tubs set up in the school yard—huge circular affairs, with rounded bottoms and sloping sides.

The POWs were still hopeful of rescue, and they had the impression that some of their guards, too, were expecting the early arrival of United Nations troops. One of them, a quartermaster, threw open a local clothing store and invited the POWs to help themselves to the stock, which consisted mainly of fine winter caps. There were enough for nearly all the POWs, many of whom thus acquired their one and only warm article of attire.

The rest of us were, if anything, even more hopeful than the POWs. Occasional booming could be heard in the distance, and many interpreted the sound as approaching artillery. From time to time, disorderly little bands of North Korean soldiers went by, often without arms. They were obviously out of the fight. Rumours of every kind were abroad, but it was difficult to get reliable news. One current theory about our journey south to Jui-am-nee was that there might be fighting and bombing on the main road along the river, and the authorities wanted us in a place of greater safety. Several of our number thought of trying to make contacts with the U.N. troops, and one night a party actually planned to leave; but a hitch occurred, and they stayed.

Such was the pitch of our excitement that every small event of our stay in Jui-am-nee was a matter of tremendous interest to us, and that made our sojourn there seem much longer. I find it difficult, now, to believe that it lasted less than a week.

It was on the following Thursday morning, October 26, that some GIs staggered us with the news that they were to leave that day. Sure enough, the POW column came marching along before lunch, passed by our houses, and went off in the direction of Kosan. When we went for water, we met orderlies who told us that forty or so sick men had been left in their care, awaiting transport.

Next came word, through our camp-leader, Mr. Moon, that we were to follow the POWs. There would be no transport. Everyone must walk or be carried. We were dumbfounded. Surely there must be some mistake? We checked again with Mr. Moon, and found there was no mistake. We pleaded and wrangled with the guards, but they were adamant. So we set about getting ready, lightening our baggage as much as possible. We improvised a stretcher for Mother Thérèse, for whom walking was out of the question. It would be very difficult for others too, especially for Sister Mary Clare, who was still lame from her fall at Kosan, and for eighty-two-year-old Father Villemot.

It was evening before we were ready to start, and it had begun to drizzle. How it would be possible for the old people, or for those who were carrying Mother Thérèse, to negotiate in the darkness winding mountain paths made slippery by the rain, we just could not imagine. After we had struggled along for a while, even the guards realized the folly of trying to proceed, and told us to return and wait till morning. This was an order we had no inclination to dispute. Tomorrow we would at least have daylight, and perhaps fine weather.

In the morning the guards revealed a still more gratifying change of mind. There would be ox-carts, they announced, for those who found difficulty in walking, and Dr. Jensen would remain behind to take charge of them. The rest of us set off again, and were halted in the evening at some houses a mile short of Kosan. There we were billeted for the night. When we retired, there was still no sign of those we had left waiting.

When folk began to gather for breakfast next morning, it was evident that some were missing. Mr. Moon did not appear, nor did Louis Dans, nor the two journalists, nor most of the diplomats. Then it got around that the missing men had left word that they were going in search of the people who had been left behind in Jui-am-nee. None of us had much doubt, however, that they were attempting to escape. Much to our surprise, they returned about four o'clock in the afternoon. They were not chatty. They hadn't, they said, been able to find the people who were supposed to be coming on ox-carts. Having told us that, they went off to get something to eat.

Long afterwards it leaked out that Mr. Moon had been informed (incorrectly) that U.N. troops were only twenty-five miles away. After the party had gone a few miles they saw Chinese troops digging in on the hillsides. For some days previously we had been hearing rumours that the Chinese had entered the war, but I think this was the first time any of us saw actual evidence of the fact. The sight of the Chinese soldiers dampened the confidence of the escape party ; it was not going to be so easy to reach the U.N. lines. They decided —wisely enough, as events proved—to turn back.

That same evening the sick POWs and the civilians we had left behind us came past in carts on their way to Kosan. Volunteers were enlisted to follow them into the town and render assistance. The party included Bishop Byrne and Father Booth, Monsignor Quinlan and Father Canavan, Bishop Cooper, Commissioner Lord, and Walter Eltringham. Ivan Kilin and Salim Salahudtin came with us, of course, to assist their wives and children, and I think Sagid Sala-hudtin came too. A walk of a mile brought us to Kosan, and we were amazed to find it a dead town. We moved through silent streets, past empty houses with their doors ajar. Here and there a heavy piece of furniture lay abandoned. Evacuation must have been hurried indeed. We wondered whether the inhabitants had fled, or had been ordered out.

The only signs of life were in the middle of the town, where we

P.A.—*Reuter*

Courageous, a fluent speaker of Korean, and well versed in Korean ways, Commissioner Lord of the Salvation Army (*above*, being welcomed home by comrades) was the obvious choice as interpreter for the group.

The Anglican Bishop Cooper (*right*), another veteran with forty years' experience of Korea, "was the scholar of the company."

Father William Booth of Maryknoll (*below*), in happier days.

[*I.N.A.*

found the carts and the POWs and civilians who had travelled on them. A jolting Korean ox-cart is no luxury vehicle at any time, and the journey over the rough mountain road had left the travellers weary and dazed. To add to their troubles, the carts were over-crowded, and some of the passengers had to toil up the hills on foot. Meanwhile the guards had badgered and bullied them, and Dr. Jensen, as leader of the civilian group, had to bear the brunt when they could not get the number of children to tally. Unknown to Dr. Jensen, some of the children had gone on ahead with their fathers, instead of waiting to ride on the carts with their mothers, as the guards intended them to do. All in all, the civilian party was far from cheerful. However, they soon recovered their good spirits when we arrived to help them find rooms and get settled in with their belongings. We got fires started to heat the rooms and for cooking, and brought water from a well.

Then we helped the orderlies with the sick POWs. Many of them were very ill, but they were bravely bearing up, and the orderlies did noble work. Catholic lads seized the opportunity of making their Confessions to one or other of the five priests working among them. I have very happy memories of that evening in Kosan. The atmosphere was free and easy ; there was cheerfulness and co-operation ; the guards were absent, and darkness veiled the dirt and squalor. I felt lighthearted, with an exhilaration that I had not known for months. The strain of our life was temporarily forgotten, and for perhaps a couple of hours my mind was free of the eternal question : " Where are we going, and how will it end ? "

At length the guards reappeared and called us together for the journey back. They seemed relieved to find no one missing. We returned to the farmhouses of the night before.

Not long after our return, Father Canavan took the stage as villain in a drama which was, for the most of us, highly diverting, but was classic tragedy for the seven Korean politicians. They had volun-teered to cook the evening meal, and had managed to procure some special kind of beans which would turn out a rare delicacy if expertly handled. With loving care they prepared the beans and set about cooking them according to a method hallowed by 4,800 years' tradition. The water was measured exactly as the sacred recipe prescribed, the heat was just right, and all that remained now was to

wait the allotted time. The critical stage was over. The experts
retired to smoke a well-earned pipe and await the portentous moment
when the beans, cooked to a nicety, would be proudly served.

At this juncture Father Canavan entered the deserted kitchen.
Ever a man of action once he had made a decision, he decided now,
and action followed. The cooks, he guessed, had gone off gallivant-
ing, leaving the beans to boil dry. To get a bucket of spring water
and pour it into the pot was but the work of a moment. He had just
accomplished this good deed when one of the cooks returned. At
first the Korean could not believe his eyes ; then, for an awesome
moment, he could not find his voice. When he did, a cry of agony
brought his collaborators running to the scene of the disaster. One
look was enough. The team rushed out to do justice to their feelings
in the open, calling heaven and hell to witness an outrage that could
evoke only mild sympathy from the other inhabitants of the
camp.

Months afterwards I was discussing old times with one of the
Koreans—a tall, stooped old fellow, known to the world as Tjo, and
to us as " Big Joe." Suddenly Big Joe lowered his voice, speaking
in the awed and reverential tones a father might use when he spoke
of a dead and dearly-loved son.

" Do you remember," he whispered, " the time Father Canavan
put water—*cold* water—on the beans ? "

Next morning (Sunday, October 29) we got orders to pack up
and prepare to move again. As usual, our destination was not
revealed, and we would have no clue till we reached Kosan. There
we would strike the main road that paralleled the Yalu, and must
either go westwards down the river, or else turn upstream in the
direction of Manpo.

Arriving in Kosan we found that the civilians and sick POWs we
had helped to quarter there the night before had already left the
town. At a street corner we recognised a suitcase which had belonged
to one of the civilians. This evidence of load-lightening made us a
little uneasy about the future. We turned eastwards out of Kosan,
and took the Manpo road.

We had not sighted the main body of POWs since we watched
them march away from Jui-am-nee in the direction of Kosan three
days before, but we presumed that they were somewhere ahead of

us. We wondered how they were faring, and hoped we would meet
up with them again.

Mr. Moon apparently still had faint hopes that we might be over-
taken by friendly troops before reaching Manpo. He therefore gave
orders, as group-leader, that we were to go slowly, and sent two
picked men to the front to set a pace that was aggravatingly slow.
The guards did not seem to mind. Mr. Moon trotted up and down
the line to cheer us up. Then his fellow politicians complained that
it was ridiculous to proceed at this snail's pace. This angered Mr.
Moon. If it was speed we wanted, speed we would get ! He took
the lead and set off at a terrific pace, and then came running back
down the line, shouting " Hurry up ! Hurry up ! "

We reached a village where the guards had evidently intended to
lodge us for the night, but it was overflowing with soldiers, and we
had to move on. It was dark when we came to another village.
Here the guards brought us to a little church. I think it was Presby-
terian, to judge from some hymn-books we found, but it was obvious
that the building had been turned over to secular uses for some time.
We pegged our claims for floor-space. Hours later a guard conducted Monsignor Quinlan and me across the fields to a house where
corn and soup had been prepared for our party. We carried it back,
but many people just went on sleeping.

Next day we resumed our trek towards Manpo. Some Chinese
army supply-carts hauled by two or three ponies passed us on the
road. There were a few Chinese soldiers to be seen, and we had
heard rumours that many more were passing at night. It was being
borne in upon us that the war had taken a new turn.

When we had gone some miles the guards called a halt. We were
allowed to go to the river to wash, and rested then for half an hour
till the order came to take the road again.

As we neared Manpo, I scanned the rolling hills through which
we had approached the town by train several weeks before. Their
summer garb of vivid green was ageing then to duller, darker hue. In
the weeks between, they had donned and doffed again their splendid
autumn motley of red and brown and yellow. Severe now in their
sombre winter dress, their gaunt lines would soon be softened with
snowy overmantles. I thought, as I trudged along, how our hopes,
too, had been bright in the summer ; had glowed more brightly still

when the land was clad in autumn glory ; had dimmed and faded with the falling of the leaves.

We were about three miles short of Manpo, and within a mile of the old quarantine station which had been our home for a month, when to our surprise the guards diverted us from the road and sent us marching off to the left across fields. We had just passed a house on the road, but we could see no others in the direction we were now taking—none, at least, but a burnt-out, roofless shell, and we dismissed that from consideration as we scanned the fields for signs of a likely lodging. Then we saw near the burnt-out house some of those who had gone ahead by cart. They came hastening to meet us. Our quarters must be near, we thought. Then, as more of our folk appeared, the truth dawned upon us. Those folk were coming from the roofless ruin. So that was to be our home for the night ! It was the remains of a two-roomed stucco house. Only the walls were standing. Inside and outside, the ground was littered with fallen masonry and charred timber.

Those who had arrived in the carts were very glad to see us, but theirs was a tale of woe ; their disappointment when they found where they had to stay, the task they had in preparing places to rest, the cold of the night. . . .

There was nothing to do but make the best of things, so we set about it. We cleared out stones and rubble from the roofless rooms, made crude flooring with the best of the charred timber, piled the rest outside for fuel. Fires were lit and a meal prepared. One of the rooms was given to the women and children, the other to the elderly men. In the lee of an outside wall we cleared a space, and built a windbreak of beams and rice bags. There the rest of us spent the night, crouching around a fire.

The sick POWs had joined up with the main body, and all were now camped by the river, about half a mile away. The main body had been there for a couple of days. They must have managed to find some odds and ends of wood or scrub, for we could see in the darkness the gleam of a few small fires—pitifully few and pitifully small for more than seven hundred men. We wondered how the sick were faring. Later we heard how the others had tried to shield them from the bitter wind by hollowing out shelters on the lee side of a slope.

Cold as it was, I realize now, looking back on that night and on other nights we spent in the open, how much worse off we might have been. I have learnt since that the weather we had in the winter of 1950–51 was moderate for North Korea. In fact that winter was one of the mildest on record.

October 31 dawned. We rose from our restless dozing by the fire to discover that George Blake, the British vice-consul, had disappeared during the night. We guessed he was attempting to escape. After a few hours he was back in our midst. He had set off southwards into the hill country, but had not gone far when a sentry challenged him in the darkness, and marched him to a house where a number of Korean officers were gathered. They were in good humour. After being questioned, Blake was lectured a little, and then given a meal. He was told to sleep till morning, and was then escorted back to us by a guard.

The officer who had so mildly lectured him belonged, Blake told us, to the penitentiary service. We would see him very soon ourselves. In a few hours' time we would all be under his command. And none of us would find him mild.

10

The Death March

" BUT they will die if they have to march."

" Then let them march till they die! That is a military order."

The first speaker was Commissioner Herbert Lord of the Salvation Army ; the second was, in his own proud phrase, " a major of the People's Army."

The major's name we have never heard. But even if we do learn it in the future it will never spring so readily to our minds, when memory conjures up his image, as the bitter name that was coined for him by the POWs. In the first few days of the unforgettable ninety-six which they and we spent under his command, one of them called him " The Tiger " ; and the name caught on all round.

This was the man who had interviewed George Blake not many hours before. Monsignor Quinlan, Father Canavan and I recognized him as the man who had come, in his white jail-governor's uniform, to interview each of us during our solitary confinement in Chunchon in mid-July. It was now the last day of October when we saw him again, and heard his blood-chilling words to Commissioner Lord.

Since early that day we had been ready to move at short notice. We waited for hours. When we were beginning to think our departure had been postponed, the officer we knew as " The Major " came to say goodbye. The " Swan Song " title that we gave to his speech at Kosan would have been more appropriate to the message he had for us now. He was handing us over, he said, to an officer of another department, and would not be dealing with us any more. His tone, we thought, was a little wistful. On our side, certainly, there was regret. We had always found The Major reasonable, and never had cause to criticize him. We were genuinely sorry to be losing him. At that moment we were mercifully unaware of how very much more sorry we would be in the hours ahead.

135

And now his successor, The Tiger, stood before us, surrounded by blue-uniformed prison warders who were to serve under him as our guards ; " Blue devils," as they became in our prisoner vocabulary. The Tiger himself wore knee-breeches and a tight-fitting jacket that gave him a lithe appearance. He was tall for a Korean, slim, quick and nervous in his movements. When he walked he leaned forward a little. His features were regular, but protruding teeth gave him a perpetual grimace. His bright eyes were keen and restless. His age we could not guess.

He told us we had a long walk before us and must proceed in military formation. His orders were to be obeyed as military commands. They would be conveyed to us through leaders whom he would now appoint. He asked us to suggest a group-leader, and we named Commissioner Lord, who had been our leader up till the time of Mr. Moon's mysterious appointment to that office by The Major.

" I have other work for him. Suggest another." (Though he did not tell us then, The Tiger had already decided to use Commissioner Lord as interpreter for the entire party, POWs as well as civilians.)

We nominated Monsignor Quinlan, and The Tiger acquiesced. Who would be the leader of the women ? Miss Nell Dyer's name was mentioned by several of the ladies, and again The Tiger agreed.

*　　　*　　　*

The burden that had now fallen to Miss Dyer was to prove heavy indeed in the grim days that lay before us. The way she carried out her nerve-racking, heart-breaking task has made her a heroine in my eyes, but I will let that part of the story unfold itself.

This tall, fine-featured woman is a native of Arkansas. Her father was a Methodist minister, and her great ambition, even as a child, was to become a missionary. This was realized around 1927 with an appointment to Korea, where she was assigned to teach in a Methodist mission school in Seoul. Later she was transferred to the large girls' school maintained by the Methodists in Kaesong, and in due course became its principal. Then orders came to leave Korea in view of the evident imminence of Japan's entry into the second World War. She volunteered for work in the Philippine Islands, and there the

Japanese war-net enveloped her after all. She spent three and a half years in internment, and then, after a period of recuperation in her home town of Conway, Arkansas, went back to her post in Kaesong. The city was overrun on the very first morning of the Red invasion, and she found herself an internee once again.

My own acquaintance with Miss Dyer began one morning in the corridor of our schoolhouse prison near Pyongyang. I had swept a portion of the corridor, and she was waiting to take over where I left off. As I passed on my collection of dust to her, I used the opportunity to pass on a few scraps of news.

It did not seem a memorable incident. But since that whispered conversation I have had more than two years in which to know Nell Dyer better, and the knowledge has made that prosaic first encounter unforgettable for me. It has been a privilege to have known her. It would be hard to find anywhere a more conscientious, unselfish or heroic soul.

*   *   *

While the appointment of leaders was under discussion, one thought was harrying the minds of all. What had The Tiger meant by his warning that our journey was to be conducted as a military march? Was he knave or fool, that he expected such people as those in our group to swing along Korean roads in military column? Did he expect it of the tottering octogenarian Father Villemot? Of frail and aged Mother Béatrix? Of Sister Mary Clare, still lame from her fall? Of consumptive Mother Thérèse? Of mothers with babes in arms?

Commissioner Lord stepped forward now to voice the consternation we all were feeling. He pointed out that many of the party would find it impossible to march like soldiers, and at military pace ; that for some, the attempt must surely be fatal.

"Then let them march," said The Tiger, "till they die! That is a military order."

There was nothing more to be said. Not, at any rate, to The Tiger. And we were too stunned to say much to each other. But I think there were few who did not breathe a prayer to their Creator, in that first shocking moment of suspicion that the man who ruled our destinies was mad.

And so we began the march of death. I do not look forward to

travelling the terrible journey again, even in memory, but if friends
of ours should follow this sketch of our weary trudgings, they will
want to follow us also through those darkest miles of all.

*   *   *

The guards made us surrender all knives or other implements
that could be regarded as possible weapons, including even the sticks
which some had hoped to use as a support in walking. We formed
up in column in such a way that the weak would have, as far as
possible, the help of the strong. Father Villemot, for example, was
between Monsignor Quinlan and Father Bulteau. Sister Bernadette,
strongest of the Carmelites, gave her arm to blind Sister Marie-
Madeleine. Larry Zellers and Nell Dyer helped Sister Mary Clare.
Father Canavan and I took charge of the Carmelite Superior, Mother
Thérèse, who had risen from a sick bed to take her place in the line.

From the direction of the POW encampment came ox-carts piled
high with supplies. As they passed we noted bags of grain, dried
fish, boxes of tobacco. If these supplies were intended for the
prisoners, many of them must have got into wrong hands. The fish
and tobacco we saw that day, for instance, were given neither to the
civilian prisoners nor to the POWs.

After the carts came the long line of POWs. I did not know many
of them then, but when they file past again in my memory, as they
often do now, I recognize here and there the officers or GIs I have
come to know since . . . Major Dunn, the senior officer . . . Sergeant
Leerkamp . . . Lieutenant Marlotte . . . Lieutenant Manietta . . .
Major Durham . . . Sergeants Knowles and Stumpes . . . and many
others whose faces I know, though some of their names I cannot
recall and some I never heard.

As the men passed by, my gaze went sometimes to their faces,
sometimes to their feet. Some of those feet were bare, and some
were already bleeding. Some feet paced steadily, if wearily, on ;
but weaker men, dragging on the shoulders of their comrades, put
ghastly, shuffling syncopation in the sombre rhythm of the march.

The civilian group fell in at the end of the POW column. None
of us were barefoot, but many were poorly shod for a journey over
stony mountain roads. Mother Thérèse, I recall, had only slippers
of cloth, made by her own hands. Norman Owen and Philip Deane

were also wearing footwear they had made themselves. Frau Gliese had rubber shoes whose soles were already holed.

On reaching the main road that paralleled the Yalu, we turned east. We knew then that our journey lay through Manpo. On the way into the town we passed our old home, the quarantine station. It was then we saw, as I have mentioned, the renovated buildings, the expensive car, the Soviet diplomat whom M. Perruche recognized.

Just short of Manpo we found the POWs moving into a field. We halted, too, and squatted on the ground for a couple of hours. We speculated on the reason for the delay. Had the officers of the guard gone off for a meal ? Perhaps there were troop movements ahead ? The rest was not altogether welcome, for The Tiger had said we must cover sixteen miles on this first evening, and we would probably pay dearly for the delay when the march was resumed.

Our forebodings proved correct. When at length word came to form up again, the guards bullied and hurried us as if we had been responsible for the hold-up.

There are many words in Korean for " quickly," but those guards of ours used only one, and used it so often that soon the very sound of it was torture. " Bali . . . Bali ! "* It was the keynote of our march. The order was hardly given to get ready to move, when the guards came shouting it, " Bali, bali ! ", and all the time we were marching, this " bali-ing," as we called it, would continue, with each guard, like a sheep-dog, running up and down and yelling it at the stragglers stumbling on.

I evolved a theory that The Tiger had worked out a schedule for the march, and had decided on specific places for our overnight stops ; that our late start, and this delay near Manpo, upset his schedule ; that the upsetting of his plans enraged him, so that he drove us mercilessly on in an attempt to catch up with his schedule ; and that his failure drove him to greater fury, and blinded him to any regard for health or even life.

Whatever be the truth of this speculation, the fact is that " Bali, bali ! " became the dominant feature of our journey that first evening, and all the days that followed. And it was this inhuman driving more than any other cause that made our march a march of death. Most of those who died were killed by the gruelling pace. The

---

* Pronounced _bahlee._

length of the journey, the lack of sleep, the bad and inadequate food, were all contributing causes ; but many, perhaps all, could have endured these hardships if they had not been continually hurried along during the hours given to travel. Many who could have walked the distance covered by the party on any one day, if they had been allowed to spread the journey over more hours of the day, were so weakened by the continual hurrying that at last they could not walk at all. This merciless pressure was especially weakening for the many who were suffering from severe dysentery, which seemed to be rife among the POWs. It was pitiful to see poor, emaciated lads who had fallen out, trying to regain their places in the lines, stumbling hurriedly and unsteadily along with a guard at their heels.

It was already night when we struggled into Manpo, and out of it by a road going east. In the gloom, there were groups of soldiers passing us, and sometimes moving across our path. But there was something different about them from all the soldiers I had seen till then. They moved at a bobbing, constant trot, long lines of riflemen and machine-gun crews clutching the pieces of their weapons. And at the rear came coolies, but not the familiar figures that plod for ever under A-frames on Korean tracks and roads ; these carried burdens swinging at the ends of poles that bobbed and swayed as they, too, moved on at a steady trot. We were meeting the Chinese.

We plodded on through the darkness, praying now for strength, encouraging one another, wondering if we could ever cover the sixteen miles The Tiger had said we must complete that night.

But we had travelled only six or seven miles when the column halted. We were told to move off the road and rest. Then word came that we would go no further that night. The guards told us we must sleep, but that was easier said than done. This was no season for sleeping in the open ; a few days later we would be marching through falling snow. We huddled close in little groups of three or four, and got what rest we could.

At daylight we were aroused, and a meal was served—of whole boiled corn, so far as I remember. We heard later that through some unfortunate blunder a number of the POWs got no food that morning.

The march was resumed. Again those strident voices were dinning in our ears " *Bali !* . . . *Bali !* "

We had covered two or three miles when there was a sudden halt. None of us will ever forget the moments that followed. When we moved on again we would be convinced beyond all doubt that we were at the mercy of a maniac who might well make us march till the last one fell in his tracks and died.

Let me tell, first, what I saw of the tragedy with my own eyes, and then add the details I heard later.

At the head of the halted column, The Tiger, a group of guards, and some GIs were talking. Commissioner Lord was there, interpreting. Presently they moved over to a knoll on the right side of the road ; they were still talking.

We saw a prisoner singled out and guards put a bandage over his eyes. The Tiger drew his pistol and stepped behind the blindfolded man. Behind me a woman sobbed hysterically. I turned my head away and began to pray for the man who stood there, motionless, waiting. A shot rang out, and its distant echoes died among the hills.

$$* \quad * \quad *$$

From Commissioner Lord and others we afterwards heard the detailed story. The Tiger had given strict orders that no one was to be allowed to fall out. After a time he had fallen back himself behind the column, as he often did. He was still absent when it became apparent that some of the GIs could walk no further, so their leaders asked the guards what should be done.

" Leave them by the roadside," the guards replied.

Swiftly The Tiger came striding along to overtake the column. The sight of men who had fallen out sent him into a fury. He called a general halt.

The POWs had been divided into sections, with one of their officers responsible for each group. The Tiger ordered every officer who had allowed men to fall out of his section to come forward. Five officers stepped out and stood before him.

" Why did you allow men to fall out against my orders ? "

" We asked the guards what should be done, and that is the advice they gave us."

" Who were these guards ? Bring them forward."

The guards could not be produced.

" I will shoot these five men," said The Tiger, " for disobeying my orders."

The group moved over to the knoll. Commissioner Lord valiantly took up the men's defence. He pointed out that they had acted in good faith, that his decision was quite unjust. The Tiger reconsidered.

" Then I will shoot the man from whose section most men were allowed to fall out. Who is he ? "

Lieutenant Thornton, of Texas, stepped forward. He was calm, master of himself. He merely whispered to Commissioner Lord : " Save me if you can, sir."

The Commissioner tried, but The Tiger turned on him in fury. " You shut up," he snarled, " or I'll shoot you, too! You're only the translator."

As he stood there muttering to himself as if in doubt, a band of soldiers passed along the road. He called to them : " What should be done to a man who disobeys the People's Army ? "

" Shoot him," they shouted back.

A moment's hesitation on their part might have saved the life still hanging in the balance. But there was none. The Tiger's hesitation ended ; but the need to justify himself still held him. Stripping off his overcoat, he pointed to the star on two bars, the insignia of a major, on the blue epaulettes of his jacket.

" I have the power," he said, " to do this."

A guard blindfolded Lieutenant Thornton. The Tiger drew his pistol, cocked it, and stepped behind his victim. Then he flicked up the back of the lieutenant's cap, and shot him through the head.

A brave man fell dead on the knoll. Down below, in the frightened hush that followed the shot, another brave man walked calmly from the ranks and began to dig a grave. It was the same tall, fair sergeant we had watched as he dug another grave two months before. He had come to us as we sheltered in the valley, to have his dead comrade buried by a priest. His name was Henry Leerkamp.

Battling now with the stony earth at the foot of the knoll, he called to the men standing petrified above : " Won't some of you come down to help me ? "

The calm words broke the spell of horror. They lifted the body of the murdered man and carried it down. It was laid in a shallow grave, and stones were piled on top. The men fell into line again. The march was resumed.

*　　*　　*

We kept on hour after hour, knowing that it would be inviting further tragedy to allow anyone to fall out now.

Our own plight was bad enough, but it was evident that the POWs were in a worse state. Again and again we heard the shout going up along the line : " Send back more strong men." As with us, the weak who could still walk were being supported by their comrades. But already many of the POWs were unable to walk at all ; they had to be carried bodily. But the pace was so gruelling, and pauses for rest so infrequent, that even a team of four could not carry a man for more than ten or fifteen minutes without relief. As each hour passed, there were more and more men to be carried, and the number of those fit to carry them was steadily reduced. If The Tiger continued to force this pace, it was only a matter of time till it would be physically impossible to obey his orders that no one fall behind. What then ?

He did press us on, all that day and for several days more. POWs first, and then civilians, we had to face the fact that some could march no longer. The Tiger and his men would deal with that situation when it came.

Some time after midday we passed through a village and stopped just beyond. The guards called for a party of men to bring food from the village. Some of us fell out of the civilian group and lined up on the road. A group of POWs formed up near us. A fair, stocky officer was beside me.

" Name is Roth," he whispered. " Lieutenant. From Dayton, Ohio. I'm a Catholic, and there are other Catholic lads who want Confession."

I waited while a guard passed by. Then I wandered out of the line and asked advice of Bishop Byrne.

" Tell the lieutenant," he said, " to try to get word to all Catholics that I'll give General Absolution just as the march begins again. The men should try to prepare themselves."

I rejoined the line, and found an opportunity to pass the bishop's message to Lieutenant Roth.

We marched into the village to collect the food, and after a long wait were given buckets of boiled maize to carry back. Our relatively small group was soon served, but distribution took longer with the POWs. Some of them were still waiting for their ration when The Tiger reappeared. He was angry at finding lunch still in progress, and ordered everyone, fed or unfed, to form up immediately. We marched away, leaving behind us by the roadside buckets of steaming maize.

For most of the afternoon we followed the course of a river that wound between sunlit hills. At first we marched along the river bank. Then, when the valley widened, our road moved out to the lower slopes of the valley's eastern wall, to continue then mile after mile through fields. The western wall was now in shadow, and still the guards pressed us on, insisting that we still had far to go. The line of shadow crossed the valley floor, crept to where we marched, passed on over us, and climbed to meet the sky. Still we kept on through the deepening dusk, hoping always that the next turn in the road would bring us to our goal. Old Father Villemot, who was being helped along by Monsignor Quinlan and Father Bulteau, collapsed from exhaustion some time that evening, and some GIs helped to carry him for a while in a blanket.

At last the moving column left the road, to halt beside a farmhouse in a field. Obviously this was not our journey's end, but it was a relief to know that the day's march was over. We had come about twenty miles since morning.

The POWs were left in the open field. The civilians were conducted to the farmhouse, where one room was found for the diplomatic group and another for the families. The rest of us slept on straw in the farmyard, as many as possible sheltering under the eaves of the house. I spent the night in the yard with Monsignor Quinlan and Walter Eltringham. Walter was suffering greatly from the cold, and we put him between us and huddled together. Even so, he could not sleep, and after an hour or two he told us he was numb with cold and must get up and move about. Monsignor Quinlan and I dozed a little from time to time.

Louis Dans and the Methodist missionary, Larry Zellers, decided it was useless to attempt to sleep that night, so they passed the hours moving among the POWs in the field, sitting now and then to chat

Walter Eltringham, ECA mining engineer from Pennsylvania, who died in captivity.

Nell Dyer, Methodist missionary from Arkansas, who survived.

Mother Béatrix (French), superior of the St. Paul of Chartres congregation in Korea, who died.

Fr. Frank Canavan, Irish Columban missionary, who died after five months' captivity.

Arthur Leopold

with sleepless men, drawing near whenever they could to the fires the guards had lit. From time to time the guards would drive back with blows any of the prisoners who had crept up to steal a little warmth, or had tried to remain near after carrying wood to feed the fires. Danny and Larry told me afterwards how they had seen men so crazed with cold that even the guards' cruel beatings failed to drive them back. They saw these poor lads lie motionless under a rain of blows, and then start to creep in again. They saw men who were themselves half-frozen trying to save others from freezing to death. Among the huddled groups men dozed, and woke to find they were hugging corpses.

By morning there were about a dozen GIs dead. Eight others or more were unable to walk, and orders were given that these should be left behind. Commissioner Lord, as interpreter, was among the last to leave. He overheard the instructions given to the local people about burying the dead. It was the number mentioned that gave that order a chilling, dread significance. It included every man we had left behind.

Dazed with cold and lack of sleep, we dragged our weary limbs to the road, and started another day's march. We travelled more than twenty miles that day, with only a few short rests. During the afternoon, Mother Thérèse, who was being supported by Father Canavan and myself, became faint. We used a blanket and two straight branches to improvise a stretcher, and all who could possibly be spared from the task of supporting others took turns at carrying the sick nun. After an hour or two she recovered a little, and insisted on walking once more.

With this exception, all of our party completed the whole of that day's journey on foot, even Father Villemot, who had collapsed the day before. The POWs were amazed at the endurance our people showed. I recall some of them asking how it was that we had many aged folk still walking, while they were carrying men of nineteen and twenty. And some of our elderly ones had kept going even without aid from others. I particularly remember two who had trudged steadily on without help since the march began, and who still showed no signs of weakening at the end of this third day. One was Bishop Cooper, and the other Miss Bertha Smith.

Miss Smith is one of the American Methodist missionaries who were arrested in Kaesong on the first day of the invasion. If she had been granted a few more months of liberty, she would have been due for retirement after a long missionary career. She had faced her disappointment with characteristic imperturbability. She was not the type to be stampeded, even by the Reds. The quiet, determined, patient way she kept going on the march was typical of how she faced every problem.

In the many months that have passed since the march of November 1950 I have come to know this lady as one whose quiet, unassuming manner covers an inexhaustible fund of kindliness and helpfulness towards others. Her fellow missionaries, in the course of the passing months, have valued her remarkable gift of memory. In their religious meetings, held without the aid of any books, Miss Smith could supply them with the words of scores of hymns.

*   *   *

If I remember that Bishop Cooper and Miss Smith still seemed fit after the third day of the march, I also remember that most of the other elderly folk, and some of the younger ones, were nearing the end of their endurance.

The Fathers Gombert, for instance, who had walked a great deal without help so far, were beginning to fail. Father Cadars had been plodding along steadily like the old soldier he was, as if the burden of seventy years sat lightly upon him ; but an infection that had developed in his hand after a heavy fall was daily growing worse, and must soon affect his general condition. Moreover, all three were suffering from dysentery, which increased their weakness. Others of the party had the same trouble, and the march was not held up to accommodate those impeded in this way : they simply had to catch up again, and it meant an agonizing effort every time.

Bishop Byrne and Dr. Jensen, who had been walking together for most of the march, helping each other, were finding it hard to keep going. Alfred Matti and Dr. Kisch were also failing. Walter Eltringham, who had eaten little since his arrest, had already been weak before the march began. He had helped Mother Mechtilde, Sister Mary Clare and others, as long as he could ; but on this third day he was barely able to keep moving himself.

Seventy-six-year-old Madame Martel was still able to walk, but

only with great difficulty ; and the same was true of the elderly
Russians, Madame Funderat, Tihinoff (Father Christmas), and Leonoff.
The Anglican missionary, Charles Hunt, a big and heavy man, was
still suffering from the gout which had attacked him in the early
weeks of internment. Bill Evans also had foot troubles, and had often
to be helped by Louis Dans, whose special duty it was to help
stragglers keep up with the main body.

Among the younger people, the worst sufferer was the French-
Korean Madame Hoang, whose plumpness was telling against her
as she toiled along, hour after hour, with her young son.

Mother Béatrix was in the worst condition of all. It had become
obvious during this third day's march that she could not go on much
longer. During the afternoon she had begun to fall behind, despite
all the efforts of her companion, Mother Eugénie. The French diplomats, who had fallen still further behind with Madame Martel, came
upon the two nuns halted by the wayside, with a guard trying to
bully them. The Frenchmen carried Mother Béatrix for a while,
but they became exhausted themselves. The presence of the French
consul, however, brought about a change in the guard's attitude.
He allowed the party to bring Mother Béatrix along more slowly,
and finally they all arrived at the school where the rest of us had been
halted for the night.

M. Perruche immediately sought out The Tiger to tell him that
many of the old people, including several French citizens for whom
he, as consul, was responsible, could walk no further, and that it was
imperative to get transport for them. The Tiger seemed sympathetic,
and promised to do what he could.

Meantime a meal was served to all of us, POWs and civilians, as
we sat in the school grounds. Then the civilians were taken into the
building. A room was set aside for the diplomats, and another for
the women and children. The rest of us civilians were put into a
corner of the one large schoolroom, and then the POWs were told
that as many as could fit in the remaining space could come in.

Exhausted men began pouring in, to sink wearily to the floor.
They sat close together, but the room was soon filled to the doors,
and there were still hundreds left outside. The guards shouted at
the sitting men to crowd closer together, and the shivering men
outside added their appeals. Tighter and tighter we were packed,

till it was impossible for any more to find sitting-space. But more kept coming, to find standing-room now along the walls. When not another man could be squeezed in, the guards closed the doors.

Then began a night that seemed an age. Soon after the doors were closed, the room became a bedlam. Cramped and twisted limbs began to ache. Men moaned with pain, tried to get some relief by movement, and were cursed by their tortured neighbours. Officers called for order, but their voices only added to the ever-growing din. Exhausted men keeled over, and were pushed aside by the stifled men on whom they had fallen. Some struggled to get out of the room, walking perforce over their comrades' bodies. Outside, others hammered at the doors and begged to be let in. Guards shouted through the windows, threatening to spray the milling prisoners with machine-gun bullets. Time stood still. One's whole world had become a chaos of noise and suffering.

Dawn came at last. The doors were opened, and men began to stumble out, bleary-eyed, light-headed, aching in every joint. When at last it was possible to leave our corner, we saw that several GIs had died during the night. Some, it was said, had died on their feet, standing against the walls.

When we had finished our morning meal The Tiger climbed on a box and made a speech. He had three main points, of which the first impressed us not at all, the second left us wondering, and the third cheered us greatly.

He told us, in the first place, that the People's Government had in mind, in all that it did for us, only the preservation of our health and our ultimate release. We should appreciate, therefore, the interest the authorities were taking in our welfare, and should co-operate with their efforts. Secondly, we need have no anxiety about people who fell out during the march. They would be taken to People's Hospitals and would be well cared for. Thirdly, from this morning there would be transport for the women who found diffi-culty in walking. We all welcomed this last announcement, and no one more than Mother Eugénie, who knew that Mother Béatrix could not walk much more.

The time came for departure, but the women were not yet ready. When the men were ready to start off, those of us who had assisted the women on previous days tried to remain behind ; but the guards told us angrily that the women would not need our help since transport would be provided. They ordered us—with the sole exception of Commissioner Lord, who was needed as interpreter—to follow the rest of the men at once. Their argument seemed not unreasonable, yet we felt some misgivings as we trudged away.

Our uneasiness was much more justified than we knew at the time. We were no sooner out of sight than Miss Nell Dyer, beset by fussing and fuming guards as she tried to marshal her party, was given the astounding news that there would be no transport after all. Everyone must walk, even those who had been barely able to complete yesterday's march with the assistance of the menfolk: Mother Béatrix, Madame Martel, Mother Thérèse, Madame Funderat and others. And there was no man to help except Commissioner Lord, who was over sixty and had a serious heart ailment.

Meantime we marched ahead, unaware of the frightful predicament in which the women had been left. We marched all morning, moving for the greater part of the journey up a long wooded slope. I do not clearly recall with whom I walked, but I have a memory of toiling uphill with little Father Christmas leaning heavily on my shoulder and puffing like a locomotive, and I fancy the memory belongs to that morning of November 3.

We came about midday to a cluster of houses at a fork in the road, and were directed into a field behind the houses. There we awaited the arrival of the womenfolk. When they came in sight at last, we were dismayed to see that they were trudging along on foot. Where was the transport The Tiger had promised? As they gradually straggled in, we found they were dazed with exhaustion and grief, hardly coherent in their account of the woes that had befallen them.

We learned how Miss Dyer, their leader, had received the cruel news that there would be no transport, and had then set about arranging the group as best she could in preparation for the journey.

They had started off in a body, the stronger helping the weak— or rather the weak helping the weaker—but they had not been able to keep together for long. Mother Béatrix, with her faithful guardian, Mother Eugénie, had begun to fall behind almost immediately. Madame Funderat had fallen behind, too, and Commissioner Lord had stayed to help her. Those four were still missing long after the rest of the party had joined us in the field and were telling what they knew of the morning's events.

Nell Dyer had borne a crushing burden of anxiety all morning. She had been scolded because her party was not ready on time, blamed for not keeping them together on the march, harassed continually by the guards, menaced by The Tiger's pistol, badgered for her inability to make exhausted people move faster, and finally tormented and bullied on her own account when she became worn out in the effort to help Sister Mary Clare.

Long afterwards Nell told me that it still made her tremble to recall the hours she spent that morning struggling along with that poor nun. They had fallen behind on the long upward gradient, and became quite exhausted. Again and again they begged the guard, who was " *bali*-ing " them, to let them rest. Finally he consented, and gratefully they stretched out on the roadside. Their spent bodies had hardly reached the ground when some local people appeared, and immediately the guard began kicking Miss Dyer in the legs and urging the two women to get up quickly and start walking again. They dragged themselves to their feet, and went on a little further till there was no one in sight. Then the guard let them rest, but warned them this time not to lie down.

" Why do you treat us like this ? " Nell Dyer asked him. " We are elderly people, and isn't it a Korean tradition to have respect for age ? "

" That is true," the guard replied ; " but now that we are in the People's Army we are not free in these matters any more."

*   *   *

We waited a long time for the missing four. Then at last a guard came into view, and with him the solitary figure of Mother Eugénie. As she came to us we saw that she was red-eyed with weeping, and soon we knew some of the tragic story that she brought. Later I heard it in detail from herself.

Mother Béatrix had begun to fail as soon as the morning's march started. She and Mother Eugénie fell behind. They had struggled on for only a mile or two when the old nun sank down by the roadside, utterly unable to go on. Guards gathered around and tried to hustle them on. They told Mother Eugénie to go ahead, and began pushing Mother Béatrix to make her get up and walk. Mother Eugénie pleaded with them. She told them the woman they were brutally treating was seventy-six years old, and had spent nearly fifty of those years in caring for the sick and the poor and the orphans of their country. Her appeals were in vain. Again Mother Eugénie was ordered away and when she would not go, the guards forcibly tore her arms away from Mother Béatrix. Calmly the old nun advised her to obey them : " Go, my Sister, go."

Mother Eugénie would gladly have given life itself for that gentle soul who now lay spent and helpless, but there was not a thing that she could do. By refusing to leave her she might even precipitate a tragedy. She went back for one last embrace. The guards dragged her away then, and sent her off, with a push, along the road. Stumbling, praying, desolate and weeping, it was two hours before she overtook the others.

Distracted though she was with sorrow, she still clung to a forlorn hope that Mother Béatrix might overtake us yet, or at least that the guards might have left her at some house where she would be cared for. Some tried to encourage her hopes, others advised her to accept the fact that Mother Béatrix was dead. Some of the women asked her had she not heard that shot back on the road.

Before another day was ended, we had seen enough to leave no doubt as to the fate of Mother Béatrix.

*　　*　　*

A life of long and remarkable service to others ended, that November morning of 1950.

Anne Marie Edouard had wished from early girlhood to devote her life to God's poor, but she had duties first to her young brothers and sisters. By 1899, when she was twenty-four, she was free to follow her chosen vocation, and in that year she entered the St. Paul of Chartres Congregation in her native France. After her religious profession, she was assigned to a home for the aged.

Her missionary career began in 1906 with an appointment to the orphanage maintained by her congregation in Seoul. Before long, the sick and the lowly in the poorer quarters of the city were familiar with her slim, upright figure, her dark oval face, her brilliant black eyes ; and they soon learned to appreciate the thoughtfulness and generosity that lay behind her shy expression. This shyness of hers made the learning of her adopted people's language a slow task, but meantime she would not let this difficulty keep her from her poor. With a Korean Sister for companion and interpreter, she went day by day on her errands of mercy to the sick and needy.

Recognition of her exceptional qualities brought her successive appointments as mistress of novices in Seoul till 1932 ; as local superior in Taikou till 1942 ; then, for the years following, as provincial superior for the whole of Korea. She still held this office at the time of her arrest. She had received instructions from her Superior-General to leave Seoul in the event of Red invasion, but had written pleading to be allowed to stay with her Korean Sisters no matter what befell. This permission had been granted.

Mother Eugénie, to whom I am indebted for these details, stresses two outstanding characteristics in Mother Béatrix : her zealous regard for the value of time, and her inexhaustible love for the poor. Never in all those years of heavy responsibilities did she cease to work with her own hands for the poor.

I have no doubt that the Korean people as a whole will blush with shame and indignation if they ever learn what was done by a few men of their race to a gracious French lady who gave to their country nearly half a century of unselfish service.

*   *   *

Some time after Mother Eugénie's arrival, the last two stragglers appeared : Commissioner Lord and the Russian widow, Madame Funderat. As they came into view, with a guard in close attendance, we saw with a shock that the Commissioner was towing the woman on a rope.

Madame Funderat was nearly seventy years old, and childless. She had been left alone in the world, by the death of her husband just a few days before the invasion began, and had been arrested in her home when the Reds arrived in Seoul.

When she could walk no further on her own on the morning of this fourth day of the march Commissioner Lord had helped her ; but his ailing heart, the uphill road, and her considerable weight soon left him exhausted. Then the guard helped her for a time, but finally got a length of rope and bade the Commissioner tie it around her waist and pull her after him.

But Lord's valiant efforts to save her from the fate of Mother Béatrix were spent in vain. The march resumed when we had eaten, and the guard insisted now that the Commissioner must leave the old woman behind. When he last saw her, the guard was helping her along. But she never overtook us.

*   *   *

I have said that I do not clearly remember with whom I walked during the morning of that day. I certainly remember my companions of the afternoon : Monsignor Quinlan and Father Villemot. During the morning, Father Bulteau and Monsignor Quinlan had been supporting Father Villemot between them. Father Bulteau had injured his knee, and was now in difficulties himself ; so I took his place as helper to Father Villemot.

The road lay at first down a gentle grade, and then along a valley. Old Father Villemot stumbled down the slope, clinging to us as we supported as much of his weight as we could. Soon after we reached the valley his strength gave out, and it was all we could do to keep him on his feet. Since the start of the forced march three days ago, those tired old feet had walked some sixty miles. He had been supported by others, it is true ; yet, except for the period of brief collapse on the second evening, when he was carried in a blanket, he had managed to keep on his feet, and to keep those feet going one after the other for sixty miles over mountain roads . . . at eighty-two ! As chaplain to the St. Paul of Chartres convent in Seoul, this frail, tottering old man had been helped up the steps of the altar each morning by the Sisters. Now he was weakened by three months of hardship and semi-starvation. What weariness and pain it had cost him to continue this killing march !

And now he was near the end of his endurance. Was his magnificent effort to be in vain, after all ? The unspoken thought agitated Monsignor Quinlan and myself as we toiled along, conscious that now we ourselves were weakening. But we were determined to use the last ounce of our strength in the attempt to save our old and gallant friend.

If we tried to rest, the guard hounded us on. We began to pray aloud, the old man joining in when he could catch his breath. After a while he told us his heel was hurting. Perhaps his sock was creased ? We stopped to look. Monsignor Quinlan supported him while I took off his shoe. There was no heel to the sock, there was no skin on the heel of the foot, and the inside of the shoe was sticky with blood. What was there to do but put in a pad of cloth and urge the old warrior to try again ? He was having spells of faintness now, but on we went, hounded by the guard, half-dragging and half-carrying the poor old man. It was pitiful. It was cruel. But what else to do ?

At last we came to a farmhouse, and there the guard let us rest a while. But soon he was urging us on again.

" I cannot possibly go any further," said Father Villemot.

*   *   *

Life had begun for Paul Villemot in 1868, in the neighbourhood of the Norvan mountains in central France. He was twenty-four when, in 1892, he began his missionary career in Korea as a newly-ordained priest of the Paris Foreign Mission Society. At that time the Church in Korea was slowly rebuilding her strength after a series of persecutions that, two decades before, had left her without a single priest for her 17,000 Christians, and without a single church building.*

The whole country (which today has eight ecclesiastical divisions) had then but a single bishop, who lived in Seoul. There were no native priests, and only about a score of foreign missionaries.

Long known as " The Hermit Kingdom " for her determined opposition to the entry of foreigners, Korea had but very recently been forced by Japan, the United States, Britain, Germany, France and others, to remove these restrictions, and she was still seething with

---

* The first known effort to introduce Christianity into Korea was made by a Spanish Jesuit at the end of the sixteenth century, during a period of Japanese occupation, but the seed was not successfully planted till nearly two centuries later. Korea in those times had to send a delegation each year to Peking with tribute for the Chinese Emperor, and it was from books and information brought back by these delegations that the first Korean Christians got their knowledge of the faith. The knowledge was imperfect, and was soon overlaid with error. But when a Chinese priest arrived at the end of the eighteenth century, he found a priestless Christian community that had developed in less than a score of years to a membership of more than 4,000, and already had its roll of martyrs. This newly-arrived priest was soon added to the roll, and thousands of Korean Christians were to die for their faith in the waves of persecution that swept over the country till late in the nineteenth century.

resentment against foreigners during Father Villemot's early years as
a missionary. To add to his troubles, Korea became a battleground
between China and Japan two years after his arrival in the country,
and he narrowly escaped the execution suffered by one of his confrères when the vanquished Chinese armies retreated through his
district in the south-west. The Bishop recalled all the missionaries
to Seoul at this time, and Father Villemot eventually arrived there
after a hazardous journey that involved, like this other, a walk of a
hundred miles.

In Seoul he had been procurator—no sinecure in those days, when
many pioneering works, including the completion of Seoul cathedral,
put a heavy strain on mission coffers. He retained this responsibility
till 1918. For twenty-five years he was in charge of the cathedral
parish. He handed over his post to a Korean priest in 1942, to retire
from active missionary life and become chaplain to the convent
and orphanage of the St. Paul of Chartres Sisters.

He had come, indeed, a long and glorious journey through life.
Was it to end now, so pathetically, in a North Korean farmyard,
this November afternoon of 1950 ?

*   *   *

"Leave me here," said Father Villemot, "and these people will
surely let me die in their yard, and then bury me."

The guard levelled his rifle and rattled the bolt. "If you don't
go on, I'll kill you."

"I'm ready," the old man replied. "You may shoot me if you
wish."

The guard looked at us. "You can't leave him here. You'll have
to go further."

We struggled on another half-mile, and rested again. The farmhouse was now out of sight.

"You can go now," said the guard to Monsignor Quinlan and me.

I remember that guard very well. In later times he has often
visited our quarters and tried to ingratiate himself with some of the
younger women. But the sight of him has always recalled for me
that afternoon when he was prepared to murder an exhausted,
helpless man of eighty-two.

We begged the guard to give us a little more time. We managed another quarter-mile, a half-mile, a mile. Then we rounded a bend, to see an ox-cart stopped with a crowd of our people round it. Perhaps we could get a ride for the old priest. We told him of our hopes, and hurried him along as best we could, watching, praying, fearing every moment that the cart would move off. We reached it at last, and found The Tiger talking with the French diplomatic group. Madame Martel had collapsed there, and The Tiger had come upon the scene. He had agreed to stop a supply-cart and allow Madame Martel to ride on it. When we came up Monsignor Quinlan appealed to him, and he agreed that Father Villemot could ride too. Joyfully we helped the two old people on to the cart.

The Tiger was almost human that afternoon. He came across a family group in distress, and found transport for them too. Later he caught up again with Monsignor Quinlan and myself as we were bathing our feet in a ditch, and stopped to chat with us.

We came up with the main body resting in a field, awaiting the arrival of the stragglers. The POWs were now marched off to a school for the night, and the civilians were taken to a small church. That day also, we had walked something near twenty miles.

Ground and roasted grain was distributed in little bags. We poured hot water over it to make a meal. Then Bishop Byrne and Philip Deane undertook to allot sleeping space, trying to ration it out so that everyone could at least lie at full length. Their task proved impossible. There simply was not enough space. Several of the party had therefore to take turns at sitting up, to allow others to stretch out for a while.

At dawn the guards came to end our uneasy rest. It was Saturday, November 4. Of all the days we have spent in bondage, none has left us more bitter, painful memories.

In the early hours of the morning it had begun to snow. Now, at dawn, the guards told us we must leave immediately, for today we would have to cross the mountain range that lay ahead, and we must hasten to reach the passes before they were blocked with snow.

Our supper of the evening before had been meagre. Now, without breakfast, we began a hurried, uphill march through snow. Mercifully, Father Villemot and Madame Martel were allowed to ride on a supply-cart. The rest of us struggled along as best we could, the stronger helping the weak.

The road, gently winding, rose gradually to the foothills, then snaked its way up the mountainside in a series of wide loops. Ahead we could see the POWs already labouring up the steep ascent. They had started—fasting, like ourselves—only a little while before our group. From the lead they had already gained, it was evident that they were being pressed hard.

I was assisting Mother Thérèse, the Carmelite, that morning, and already we were lagging behind the rest. Beside us, Sister Bernadette was toiling along through the thickening carpet of snow with blind Sister Marie-Madeleine. Just ahead, Larry Zellers was supporting Sister Mary Clare.

Shots sounded somewhere near us, but caused us no alarm. We had often known the guards to amuse themselves by firing off their rifles. As we passed the mouth of a ravine we saw an officer and some guards returning toward the road. Larry remembers distinctly that they were laughing, but like myself he thought nothing of the incident at the time. Somewhere ahead of us more shots sounded. If the thought entered our minds that there were more shots than usual, it was soon dismissed from our attention as we laboured on, anxious to overtake the others.

We came upon an exhausted GI sitting by the roadside, then another. Beside each of them a guard was standing. We passed around a bend, and then two shots rang out behind us. We knew at once that they had been fired by the guards we had just passed. I remember still how my head reeled and my knees went weak as the shocking truth came home to me. We recalled now the first shots we had heard, remembering the guards emerging from the ravine. We recalled, too, the shots that had sounded ahead ; fired perhaps in another ravine.

Our hearts ached with helpless pity as we came upon more and more men sitting or lying exhausted by the roadside, attended always by guards, who waited ominously till we stragglers passed. Then, each time, we listened in dumb anguish for the sound that always came—the sound of a shot behind us on the road.

Never before had I witnessed such tragedy as this, and I had never before felt so utterly helpless in face of others' need. Even the task of helping Mother Thérèse was taxing all my strength, and if we tried to rest, the guards roared us on.

I had no help to give the men who fell and lay beside the road, exhausted, doomed. A few months ago they could have made this march with ease. Captivity had transformed their vigorous young bodies into feeble, tottering skeletons. Half-starved and ill-clad, they had lived in almost arctic cold, sometimes in unheated buildings, sometimes under the open sky. They had covered the miles behind us in long, forced stages, with sleepless nights and all but foodless days. And if they weakened now, they would have gone through all this in vain ; for the penalty for weakness was death.

We passed them by as closely as we could and as slowly as we dared, and I spoke a few words about God's love and mercy. God was near to us in this dark hour . . . beyond this night of pain and hate. His love was real . . . His mercy . . . His forgiveness . . . His reward was waiting for us . . .

Some nodded as if they understood. One poor lad just looked blankly up at me, and asked me if I had a cigarette. I remember the trickle of blood that ran from one man's mouth. There was one, with eyes wide and bright, who stared defiance at the guard standing over him. I watched another struggling to his feet, to stagger a few paces and then sink down again. One boy sang *God Bless America* as he waited for death by the roadside. The brave voice was stilled before we reached him ; it was one of the women in advance of us who told me later.

The marching POWs were well ahead of us now. Above us on the mountain face I watched the column vanish round a bend to reappear on a higher loop of the road. Higher and higher they climbed, vanishing, reappearing. It was obvious that they were being forced on at a gruelling pace, and more and more must be falling by the wayside.

My eyes fell again to the road beneath our feet. The white carpet of snow was flecked with red. Blood on the snow . . . Other sights of that morning may fade from memory with the passing years, but the picture of blood-flecked snow is etched too deeply ever to be erased.

Twenty-two men fell out that morning. Knowing what had been their fate, we had no doubt now of what had happened to Mother Béatrix and Madame Funderat and the eighteen soldiers who had fallen out the day before, and the sick men who had been left behind on previous days. And we knew now what "People's Hospitals" meant in the language of The Tiger.

At last I arrived with Mother Thérèse at the top of the mountain. Most of our group were assembled there already, but Commissioner Lord was not among them, nor Sophia Sultan. Soon the Commissioner joined us, with the alarming news that he had been forced by a guard to leave Sophia by the roadside when she refused to walk any further. Then, to our great relief, Sophia came into view, all smiles, riding atop a load of supplies. On another cart came Madame Martel and Father Villemot.

For the downward journey some others were allowed to ride along with Madame Martel and Father Villemot; the rest of us began the descent on foot. Larry Zellers was helping me now with Mother Thérèse. The steep, tortuous route through slippery snow proved difficult and dangerous. Mother Thérèse became faint before we reached the foot of the mountain, and Larry and I half-carried her.

The POWs had already started down the mountain before our party reached the crest. None of them, thank God, fell out during the descent.

From the foot of the hill the road wound into a town whose name we found to be Chasong. As we walked along a street, Bishop Byrne stepped aside to tie a shoelace. A bellowing guard rushed up and gave him a violent shove, ordering him on. The Apostolic Delegate went sprawling in the snow. Someone helped him up and he went on, his expression as placid as ever.

It was still mid-morning, perhaps ten o'clock, when we arrived at a schoolhouse and learned to our joy that we need march no more that day. Whether The Tiger's lust for blood was sated, or whether he had at last caught up with his schedule, or whether higher authority intervened to give us some relief from the relentless daily marches, we never knew. Whatever the reason, we were told we could rest at Chasong for the remainder of that day and part of the next. Moreover, when we did resume our march, we found a change; the treatment was a good deal more human.

We were shown into a classroom of the school—and saw a vision that we feared could not be real : a vision of straw laid out in bed-sized lots upon the floor. We confirmed with eager hands the evidence of our eyes. Yes, there was actually soft straw waiting to cushion our weary, aching bodies ! To us, on November 4, 1950, those heaps of straw seemed the most luxurious couches in all the world.

Soon after our arrival, Monsignor Quinlan and Commissioner Lord renewed their pleas for transport for the weak, and finally they were told that vehicles would be found. And so they were. That evening a truck and a bus carried off the women, the children, the old men, and five very sick GIs.

The rest of us stayed at the school till the following afternoon. We left then in two groups. Civilians marched with the main body of POWs. Behind us followed, at an easier pace, POWs who were sick or weak. Father Booth accompanied the slower group as interpreter.

That evening we travelled about ten miles. For our group a fierce enough pace was set, but we were all able to keep up except Charles Hunt. When he began to lag behind, Monsignor Quinlan and I went to his assistance. His strength had failed completely, and we found ourselves getting weak in the effort to support him. He was, as I have mentioned elsewhere, an unusually big and heavy man. Seeing our plight, a guard said he could wait for the slower group and ride on one of the supply-carts.

The Monsignor and I were sent on to rejoin the men ahead. We overtook them as they were entering a schoolhouse in which we were to spend the night. When the others arrived, we were glad to find Charles Hunt rested and somewhat recovered. But he was still far from well.

Next day we set off again in our two groups. As on the previous day, we covered only ten miles. It was a short stage compared with some we had made earlier, but many of the party were nearing the end of their endurance, and were able to complete it only with the greatest difficulty. This was true, I remember, of Bishop Byrne, Dr. Jensen, Bill Evans and Dr. Kisch. I was in trouble, too, with an infection in the sole of a foot. I was demoted from the rank of helper, and had to be helped myself. Monsignor Quinlan lent me his strong shoulder from that day till we reached the end of our journey two days later. The foot infection, fortunately, did not spread, but it remained with me for months.

On the night of the 6th our lodging was again a schoolhouse.

The civilians were given two small rooms at the back of the building. They were *ondol* rooms, and we had them nicely warm when one of the misguided Turks found a pile of wood in the yard and decided to feed the fires to capacity. He meant perhaps to provide in one splendid feast all the warmth we had hungered for in more than a week ; or perhaps to ensure that we would not feel cold again for several days to come ; or, very possibly, both. However admirable his intentions, he made an oven of the ten-foot-square room in which eighteen of us had to spend the night. I escaped from that room in the morning with a more vivid idea of purgatory than I ever had before.

Walter Eltringham emerged to find that his shoes had been roasted even more unmercifully than himself. We had all left our footwear in the hall between the two rooms, and unfortunately someone had moved Walter's shoes and left them on top of a firebox. By morning they were so shrunken and hardened as to be unwearable. This was a serious disaster, for Walter had to march from that day on in crude sandals of rice-straw. Certainly, abnormal living conditions can have a magnifying effect on minor inconveniences, and we experienced many instances of this.

*   *   *

Of these small accidents of ordinary life, perhaps the most serious in their consequences for us, were those that made eating difficult.

Commissioner Lord, for example, had broken a denture in Manpo. Ordinarily this would have meant a few days of discomfort, and of restriction to soft foods till the denture was repaired. But the Commissioner could not get repairs made, and so had to resign himself to the prospect of remaining toothless for the rest of his internment, and going unfed when no soft food was available. Old Father Villemot and Mother Béatrix, who had come toothless into internment, had endured since July the afflictions which began at Manpo in September for the Commissioner ; and later on Monsignor Quinlan and Sister Marie-Madeleine were to suffer in the same way.

This was a serious matter indeed, for in these days of forced marching, nourishment was simply vital. Besides, the two (sometimes three) daily meals often consisted of nothing but whole corn, and that is no food for people without teeth. It was important to The

Tiger that his official interpreter should keep going, so occasionally he saw to it that Commissioner Lord got food he could eat. But The Tiger had no such interest in the survival of Father Villemot or Mother Béatrix, or of anyone else who found the corn uneatable. The Commissioner, joined by Monsignor Quinlan and Miss Dyer, tried again and again to get better food for those who were failing through malnutrition, as he had also tried to get transport for the weak. The latter plea had at length produced some result, but no amount of begging brought the sufferers food they could eat.

Mother Béatrix had been executed as the penalty for exhaustion on the fourth day's march. Her exhaustion was largely due to the virtual starvation imposed upon her by the lack of food she could eat. Father Villemot would die before another week had passed, less violently, but from the same cause, virtual starvation. Both were victims of a circumstance that would, in normal life, be trivial ; they had starved because they could not eat hard food.

*   *   *

We laboured through still another day, but this was uneventful. Again we were brought to a schoolhouse for the night.

That evening Major Dunn, the senior officer of the POWs, came to our room with a Korean officer, looking for Commissioner Lord. The Korean officer was compiling a record of dead or missing prisoners, and the Commissioner was needed as interpreter. For hours the three men struggled with figures and dates, trying to get the record straight. It would be interesting to see the report that was finally drawn up by that Korean officer. Did it mention, I wonder, that The Tiger, at some point during the march, had ordered the guards to take all identification discs from the POWs ? Did " missing " and " dead " have separate meaning in the report of the march itself ?

Next day (November 8) a short march brought us to the town of Jungkan-jin. We were taken to a large school building, and there we found the folk who had gone ahead by bus and truck. They had sad news for us. They had arrived three days before, on the morning of Sunday, the 5th. The following morning they had found that Sister Mary Clare was dead, having passed away quietly in her sleep.

They laid her to rest in a simple grave on a hillside behind the school.

The five sick soldiers who had travelled with them were in a bad state, and they had been giving them such help as they could. One in particular had won their sympathy—an unfortunate lad who had undergone, without anaesthetic, an operation for appendicitis, and had been convalescing nicely when the order came to march. The incision had soon opened up, and he must have suffered agonies during the five days he was forced to keep going on foot. He was now very ill, but showing the greatest patience, courage and cheerfulness. Unfortunately he was to die before the winter passed.

We had begun the forced march from near Manpo on October 31. Our arrival at Jungkan on November 8 completed a journey of more than a hundred miles. We had left almost a hundred dead along the way.

Jungkan and Halang

November 9, 1950 to March 28, 1951

THE death march was over, but it had not yet taken its full toll of lives. It had cost the POWs ninety-six of their number. We had lost Mother Béatrix and Madame Paradget, and now Sister Mary Clare had died of its effects. Fourteen more deaths at the civilian party were soon to follow, three at Jungkan and eleven in our next camp at Halang, all caused or hastened by the effects of the gruelling trek. We stayed a week in Jungkan, and nineteen weeks in Halang. How many of the POWs died during those twenty weeks I do not know, but the number must have been very high: over two hundred, I would estimate.

I can deal only in a fragmentary way with the fortunes of the POWs, for their story and ours have run on different paths, converging briefly at irregular intervals. But from those occasional contacts it appears that if their story is ever told in the free world, it will make far grimmer reading than ours. During the forced march itself, we civilians received some quarter in that the weak were sometimes allowed to fall behind without incurring the death penalty; whereas the POWs were driven on without mercy almost to the end, and none that fell were spared. Here in Jungkan, too, where they were accommodated in the same schoolhouse as ourselves, even such niggardly efforts as were made to lighten our discomfort were denied to them. They slept on the bare wooden floors. We at least had rice-straw mats. We were also given a heating-stove. It was placed in the open doorway of the partition that divided our room into men's and women's quarters. It behaved erratically, sometimes making the room too hot, sometimes leaving us icy cold; and the supply of wood was irregular. Nevertheless, it helped to make the draughty room more habitable. The POWs had to suffer the biting cold and the constant draughts with no heating at all.

11

Jungkan and Hajang

NOVEMBER 9, 1950 TO MARCH 28, 1951

THE death march was over, but it had not yet taken its full toll of lives. It had cost the POWs ninety-six of their number. We had lost Mother Béatrix and Madame Funderat, and now Sister Mary Clare had died of its effects. Fourteen more deaths in the civilian party were soon to follow, three at Jungkan and eleven in our next camp at Hajang, all caused or hastened by the effects of the gruelling trek. We stayed a week in Jungkan, and nineteen weeks in Hajang. How many of the POWs died during those twenty weeks I do not know, but the number must have been very high : over two hundred, I would estimate.

I can deal only in a fragmentary way with the fortunes of the POWs, for their story and ours have run on different paths, converging briefly at irregular intervals. But from these occasional contacts it appears that if their story is ever told in the free world, it will make far grimmer reading than ours. During the forced march itself, we civilians received some quarter in that the weak were sometimes allowed to fall behind without incurring the death penalty ; whereas the POWs were driven on without mercy almost to the end, and none that fell were spared. Here in Jungkan, too, where they were accommodated in the same schoolhouse as ourselves, even such niggardly efforts as were made to lighten our discomfort were denied to them. They slept on the bare wooden floors. We at least had rice-straw mats. We were also given a heating-stove. It was placed in the open doorway of the partition that divided our room into men's and women's quarters. It behaved erratically, sometimes making the room too hot, sometimes leaving us icy cold ; and the supply of wood was irregular. Nevertheless, it helped to make the draughty room more habitable. The POWs had to suffer the biting cold and the constant draughts with no heating at all.

Many of both POWs and civilians were already seriously ill. It is sad to think that even at this stage many of them could have been restored to health, if only they had been reasonably fed and housed. Proper medical care would probably have saved most of them. Whether our immediate custodians could have provided better medical facilities or not is debatable. But to those of us who watched Death's sickle reaping during those days, it remains a bitter memory that they withheld from the sick the ministrations of two qualified physicians who were present in the camp—Captain Boyson with the POWs and Dr. Kisch with us. Both were only too anxious to do what they could, but they were hopelessly handicapped. Captain Boyson was put in the position of lackey to a Korean nurse, carrying the medical kit for her as she tended the POWs. When serious illness among our group was reported to the guards, a Korean doctor would appear. I use the title " doctor " because that is how he described himself. In reality he was, I think, a medical orderly with some practical experience of doctoring. Occasionally Dr. Kisch was consulted, and sometimes he was even allowed to borrow the Korean's stethoscope, but he was never given charge of a case. Drugs were always in short supply. The Korean had a little sulphadiazine or penicillin now and then, but usually his treatment was restricted to painting external lesions with mercurochrome, administering a powder of some kind for internal disorders, and quieting the dying with a camphor injection.

It would be interesting to know how the medical care provided for the prisoners of war and civilian internees is described in the official records of the North Korean régime. If " People's Hospital " is official terminology, we had some experience of how The Tiger interpreted it. In the coming weeks we were to see some less imaginary institutions described as " hospitals " by our captors, but the term was still illusory. Those " hospitals " were hovels where sick prisoners shed the last remnants of their morale. Half-naked, lice-ridden, blanketless, the starving skeletons lay on the floor awaiting death. Dysentery patients staggered out, while they could still walk, to latrines in the arctic cold.

Adding insult to injury, The Tiger told the sick that their afflictions were due to their failure to take care of their health. To that insult he proceeded, incredibly, to add further injury.

The remedy for our health troubles, he announced, was fresh air and exercise. A day or two after our arrival, he gave orders that everyone must turn out for physical exercises before breakfast. In consternation we protested how sick many of our folk were, but we could get exemption for only three—Father Villemot, and the Carmelites, Mother Thérèse and Mother Mechtilde. Bishop Byrne, Father Canavan and Walter Eltringham were on the verge of pneumonia, but they were ordered out to the freezing air of the yard. So, too, were the septuagenarian Gombert brothers, both of whom would be dead in a few days. Father Antoine was unable to walk alone. Someone helped him to his feet and brought him as far as the outer door. There he collapsed, and had to be carried back.

Apart from the padded jackets issued to us five or six weeks before in the Manpo camp, many in our group had only light summer clothing. As for the POWs, almost all were clad merely in the remains of the summer uniforms they had been wearing at the time of their capture. In the compulsory exercising, too, the POWs fared worse than we, for The Tiger climbed on a rostrum to direct them, whereas we were left to ourselves. Those early morning parades in the November cold were death sentences for many.

The death rate was further accelerated by the inadequacy of our food, in quantity and quality. It consisted mostly of maize or millet ; and these insipid meals were rendered even more unsatisfactory in the first few days by bad cooking. The POWs did the best they could with an improvised kitchen, but their facilities were poor. After a day or two some of the women were allowed to help, and the cooking showed a little improvement. Even so, we were desperately ill-fed. Writing these lines more than two years later, under conditions long since improved, I find it difficult to realize the atrocious hunger of Jungkan in November of 1950. One significant recollection stands out : it was at Jungkan that I watched POWs stealing leaves of frozen cabbage—and watched them, not with pity, but with envy.

We suffered also from continual shortage of water. There was a well in the school grounds, but it was dry. Water had to be hauled from elsewhere by the POWs. It would not have taken much to satisfy our thirst in that bitter weather (so cold that the water-carts always came in festooned with great icicles), but we never could get enough.

★   ★   ★

Old Father Villemot was nearing death. Clearly, his frail body could not endure much more. On November 11, while the Catholics gathered round him were reciting the rosary, he passed quietly away. Some of the GIs buried him, and Monsignor Quinlan was permitted to go along.

In the next two days, the two Fathers Gombert were laid to rest beside Father Villemot. Father Antoine died at 4 p.m. on November 12. In his last moments he had received a request from his younger brother : " When you are with God, call me." The call came for Father Julien at 8 p.m. next day. Even Death's strong arm could not long keep apart those two whose lives had been practically one.

★   ★   ★

The Gombert brothers belonged to a family of seventeen children. Together they entered the Paris Foreign Mission seminary, and together they were ordained in 1900. They left France on the same ship for Manchuria, but before the ship reached Hongkong the Boxer Rebellion had broken out, so they were diverted to Korea.

Father Antoine, stationed at Ansong for thirty-three years, had built up a flourishing parish by the time he was transferred to the major seminary in Seoul, where he served first as spiritual director and later as procurator. Eventually he retired from active missionary work to become chaplain to the Carmelite Sisters in Seoul.

Father Julien had developed two districts into fine parishes when, with the outbreak of war, he was called in to Seoul cathedral in 1942. In 1946 he went to Inchon as chaplain to the convent and orphanage of the Sisters of St. Paul of Chartres.

The districts that these men took over are now prefectures embracing a dozen large parishes. Yet in those pioneering days they both made regular visitations of all the territory under their care, travelling sometimes on horseback but mostly on foot. Truly " there were giants in those days."

★   ★   ★

The day we had marched into Jungkan, B.29s had been droning overhead. Chinese troops were now continually passing by, and

one morning some of them stopped to dig in around the school
and on the mountainsides. Fighters came over occasionally and
strafed, and on one occasion light bombers made an attack on the
town.

We were still hopeful, but it was becoming more and more difficult to know what it all added up to. Some of the group were losing
heart, and more were falling sick. Many had alarming coughs.
Mother Thérèse, I remember, was seriously ill; yet she was still
sewing for others.

Late on the evening of November 15 a Korean officer came to
say that we must be ready to move next morning at five o'clock.
Move where? And why? Our hearts sank again.

The women had to go to the kitchen that night to make remote
preparations for breakfast before snatching a few hours' sleep. Then
in the early hours they had to face the cold of the kitchen once more.
They had breakfast ready for us at 3 a.m.

Some time before daylight guards came to warn us to be on our
toes. Should we take our packs? No, they told us. We sighed
with relief and breathed a prayer of gratitude. Then an officer came
and ordered us to assemble in the yard—and to bring our packs.
More heartburnings, more discussions, renewed inquiries. Finally
all of us, POWs and civilians, were lined up in the yard with our
packs. The very sick (among whom was Bishop Byrne) could
remain at the school, we were told, but the rest of us must take shelter
in the hills for the day, and would return to the school at evening.

But we didn't get to the hills. We went to houses on the outskirts
of the town. Some time after the civilian men had been settled in
a house, a dispute arose outside between the guards and some local
women who objected to our being there. To our surprise, the guards
yielded to their objections, and we had to move to a derelict place
some distance away. We spent a couple of hours cleaning it up,
and then set about preparing lunch.

Walter Eltringham was so ill that permission had been given for
him to remain at the school, but he insisted on coming with us. For
several days now he had not been his usual cheerful self, and today
he was quite abstracted. After we moved into this second house,
he sat down on the floor with his back to the wall and proceeded to
empty out the contents of his pockets, saying he had no further use

for them. A day or two earlier, he had told Father Booth he had squared his accounts with the Lord and was ready to face the end. Now, soon after he had transferred everything from his pockets to the floor, he fell into a coma, and we were unable to rouse him when the meal was ready.

Later that day, when our evening meal was already cooking in the pots, we received word that we must move out of Jungkan immediately. Dear God, how far? Were we facing another death march?

We gathered up our belongings. Walter Eltringham was still unconscious. We asked the guard what we should do with the sick man. After pondering a while on the problem, he bade us carry him back to the school. We placed Walter on a blanket, and four of us— Ahmet the Turk, Larry Zellers, Louis Dans and I—took a corner each. Bishop Cooper followed behind, supporting the sick man's head. As we emerged into the street, we saw trickling lines of POWs moving from neighbouring houses to join their comrades who were already streaming out of the town. The women and children were lined up, waiting patiently.

We had carried Walter Eltringham half of the mile back to the school when we encountered a diminutive captain armed with a tommy-gun.

" Where are you going? " he demanded.

" This man is sick, and we are taking him back to the school."

" Turn around and go with the others."

" But this man is very ill. He is in a coma, and will only get worse if we have to carry him far."

The tommy-gun swung up and menaced each of us in turn.

" Then carry him till he dies."

The words had a grimly familiar ring. The man who spoke them was second-in-command to The Tiger.

Walter, even in his emaciated condition, was a heavy burden for the five of us, and there was no hope of assistance at this stage. Eleven other able-bodied men, unaware of our plight, were marching ahead of us through the darkness. We stumbled along, grew desperately weary, and at last were completely exhausted. The guard who accompanied us was not unsympathetic, but he felt alarmed now that we were so far behind the main body of prisoners and were falling further behind all the time. He urged us to hurry, now threatening, now entreating. We rested, tried various methods of carrying, but the pace got slower and slower and we stumbled more and more. We talked when we rested. We didn't see how we could keep on indefinitely, but we were determined not to leave Walter by the roadside.

Just when our strength was almost at an end, the sick man made a move as if to stand. We lowered his feet to the ground, and two of us took his arms over our shoulders and supported as much of his weight as we could. Then the great-hearted man began to walk between us. Even now I cannot think of that moment without emotion. Though he seemed unconscious and never spoke a word, Walter must have sensed what was happening, and summoned the last ounce of strength left in his body, forcing it to walk once more.

Our journey ended about five miles from Jungkan at a hamlet called Hajang-ree, where we found the rest of our group waiting near some houses by the roadside. We could hear the muffled steps of the POWs, the shouting of their guards, the voices of section leaders issuing instructions. Cold, dispirited, weary to death, we waited in the darkness, talking in low tones. After a time the sick arrived in ox-carts.

It was nearly three o'clock in the morning when guards came shouting through the gloom to conduct us to our quarters. The Korean politicians, the two journalists, the diplomats, and Mme and Mlle Martel were taken away separately, and we found later that they were accommodated in a house about a hundred yards behind ours.

The rest of us, fifty-one in number, were brought through a roofed gateway into a small yard. Disposed around the yard were a store, sheds, and a Korean-style house consisting of three rooms and a kitchen. The rooms were about ten feet square. The twenty-seven men of our party were put into two rooms, the twenty-four women and children into the third. It was an *ondol* house, and the floors were still warm. This was a blessing for us, but we felt for the unfortunate family who must have been turned out of their home but a short time before. The guards tied the doors, and did not let anyone out till daylight came.

All that day (November 17) Walter Eltringham lay on the floor, breathing heavily. His breathing became quieter in the late afternoon, and finally ceased. We buried him next morning in the frozen earth, on a slope not far from the house.

Another grave was needed next day for the Carmelite, Mother Mechtilde, who passed to her reward on November 18. That reward must be very great. The patience and courage she showed in her ordeal proclaimed that she was close to the Giver of Grace.

*   *   *

For one who had planned a life in the retirement of a contemplative order, Mother Mechtilde had certainly been in plenty of big trouble. Godelieve Devriese was born at Ypres, Belgium, in 1888, and in time she became Sister Mechtilde in the Carmelite convent in her home town. When the Germans invaded the country in 1914 she had to return home, but three years later she was able to re-enter Carmel at Aire-sur-Adour, in south-west France. Soon afterwards she answered a call from the Middle East for Sisters and found herself a member of the Carmel in Smyrna, Turkey. She was but a few years there when the insurrection of 1923 broke out. Many foreigners were killed, and the Sisters only just succeeded in escaping on a French naval vessel. Back again in Aire-sur-Adour, and now prioress, Mother Mechtilde listened to Bishop Larribeau of Seoul as he pleaded for Sisters to open a Korean Carmel. The Prioress resigned, and volunteered for Korea. Her first convent was washed away by a flood, and another had to be built. Then came the difficult years of the second World War and, hard on them, the shattering of the peace in Korea.

*   *   *

One evening the Korean doctor sent orders that four of our sick— Bishop Byrne, Father Coyos, Father Canavan and Bill Evans—must be transferred to a " hospital." When we asked the messenger where this hospital was, he pointed to a nearby cottage. Wouldn't it be better, we suggested, to leave the patients where they were ? He went off to consult the doctor again. There had been some suggestion that Father Canavan's symptoms indicated meningitis. We concluded that our medico had meantime discovered from his books that meningitis could take a contagious form ; hence the decision to isolate Father Canavan and his three sick companions. The messenger returned to say that the doctor insisted on the men being taken to "hospital." It was now midnight. We pleaded again. Couldn't we wait till morning? The obliging orderly agreed to consult the doctor once more, but returned with another order that the patients must be transferred immediately.

We took the four men out into the icy night, across a field to the ruined cottage. Bishop Byrne had to be carried in a blanket. The others were able to walk with assistance. The room allotted to the patients had no door, and we could only curtain the opening with a rice bag. For beds, we got some rice straw and spread it on the earthen floor. The moment we had the sick men settled the guards ordered us away. During the following days we were allowed to bring them meals, mostly dryish millet which they could not eat. Some GIs moved into the other room of the cottage and tried to tend the sick men. But there was little they could do. The cottage, in better days, had been heated on the usual *ondol* system; but when the GIs tried to give some comfort to the patients by lighting the fire, so much smoke poured up through the broken floor that the experiment had to be abandoned.

Bishop Byrne worsened rapidly in the cottage, and finally became delirious. He never complained or seemed dissatisfied. On the morning of November 25 Monsignor Quinlan, who had gone to visit him, returned to announce that Bishop Pat had gone to heaven. There was not a soul in camp who heard the news without a leaden sense of personal loss.

The bishop was buried close to our other dead, with a ceremony very brief for a dignitary of the Church. The only sign of his rank was a light cassock of black silk, with red buttons and piping. Monsignor Quinlan had been wearing this when he was arrested, and with it he now clothed the body of the Apostolic Delegate. The buttons, under their covering of red cloth, were of metal, and the Monsignor hopes that they may help, some day, to identify the remains.

A few days later, the other three patients were allowed to come back to us. Father Canavan's trouble had been finally diagnosed as pneumonia, but he now seemed to be over the crisis.

Meantime I had fallen ill myself. Dr. Kisch, examining me with the aid of the Korean doctor's stethoscope, diagnosed pneumonia.

The Korean had some sulphadiazine at the time, and his ten or twelve tablets helped me through the crisis. I was delirious for a time, but in Monsignor Quinlan I had a devoted nurse. To his constant attendance I largely owe my recovery.

Father Coyos developed a cough that seemed to indicate the return of his former tubercular trouble, and he became so thin that his limbs no longer had shape. On top of this, he caught a throat infection that rendered him almost speechless. However, he fought the battle for recovery with characteristic determination, and finally won.

Dr. Jensen was seriously ill for most of the winter with dysentery, a most debilitating and dispiriting malady. Later on, when we could afford to be jocular about events that had been deadly serious at the time, he confided to me that on one of his worst days he heard someone remark that Kris Jensen would be the next to go. Even in his extreme depression he felt so riled by this cool forecast that he determined, then and there, to prove the prophet wrong.

Another who recovered from a serious complaint was Father Booth. A carbuncle developed on his back and spread alarmingly. He was left without treatment for periods of as long as five days, and when the Korean doctor or his assistants did come to change the dressings they usually had nothing but mercurochrome. On a few occasions they brought a small supply of one of the sulphonamide drugs. But Father Booth's carbuncle inexplicably stopped spreading and gradually disappeared.

Many of our sick never recovered. Mother Thérèse had been ailing since the days of Manpo, and M. Matti since the end of the long march. On November 30 their sufferings ended ; and Charles Hunt and Bill Evans soon followed them through the gates of death.

Father Canavan had a serious relapse after his apparent recovery. When someone tried to cheer him with the hope that we might eat our Christmas dinner in freedom, his reply was : "I'll have my Christmas dinner in heaven." For that celestial banquet he left us on December 6.

Among the Russians was a quiet, courteous old fellow named Leonoff, a close friend of Father Christmas. He was about seventy, and it was amazing that so frail a man had survived so long. He failed rapidly at Hajang, and on December 9, died quietly in his sleep.

Then Fathers Cadars, who had won the admiration of all by his fight against a severe infection in the hand, began to fail, and death came to him on December 18.

Father Bulteau, who had helped to nurse Father Cadars, was finally in need of nursing himself. He had looked as strong as an ox, this fifty-year-old bearded giant, when first we met him, though actually he was in poor health. Now his endurance was worn right down, and God called him home on January 6, the feast of the Epiphany. He was the last of our group to die in Hajang.

Born in 1901 in the department of Vendée, France, Joseph Bulteau was ordained for the Paris Foreign Missions in 1927. He went to the vicariate of Taikou, Korea, and was sent to Pusan, where he built the church that still stands there. Failing health sent him back to France. Conscripted into the army on the outbreak of World War II, he was taken prisoner by the Germans and subsequently released because of illness. Then he returned to work in his native diocese till the war should end. When the Church and the civil authorities came to grips over the question of private schools, Father Bulteau— always in the thick of the battle—was arrested, tried and fined. After the war he took a brief course in medicine, and returned to a parish in South Korea. He had been there only a few months when the invasion began, but in that short time he had already established a flourishing dispensary. The Church Militant lost a very zealous member when Father Bulteau was laid to rest in Hajang.

These days, Chinese troops were passing frequently through the village, and we used to debate whether they were going to the front or returning from it. Not until the New Year did we give up hope of being rescued, and it was months before we were convinced that the Chinese had pushed the U.N. Army far to the south.

Soon after our arrival at Hajang, Commissioner Lord was placed in solitary confinement in an empty and unheated house. He received frequent visits from The Tiger, who would begin by drawing his pistol and placing it on the table, and would then badger Lord with interrogations and repeated demands for a " confession." This went on for a fortnight. It was a very anxious and trying time for the unfortunate prisoner, who had not the least notion of what he was expected to confess. Eventually The Tiger abandoned whatever suspicions he had entertained—perhaps, as it was rumoured later, that the Commissioner was organizing a conspiracy in the camp. The prisoner was sent back to us, a very relieved and happy man.

In those days we were very hungry, and food became a universal thought-object. So at this point I must again discourse on food and cooking, with special reference to the subject of millet. This is a small, yellow grain, not much bigger than the head of a large pin, and thoroughly deserves the title we gave it, " bird seed." (I believe you will find it, as a matter of fact, in standard canary feed.) Even the Orientals rank it low in the scale of grains. Millet is not the food of the gods. We found it unpalatable, especially if it came too dry from the cooking-pots. Up till New Year, we ate millet at least twice a day. With it we had corn, beans, Chinese cabbage, bean paste, salt, and occasionally bean oil. The daily grain ration was 600 grams per man. Its adequacy naturally depended on the amount of auxiliary rations. According to regulations we were to receive a regular ration of meat, bean oil and bean paste. In practice, one or all of these would be missing. During the whole of the winter we received meat only three or four times, and then a very tiny piece each. Fish we had twice. The first time it came steamed on rice, and provided a subject of delightful conversation for days. We received rice again at New Year, and thereafter we usually got enough rice for one meal a day.

If I condemn millet, I pay tribute to our friend the soya bean, which undoubtedly saved our lives. Each time beri-beri appeared it was because soya beans had disappeared from the menu. The authorities seemed to have trouble in obtaining supplies of these beans, despite the fact that they were grown locally. Consequently they were rather strictly rationed, and at times not available. These hard, round, yellow beans can be prepared in a variety of ways, and are quite palatable in any form if sufficiently cooked. They can be simply boiled ; they can be soaked and ground to obtain a white cream, which produces " bean milk " when diluted with water and boiled ; or they can be boiled and ground and then have water added, to make a thick brown soup. The oil most commonly used in Korea is bean oil. There is also bean sauce, a black, salty liquid.

When we reached Hajang, The Tiger had placed the parents of the White Russian family in charge of the kitchen. Ivan Kilin was at that time thirty-six and his wife Marusya was twenty-nine. Ivan is a

The first group freed arrives in Berlin *en route* to England : *(left to right)*, George Blake, Bishop Cooper, Commissioner Lord, Norman Owen, Monsignor Quinlan.

stocky, hardy fellow, and very cheerful. Marusya, an excellent wife and mother, is a capable, industrious, buxom lady, with long and beautiful fair hair.

Madame Kilin soon found that the kitchen work left her insufficient time to care for her three young children, so her place was taken by Salim Salahudtin, the father of the Turkish family. Ivan Kilin and Salim Salahudtin remained in charge for more than twelve months, till a team of cooks recruited from among the womenfolk took over early in 1952.

At each succeeding camp we have had to undertake more and more work to help ourselves. At Manpo there was little to do except carry water and run the kitchen. Here in Hajang we had in addition to carry rations and wood from the quartermaster's stores, and grind grain. There was a walk-around mill in the yard, where the grinding of corn and beans for the evening meal went on every morning, the able-bodied men taking turns at the job.

Every few days a party of men went off with empty sacks to the storehouse to collect rations. The going and coming didn't take long, but the waiting often took three hours, and in that sub-zero weather it seemed to us, ill-clad as we were, like three weeks. Distribution of rations took place, not in the hours of sunshine, but late in the afternoon when it was already intensely cold.

But bringing rations had compensations. We could meet groups from other houses—the POWs, the diplomats, the Korean politicians —and exchange news and views. I remember a conversation I had, on one of these occasions, with M. Perruche. By now the mountains were blanketed under heavy snow, and he told me the scene reminded him vividly of a place in the Alps where he and his wife had spent a holiday ; but there were differences which I felt my imagination could not bridge.

The nefarious activities of which we have been guilty in later camps, and which will be referred to in due course, had their small beginnings at Hajang. Handfuls of beans, corn, salt, and bunches of leeks and the like found their way into our pockets when the quartermaster's back was turned. It was my pious ambition to steal a whole bag of grain, but I never managed more than a few bowlfuls.

At Manpo, carrying water had been a good form of exercise. At Hajang it was very different. The able-bodied were paired off, and each pair carried for a day. It only involved two hours' carrying after breakfast and one after lunch, but the cold of the winds that blew over that village from the north could penetrate to the marrow of one's bones. I could gauge the temperature fairly accurately by the rate at which my beard iced up. Water trickling from the leaky bucket formed lines of ice on the path, and the lines multiplied till they joined to form a sheet. Skating on ice can be fun—but not when you are carrying water. The mouth of the well, too, would slowly ice up until the bucket would scarcely fit through the opening. We would then de-ice it with a pick.

I never think of water-carrying at Hajang without recalling Kijikoff and his friend Smirnoff, the stout Russian with the round face and baby blue eyes. They had been allowed to bring some clothes into camp, and each managed to retain a good overcoat. When their turn for water-carrying came, they solemnly donned overcoats, then put their shirts on over the coats, stuffed both into their belts and went out into the arctic weather apparently clad in shirt and pants. It was a laudable precaution against the taking ways of the guards, who must have wondered that they thrived so well on the slim diet of the camp.

Most of us were now a little better clad, for we had inherited some of the clothes of our departed. After my sickness, my friend Lieutenant Peppe, who was in charge of the laundry, where vermin-infected clothes were steamed in drums, sent me a light quilted suit, and life thenceforth became much rosier. Near the end of the year, some of the others received new light quilted suits, pale blue in colour. In January, a supply of heavily-quilted khaki suits arrived in the camp, and each prisoner received one. They were not made to order : the children needed only the jacket to cover their tiny frames, while some of the bigger men now found advantages in the dieting that had been forced upon them. But the clothes were clean and, what was even more important, they were warm.

We had to go each day to bring bundles of wood from the quartermaster's yard. This daily chore brings to mind a certain guard to whom we gave the name "Helpful." Many of the guards were arrogant bullies, but there were some who were thoughtful and obliging. "Helpful" was one of these. We received a ration of so many bundles of wood. If carefully used it was barely sufficient.

The quartermaster usually allowed us to add loose sticks to our
bundles. If some of the party had a free hand for half a minute
when the enemy wasn't looking, there would be no shortage of loose
sticks that day. Most of the guards would assist the quartermaster
to keep an eye on us, but " Helpful " aided and abetted our activities.
Not only did he look the other way when our extra carriers picked
up bundles, but he often carried back a bundle himself. " The day
will come," he told us, " when there'll be a shortage of firewood ;
so you should try to store a few bundles in a shed." And he was
right. There came a two-day period when there was no wood in
the yard, but we carried on without missing a meal, and were even
able to present some bundles of wood to the POW officers.

*   *   *

At Hajang we had some contacts with the POWs. Some of the
officers used to come to our house, with their guard's permission, to
use our mill-stone. Among the GIs, we came to know those who
were barbers, and those who worked in the sanitary squads. One
GI of whom we saw quite a lot was Tex Kimball, who had shared
some of Philip Deane's adventures back in July. Tex was in charge
of a disinfecting team, and the authorities must have concluded from
his assiduous attentions to our house that it was in a particularly bad
condition. He came to spray it quite often, and always managed to
spread this operation over three days. He would come on the first
day to survey the situation, on the second to spray, and on the third
to inspect the work done. We found him cheerful company.

Another whose visits were always enjoyable was a lad who ran
the hospital just across the field—or so we gathered from his first
visit to us. When, on subsequent visits, he gave us the impression
that he had at one time or another run practically everything in the
United States and elsewhere, we began to value him as a real discovery—a new Munchausen. We could not check on his wider
claims, but were sufficiently intrigued to inquire about his position
at the hospital, and we found that his responsibilities began and
ended with the kitchen fire. We became quite fond of this garrulous
boy, and were very sorry when we heard that an officer of the guards
had battered him badly with a rifle-butt, and still more sorry when
news came that he had died in the hospital from his injuries.

The officer responsible for this boy's death was a young, handsome fellow whom the POWs knew as " Burp-gun Charlie." He later beat up a POW officer, who was also taken to hospital and eventually died. I have previously mentioned an incident that occurred on November 4, that unforgettable fifth day of the death march, when so many exhausted POWs were shot. I told of how we had heard shots fired, and seen an officer and guards coming out of a ravine afterwards—laughing, Larry Zellers noticed. The officer was Burp-gun Charlie.

*   *   *

Attempts were made from time to time to "indoctrinate" the prisoners, and perhaps the most determined efforts were made at Hajang. Soon after we arrived, the whole camp was assembled in the school grounds to listen to a fanatical denunciation by The Tiger of the capitalistic countries and especially of the United States. His indictment of America's iniquities included the statement that her people were the filthiest in the world. Why ? Because most Americans actually had toilets *inside* their houses.

Thereafter the POWs had to listen to a whole series of lectures—two a week, usually—prepared for their edification by a fiery little lieutenant. We civilians were evidently regarded as hopeless reactionaries. We did get a few lectures from a tall, earnest captain, but after that we were left in peace.

The POWs learned some surprising things about their native country from the lieutenant's lectures : that women, for instance, were downtrodden ; that only a few favoured citizens could receive a college education or own a car ; that free elections were unknown. When the men protested that the lecturer's statements were not borne out by their own experience of life in the States, he would airily wave their objections aside, and carry on.

Commissioner Lord, who usually acted as the lieutenant's interpreter, gave us many a laugh with his reports of the lectures, of the POWs' objections, and of the "examinations" that were held from time to time. By way of diversion, the Commissioner would sometimes feed back to the examiner a highly satisfactory version of the POWs' replies. An examinee might very possibly have been engaged during the lecture in roasting a chicken surreptitiously at a stove at the back of the room, but provided he would co-operate by talking for a sufficient length of time on any subject that occurred to him, the Commissioner could present on his behalf an answer that made the lecturer purr. The examinee would get a pass with honours, and the lecturer would feel that he must be doing fine, and a good time would be had by all.

*   *   *

It was at Hajang that I first became a stoker in the kitchen. Previously the job had been done by Dimitri Vorosiff, a lean Russian endowed with unusual gifts as a handyman. He was fifty-nine at this time. When he fell ill in December, Larry Zellers and I took turn about as stokers.

We found the job no sinecure. The wood was so green that sap hissed and boiled from it for a long time after it went into the firebox. It was soon borne in upon us that making fires with such fuel was quite a science, and I fear our apprenticeship cost the fence around our house not a few dry poles.

It was necessary to start work about 4.30 in the morning, and the kitchen was not inviting at that hour. Temperatures of minus 35° Fahrenheit were not unusual, and when the wind was from the north an icy blast came through the back door. Each night we banked a fire, but on some mornings we found only cold ashes left. This meant asking the guard's permission to get some live coals from a neighbouring house, for we had no matches. I have vivid memories of pre-dawn excursions through the silent cold to a house where POWs were billeted. I can still see their faces lit by pale flickering light as they crouched around their fire.

*   *   *

The feast of Christmas came. We were at pains to appear bright and cheerful, and each one's " Merry Christmas ! " was given out with zest. But most of us, I think, were sad at heart. There were few in camp who had not lost a friend in the preceding month, and at such a time we were keenly conscious of the gulf that separated us from friends at home, now exchanging presents and making merry. There were hymns and carols on Christmas Eve and again on Christmas Day. A couple of officers of the guard heard about the singing and came to make inquiries. They were courteous fellows, and they returned in the evening to listen.

From time to time the guards or officers were transferred, and new
ones came to take their places. We all waited for the day when The
Tiger would pass out of our lives. He did at length go away for
some time, and we didn't know he had returned until he appeared
at our house on a tour of inspection shortly before New Year. For
the first time since we had met him he wasn't carrying a pistol, and
he seemed to lack his usual fire. He told Monsignor Quinlan he
had been sick. He left the camp again, and then we heard with great
joy that he was not returning.

To our further joy and relief, the new camp commandant was a
kindly, courteous man. In so far as he could he improved conditions in camp, and he was always fair and reasonable when an
appeal was made to him. He couldn't give us supplies that were not
available, nor change overnight these Tiger-trained guards ; but the
cruel beatings of the POWs did stop, and we never afterwards feared
that a life would be suddenly and unjustifiably taken.

The Tiger's former disciple—the little captain whom we had encountered the night we were carrying poor Walter Eltringham—
departed too, and the womenfolk especially heaved a sigh of relief.
He used to take delight in going into the rooms of these poor, helpless
creatures and baiting and badgering them about their religion, their
countries, and the unmarried state of the Sisters and missionaries.

His successor was a tall, unpleasant-faced officer. I could not
easily describe how his head and neck sat on his shoulders, but the
POWs' name for him, " Gooseneck," was not purely arbitrary.
He wore no insignia on his uniform, and it was a long time before
we discovered his rank and position. For that reason we called him
the " Mystery Man," soon shortened to " M.M."

" Do you believe in God ? " he asked Commissioner Lord on his
first visit of inspection to our house.

" I do," the Commissioner told him.

" Then from now on I'll be your god," he sneered, " and you can
thank me for the benefits you receive."

I have mentioned that some of the POW officers had permission
to visit our house to use our mill-stone. When the Mystery Man
discovered them one day sitting in a room engaged in conversation
with us, he was really annoyed. He locked Commissioner Lord in
an unheated room, took Major Dunn, senior POW officer, away

for interrogration, and then returned to question the Commissioner. But neither was simple enough to be caught by the statement that the other had confessed to discussing political and war news. They both insisted that the subject of conversation had been the menu of the dinner with which we were going to celebrate our release. This was the truth, but (as the Mystery Man suspected) not the whole truth.

He was bested, and he knew it. But he was quite observant and noticed when he returned to question Commissioner Lord that he was no longer bare-headed. Who had passed in a cap to him? Father Booth confessed to the crime. Interviewing the culprit, the Mystery Man was so enraged at his calm statement of fact that he gave him a kick as he lay on the floor, and departed breathing threats.

I had an encounter with the M.M. on St. Patrick's Day. The Sisters, with their amazing ingenuity, had snatched some green material and thread out of the air, and had made shamrock-and-harp badges for Monsignor Quinlan, Father Booth and me. I was standing with a crowd near the front gate when the M.M. came along and spotted the little green badge on my jacket.

" What's that ? " he asked.

Someone explained.

" We don't need that sort of thing in North Korea," he snapped, and his hand shot forward and tore the emblem from my jacket.

" Thank you," I said. " I'll always remember you by that."

" What did you say ? " he demanded.

I repeated my statement. He seemed a little taken aback, and went off muttering. When he found Monsignor Quinlan with a similar badge, he was less hasty and asked for explanations. Finally he consented to allow the Monsignor to wear his emblem, and gave him mine, asking him to return it to me and say that he hoped I would not harbour ill feelings.

This morning the faithful Mother Eugénie came to pin a shamrock on my jacket. It is two years later, and again St. Patrick's Day.

*   *   *

At Hajang there were the inevitable interviews, but fewer of them. Near the end of January a tall, grey-haired major, almost European

in appearance, came and spent part of a day and all of a night record-
ing our life-histories. Then he moved over to the house occupied
by the Korean politicians and the diplomatic party. A vehicle was
heard chugging into camp that night, and next morning the diplomats got word to us that they were leaving in a bus at eleven o'clock.

Excitement ran high in our group at this move, and the rumour
spread that we would follow them in a few days. An officer of the
guard, returning after a temporary absence from the camp, said the
diplomats had left by train from Kangyi for Pyongyang. We had
no further news of them till twelve months later when members of
our group saw some of them in Manpo.

The Mystery Man came to tell six of the men of our group to
move over to the rooms vacated by the diplomats. The six who
moved were Commissioner Lord, Dr. Kisch, Louis Dans, Larry
Zellers, Smirnoff and I. Our departure enabled the remaining men
to move into one room, and the women and children, who had
been all this time crowded into one room, were able to take over a
second. None of us hoped any longer that we would be following
the diplomats out of the camp. Our orders to change house
dispelled that rumour.

We were comparatively comfortable in the new place. The
Korean family who owned the house still lived there, and the lady
of the house did the cooking. We were able to wash every day and
do laundry frequently—luxuries unheard of in the other house,
where there was but one cracked wooden wash-bowl for the whole
community.

We were quite cut off from our former quarters, and we could
meet our late companions only when we went for rations. At least
that was the M.M.'s ruling, but the M.M. was not always there, and
not all the guards were strict.

All this time Monsignor Quinlan had been our group leader.
That position meant for him not only responsibility, but also extra
work, because often his method of getting community work done
was to do it himself. The departure of six of us accentuated his
labour problem. However, the women fell to and helped, and life
went on.

The farmers whose houses we occupied had been told, we heard,
that they would have their homes back before the farming season

began. Hence it is not surprising that there were constant rumours about the prisoners moving away. It seemed fairly definite that the POWs were going to move to former Japanese barracks a few miles away. Carts carrying supplies left the camp, and finally a small group of prisoners went to prepare the place. Rumours had persisted that our group was not going with the POWs, but on the evening of March 28 a Korean officer came to tell us to be ready to move with them next morning.

12

Better Days at Ando

MARCH 29 TO OCTOBER 8, 1951

THE POWs marched out of the village and the civilian group fell in behind them. How different from the last time we had marched! The day was fine, the guards were not hurrying us, and we were at ease. But there were many of our friends who were not marching out of the village, and we could not but think of them as we left. They were sleeping over there on the hillside and back along the trail. What divers paths had brought them—aged priest and tow-haired private, miner and lumberjack, world-citizen and cloistered nun—converging from the world's wide corners, to leave them, in silent, close fraternity, awaiting the Day of Resurrection among the wild Korean hills!

We went back the way we had come, into Jungkan-jin. Over to the left was the school we had occupied for a week, and a little further on we saw a small, steep-roofed church with a cross above. It had been built by Father Cleary, one of Father Booth's confreres, when the Maryknoll Fathers had charge of this area.

We kept on through Jungkan and out along the Manpo road for a mile or two until we met a lesser road going off to the left. A couple of miles along that road we came to a cluster of stone buildings at the foot of a mountain rising sheer from the valley. We learned that these had been barracks, built by the Japanese, and that they had been used later as a school. The name of the district, we found, was Ando-rec.

The road ran between the buildings. To the right were some small stone cottages that had probably been officers' quarters. To the left, in a barbed-wire enclosure, were a number of large stone buildings which formed the limits of a rectangular parade ground.

To the right of the gate was a building containing a dozen or more small rooms. This was the hospital, and here our group was put.

12

Better Days at Ando

MARCH 29 TO OCTOBER 8, 1951

THE POWs marched out of the village and the civilian group fell in behind them. How different from the last time we had marched ! The day was fine, the guards were not hurrying us, and we were at ease. But there were many of our friends who were not marching out of the village, and we could not but think of them as we left. They were sleeping over there on the hillside and back along the trail. What diverse paths had brought them—aged priest and tow-haired private, miner and lumberjack, world-citizen and cloistered nun—converging from the world's wide corners, to leave them, in silent, close fraternity, awaiting the Day of Resurrection among the wild Korean hills !

We went back the way we had come, into Jungkan-jin. Over to the left was the school we had occupied for a week, and a little further on we saw a small, steep-roofed church with a cross above. It had been built by Father Cleary, one of Father Booth's confrères, when the Maryknoll Fathers had charge of this area.

We kept on through Jungkan and out along the Manpo road for a mile or two until we met a lesser road going off to the left. A couple of miles along that road we came to a cluster of stone buildings at the foot of a mountain rising sheer from the valley. We learned that these had been barracks, built by the Japanese, and that they had been used later as a school. The name of the district, we found, was Ando-ree.

The road ran between the buildings. To the right were some small stone cottages that had probably been officers' quarters. To the left, in a barbed-wire enclosure, were a number of large stone buildings which formed the limits of a rectangular parade ground.

To the right of the gate was a building containing a dozen or more *ondol* rooms. This was the hospital, and here our group was put.

187

The sick POWs arrived next day on ox-carts. They were excited and had a tale to tell as we helped them down. We had seen the B.29s that had flown over that morning, hadn't we ? We told them we had seen the bombers and heard booming in the distance. There had been much speculation over the affair. They told us they had been passing near one of the Yalu River bridges just as bombs began to fall. They took shelter, but not before one guard was struck in the face by shrapnel. A couple of spans of the steel bridge had been blown out. This news caused a lot of excitement in the camp. Probably that was not the only bridge on the Yalu bombed that morning, and it looked as though the U.N. forces meant business. But again our hopes of liberation were doomed to disappointment.

The hospital became crowded out, so the civilian men were moved over with the POW officers, who seemed glad to have us. We talked interminably with them and played bridge and chess. In the evenings the Catholics gathered at one end of the room for a rosary, and the Protestants at the other for prayers.

If the story of those POWs is ever told, Major Dunn, the senior officer, could well be cast in the role of hero. He is quite sufficiently tall, dark and handsome, and he has more than the desired physical qualities ; his courage and selflessness, his fairness and forbearance, his calm and dignified bearing, have won him admiration on all sides. In spite of sustained Communist efforts to belittle the officers, Major Dunn's men never lost their respect for his sterling character.

Major Dunham was another we all admired. This plucky little man waged a stiff fight against beri-beri, and was ready to try anything the doctors suggested. He never lost his cheerful spirits, but he did finally lose the battle, much to the sorrow of us all.

Our quarters were separated from the officers' by just a partition. I remember how Lieutenant Marlotte's clear rich tenor would respond to Monsignor Quinlan's requests for an Irish song. And I recall long talks with Lieutenants Peppe and Manietta, Sergeants Knowles and Stumpes, and P.F.C.'s " Doc " Albranski and Arthur O'Keefe. Then there was Henry Leerkamp, the tall, fair sergeant who had dug graves. Nearly all these men were veterans of the Second World War and had a rich fund of experiences. Albranski had been a medical orderly with 180 prisoners in New Guinea. When they were rescued after twelve months, they had not lost a man. We liked O'Keefe for the way he embarrassed the Korean officers and guards when they gathered the men for a political meeting. When Arthur rose to ask questions he didn't beat about the bush.

Each day the guards escorted a large party to the hills to carry firewood, and after the confinement of the winter, it was a wonderful relief to be on the mountains again. The shouting and bullying of the guards, however, did not add to the enjoyment of the day : weak men were often forced to carry heavy loads. I was recovering my strength and usually carried a fair-sized section of a tree trunk, but I came under the guard's stick one day for declining to take a load he indicated. Sometimes it is a disadvantage to know Korean. The POWs can converse with friendly guards quite ably with scraps of Korean and Japanese and signs, but if a guard gives an order they don't like, they simply can't understand unless it is clearly translated into English.

In point of fact, the POWs were recovering their strength and spirits, and a quiet battle was going on between them and the guards. The guards were losing ground all the time, and we quite enjoyed the situation. Had the authorities been shrewd enough to withdraw from the compound and make the POW officers responsible for discipline, their worries would probably have ended. Instead, they tried to discredit the officers and to control the men themselves. A meeting was called to reorganize the camp. It was divided into sections, with a guard as section leader, and a POW (usually a sergeant or private) as sub-section leader. The only POW officer with authority was the sub-leader of the section composed of officers. The civilians formed another section. In the eyes of the authorities, age and experience were not necessary, or even useful, qualifications in a leader, and so, passing over men like Monsignor Quinlan and Commissioner Lord, they made Sagid, the eighteen-year-old Turkish lad, our sub-section leader.

The guard in charge of one section was a cocky little sergeant whom the POWs called "The Whip." He decided that an outfit led by him should be a smart one. He taught—or tried to teach—his men words of command in Korean. He had them learn Korean songs, and when we went for wood they sat and sang them, with hand-clapping accompaniments that reminded one of pupils in a kindergarten. But the outfit just couldn't learn to be smart. When

The Whip gave a snappy Korean command the men either looked blank or very snappily did the wrong thing. I fancy The Whip decided that they were so dumb that not even the regenerating powers of Communist discipline could do anything for them.

The Korean quartermasters were almost in despair. Supplies were disappearing from the store-sheds. The quartermasters obtained new and larger locks, but finally relied on large nails driven into the door frame. It took at least a solid piece of iron to bend the nails, whereas a tiny piece of wire, in the hands of the more expert prisoners, would open any North Korean lock. On the rare occasions that tobacco arrived, there was often none for distribution because it disappeared before it could be given out. Suckling pigs came to be reared, but they died untimely deaths in the small hours—and the corpses were never found. The prisoners had to count ears of corn under the watchful eyes of guards. A shortage. Count again. A still greater shortage ! . . .

Guards were put near the store shed. Just one guard during the day, because surely a roving guard can keep the contents of one small shed intact in broad daylight. One day two men came near the shed to shoot small birds with a catapult. It was apparently a very interesting pastime and they were enjoying themselves thoroughly. The guard felt envious. They were nice friendly fellows too, because when the guard showed an interest in the proceedings, they demonstrated the use of the catapult and let him try his skill. They found stones for him, and birds to shoot at. The best targets always seemed to be further and further from the storehouse. And the birds that were just asking to be shot were round the corner, where a building blocked the view of the storehouse. . . .

But, it must be added, life was not yet all fun and frolic. These activities of the POWs would indicate that there was still room for improvement in the menu. There were still a great number of pale, gaunt men in hospital, and from time to time deaths occurred.

*   *   *

At the barracks at Ando we were able to talk more freely to the Sisters, with whom, up to that time, rules or circumstances had prevented us from associating. I often walked up and down the parade-ground with Mother Eugénie, blind Sister Marie-Madeleine between us.

This is an opportune moment to say a little more about these Sisters. In the world, Mother Eugénie had been Yvonne Demeusy. She had delayed entering the convent of St. Paul of Chartres till she was twenty-three, as she had been needed at home. At Manpo in February 1952 Mother Eugénie celebrated the Silver Jubilee of her entrance into religion. After profession she had trained as a nurse, and in 1932 she came to Korea to take Mother Béatrix's place as mistress of novices in the convent at Seoul. She was still holding that position when the Reds came. Other members of the family had entered religion, too, and an elder sister is the present Mother General of the St. Paul of Chartres Congregation.

So intimate was the life in camp that it seemed your neighbour knew, not just what you were doing, but what you were thinking. He was soon aware that you possessed your share of human frailty— and you could have told him that he wasn't perfect either. In these circumstances, it says much for Mother Eugénie that no one has ever heard her criticized. She says that it is her vocation to work for others—a vocation literally and heroically fulfilled, surely, by this nun so patient, so gentle and retiring, so industrious, so full of selfless devotion to others. At Hajang, what she did for the sick French priests is beyond telling, but she never spoke of it, nor asked for help, nor complained. In later camps there have been few for whom she did not wash or sew at one time or another. Hour after hour her needle would fly, making socks and gloves, patching and altering garments ; or her hands have been busy washing clothes in ice-cold water. She was seldom unable to carry out a request, and when you thanked her for fulfilling one, she would say simply : *"A votre service."*

Sister Marie-Madeleine has been admired for her gentleness and for her patience and fortitude under a great affliction. At a later camp than Ando she was to prove herself a gifted teacher. The children would flock around her to learn French, and she spared neither time nor effort to help them.

She was born nearly sixty years ago at Marmande, near Agen, in south-west France. Her name was Henriette Marquier. As a young girl she attended a training college for teachers, and while there fell away from the practice of her faith. Only the college discipline kept her attending Mass. She left the college and began teaching, and subsequently became engaged to a young man whom she loved deeply. Then her fiancé disappeared, and the blow left the young teacher nervous and distraught. Then she met a young widow of great faith and fervour, who had recently lost a devoted husband. This lady's resignation and peace of mind greatly influenced Henriette, and she began to pray again and read spiritual books. Ernest Psichari's *Voyage du Centurion* was a landmark in her life. She joined the association " Universitaires Catholiques," and was soon writing fine articles and poems for its magazine, *Davidées*.

Henriette's rediscovered faith was bringing her untold happiness, but she could not forget the past. It was not that it worried her. She understood the divine mercy too well for that. But she wanted to demonstrate by sacrifice her regret that there was a past to be forgiven, and her appreciation of God's generosity in overlooking it. Hers was not a nature to be satisfied with half-measures. She walked out of the life she loved so much, to become Sister Marie-Madeleine in the Carmel of Aire-sur-Adour.

In time, Sister Marie-Madeleine became mistress of novices. Her eyes were very weak, and doctors repeatedly ordered her to be careful. Then she volunteered to help the new foundation in Korea, and in 1938 went to become mistress of novices in the Carmel at Seoul. She found her Korean novices very poorly supplied with religious books in their own language. They had only one copy of the Rule, few suitable spiritual books, no manuals to guide them in their meditations. Translations and transcriptions were urgently needed. How could she spare her eyes ? In 1948 she went completely blind.

Another Carmelite who has shared our captivity is Mother Henriette. Since the death of Mother Thérèse she has been called " Mother Superior " by the other Sisters, and most of the people in camp have adopted that title for her too. In the world she bore the noble name of De Lobit, a name well known in France, and renowned in its army, where it was always represented through the years. In the first World War it was a General de Lobit who liberated Yugoslavia, adding more lustre to the family name. And in the early 1920's one of the General's nieces entered Carmel at Aire-sur-Adour to become Sister Henriette. She volunteered in 1938 for the

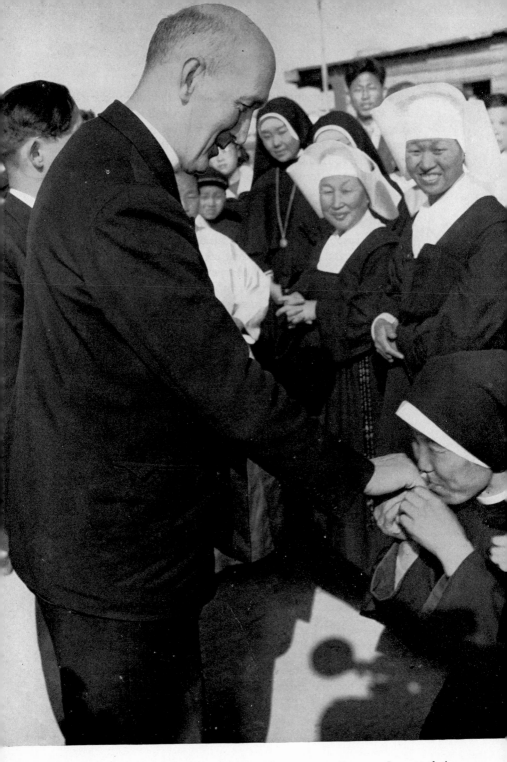

Monsignor Quinlan being greeted in Seoul on his return to Korea as Regent of the
Apostolic Delegation (April, 1954).

Carmel in Seoul, and was assigned the difficult task of making ends
meet for the young and struggling community. In 1948 she became
sub-prioress.

I wonder how many graces have been won for our camp by the
prayers of Mother Henriette. She does not enjoy good health, and
hence has not been able to take an active part in our common life.
But late at night and again early in the morning you may see her
sitting quietly among her sleeping companions, and the expression
on her face tells you that her thoughts are with God.

★   ★   ★

One day, I think it was May 10, we were waiting for an orderly
to appear and bellow " Civilian che-o-ow ! " at the mess-hall door.
And then suddenly word came for the civilian men to pack up and
be ready to move in twenty minutes. No indication of where we
were to go, nor of the length of the journey. We protested that we
were about to have our meal, so the order was changed to " as soon
as you have eaten." We ate, packed, and assembled before the gate.
The M.M. was there. He drove away the women when they came
to say goodbye, overloaded us with rations, and ran about kicking
people in the shins.

We filed out the gate, over the road, and across the stream. There
was a valley before us, rising gradually to the foot of a mountain
a mile distant. A few hundred yards across this valley were some
Korean houses, and one of them was empty. This was to be our
new home.

The place was in the usual state of unpreparedness. When we told
the guards there was no means of preparing supper, they shrugged
and said : " That's your responsibility, not ours." But they were
embarrassed, and changed their tune when we told the people next
door about our needs. Finally we obtained enough utensils to cook
supper, as well as some rice bags to cover the mud floors.

The guards also yielded to the demands of Ivan Kilin and Salim
Salahudtin that their wives and families be allowed to join them. It
was not long till these folk arrived, accompanied by Maisara, the
Turkish girl.

An incident that was rather significant occurred next morning. We
had not been accustomed to fall out for roll-call with the POWs. This

morning an officious guard came along quite early, shouting for us
to line up in the yard and number off. We didn't jump to it with
the alacrity he expected, and he was annoyed. Finally he had everyone there except Madame Kilin and her children. Exasperated, the
guard went to bring them. Madame Kilin was not lacking in courage,
and she calmly went on taking her time. The guard levelled his
rifle and rattled the bolt. Madame Kilin sneered at him. " Go on ;
shoot me," she said. " Shoot me and these innocent children ! "
The innocent children, meanwhile, frightened by the rifle, were
howling their heads off, and the discomfited guard had to retire,
breathing threats. He reported the matter to the camp commandant,
but was reprimanded ; and we were assured that there would be
no more such incidents.

The official policy towards us, we sensed, was changing for the
better. Before long, the wood-getters were going to the mountains
unescorted, and finally others were allowed to go searching for
mushrooms, edible plants and fruit. As the season advanced, rasp-
berries were brought back from these excursions, then wild grapes,
and finally a delicious fruit which the Koreans call *ta-ray*. It is a
small, green fruit, with a soft, seed-filled flesh, and grows on a vine.
I have never seen it in any other country, but the Russians knew it
and called it *kish-mish*.

Every few days we went over to the barracks to bring rations.
Our diet still left us hungry, but it had vastly improved, and we
were slowly regaining our health. We had passed through the lean
season for food which all Koreans, but especially the poorer folk,
know so well. It occurs in early spring, when winter stores of pickles
and frozen vegetables have disappeared, and early crops have not
come in. But we were now receiving Chinese cabbages, turnips and
leeks, and later we would receive foreign cabbages and potatoes and
cucumbers. Imagine fresh, green cucumbers ! The whole camp
went wild the first time they arrived. Later on, for a celebration in
August, we even received one tomato each !

At Ando we became acquainted with a new type of grain. No
one seemed to know quite what it should be called in English. Some
called it *sorghum*, but Miss Bertha Smith, who was quite a farmer,
thought it was the same as the *Kaffir corn* grown in her native Missouri.
In Chinese it is *gao-liang*. We mostly called it by its Korean name,

su-su. The plant grows very tall, and the grain is the size and shape of rice, but pinkish in colour. The first shipment we received at Ando was not pure *su-su*, so in those days we were not really in a position to make a pronouncement about its flavour. It had come, at some stage of its history, into rather too close contact with kerosene.

Our experiment in the primitive mode of life had interesting aspects, if one had a mind to view it in that light. It took the combined efforts of most of the able-bodied people in camp to provide three not very elaborate meals a day. Wood had to be cut on the hills and hauled to the house, water had to be carried, rations brought from the barracks, and corn ground at the ox-mill with ourselves for oxen. Grain had to be washed and beans soaked and ground. Finally there was the cooking to be done.

*   *   *

We lost two of our number in the month of June. Smirnoff, the big Russian, was fat no longer. The poor man had been failing, and finally he was sent back across the river to the hospital, where he died in the first days of June. Dr. Kisch was sick. He couldn't eat the food, and took only a little rice each day. We gave him extra rice, and tried to induce him to take more than rice, but he said it only made him worse. He too went to hospital, and died there on June 29.

Men were still dying at the barracks, and there was one death that was more tragic than most. We heard a shot from the barracks one night, and next day received the news that Lieutenant Sirman, a young airman whom we respected and admired, had been shot dead by a guard the night before. The camp authorities claimed that he had been caught passing through the fence from outside and had failed to halt when challenged. His fellow-officers said he had merely gone to get a drink of water and had remained inside the fence.

Father Booth met someone who had access to a radio, and through this channel we heard news of a proposed peace conference. Then the commandant of the camp told the POWs about the conference, and said he would keep them informed on its progress. There was excitement in camp, and the optimists planned dinners in the free world for the end of July. But we heard no more, and concluded that the conference had not been a success.

The camp authorities had been promising us clothes for a long time, but spring slipped into summer, and still they never came. Many people, therefore, continued to wear winter clothes long after spring fashions had come in. When these clothes became unbearably warm, they removed the cotton-wool padding and went to work on the material with needle and thread. The thread was usually pulled out of blankets. Larry Zellers made a very creditable needle from a piece of barbed wire, ground down on a stone picked up on the hillside. The coming of summer found, too, many of us going barefooted.

Finally the camp commandant himself went off to get supplies of clothes, and at length returned to say they were coming. One day when we went for rations, we found the POWs proudly wearing khaki overalls and canvas shoes. One lad called us aside and took out of his pocket a cloth wallet, from which he extracted a package. He removed an outer wrapping of paper, then an inner one of cloth, and finally revealed the treasure. His face shone with the pride and joy of ownership as he handed it carefully to us for examination. " Smell it ! " he said. It was a cake of faintly perfumed toilet soap.

Soon we were decked out like the POWs. Besides the overalls, shoes and socks, there was for each of us a set of white cotton under-wear, a toothbrush and toothpaste. Larry Zellers had to cut the toes out of his shoes to get into them, and so much of his feet protruded from the shoes that he soon laid them aside, saying that they only gave him a sense of security without the security. To this his mangled toes bore witness.

★   ★   ★

Most of the able-bodied men among the internees gave thought from time to time to the possibility of escape. But there were three hundred miles of mountains between our camp and freedom, and very few people who could afford to run the risk of helping an escapee. Taken all in all, it wasn't easy to escape. But Louis Dans decided to try. He made haversacks, obtained boots and water-bottles from POWs, and collected food. He hid his equipment in the mountains, and one morning he went to cut firewood and did not return.

When he had not appeared by dusk, the guards sent us to scour the nearby mountainsides, calling his name. Then all the guards from the barracks went dashing off into the night, and next day they

widened the net through police and village leaders. Heavy rain fell
at night. We knew that would be a serious blow to the man on the
run. Three days later a guard told us that Dans had been captured,
and soon he was back at the barracks. The authorities were pleased
with themselves. They knew this unsuccessful attempt would deter
others. Dans was interrogated at length, and he lost a diary and
some valuables he had retained up till that time. He was nominally
punished by a period of hard labour, which was not much more
than the others were already doing. But he was kept over at the
barracks.

An officer brought him over to collect belongings he had left
behind, and had him tell us his story. His plan had been to keep to
the mountains, away from frequented roads. But he had encountered
country that was far more rugged than that around us, and found
peaks he couldn't scale and precipices that forced him to retrace his
steps. He had spent a couple of nights in pouring rain and grew cold
and weak. He decided his plan was not feasible and took to the
roads. The villagers were on the lookout for him, and before long
he was stopped and handed over to the police. In the three days he
had gone thirty miles.

With Louis Dans, all the non-European men in camp were taken
to the barracks with the exception of the two fathers of the families.
We were never quite sure what was the reason for this move. The
womenfolk who had been at the barracks were brought to join us.
Ivan Kilin and Salim Salahudtin were still the cooks. That left only
three of us—Monsignor Quinlan, Larry Zellers and myself—for heavy
work, and our days were very full.

One day a sedan car arrived at the barracks and in it were three
Russians and a Korean nattily dressed in Western clothes. One of the
Russians was a tall, fair, handsome young fellow whom we named
"Blondie." He spoke English, and seemed to be translator and
secretary to the Korean, who spoke fluent Russian and must have
been an official of some standing.

The other two Russians seemed to be officials in their own right.
One was quite fat, and the other a dark individual with rugged
features. Their dealings were mostly with the White Russian and
Turkish people of our group. These they interrogated, urging them
to go to China to live, and to take out Chinese citizenship. They also

interested themselves in those POWs who were of East European descent. But none of those interviewed were enthusiastic about the proposals put to them.

The Korean and Blondie interviewed the remainder of our group and a good number of the POWs, along the usual lines. Most of our group came in for a second interview, some for a third. They seemed to be very intent on finding out what we thought about the war in Korea. The party never overworked themselves, at least around our camp. They lived across the river on the Chinese side, and drove into the camp now and then to continue interviews.

In early October a major, accompanied by stars of lesser magnitude, arrived to inspect the camp. Though the major didn't seem to know it when he came, the end of our stay in this camp was at hand. We might have known it because the POWs had really been working hard, turning the mess hall into a huge *ondol* heated by the kitchen fires. They now had winter quarters that promised to be comfortable, and experience had taught us that when we made a camp comfortable, it was time to move on to the next.

I have many other memories of that camp which will not quickly fade. Memories, for example, of pre-breakfast excursions to the copses to haul back bundles of firewood, when the air was fresh and exhilarating, when bare feet that had been so hesitant on the hard, pebbly path stepped confidently and gratefully on to the cool, wet, luscious grass where the path entered the copse. Memories of Larry Zellers and myself crossing the stream, turned into a waist-deep mountain torrent by recent rains, carrying between us a bag of potatoes slung from a pole, both of us doubting if we could reach the far bank without being swept off our feet. Memories of moon-rises that we all went out to see. Memories of the beautiful wild flowers that we found on the hillsides.

Of all the places we have known in North Korea, the picture of that valley and the houses where we lived will fade last from my mind. There, for the first time, after months of confinement under strict supervision, we could wander abroad at will.

On Sunday mornings Monsignor Quinlan and I often climbed up the path that led over the mountain to the Yalu. We sat on the mountainside, said the rosary together, then chatted till it was time to return for lunch. When we reached the crest on the way back,

our valley lay in full view below. Over a mile away was the tall
mountain that formed the far wall of the valley and rose sheer from
its floor. The grey cluster of barrack buildings, dwarfed by the
distance, lay up against the mountain wall, surrounded by fields.
Two lines cut the scene, the thin brown strip that was the road, and
the broader silver strip of the river. On our side of the river, wooded
slopes, rising to left and right, framed the valley that lay directly
beneath us, with its cluster of buildings, of which the nearest was
our house.

In this valley, for six months, we had lived and worked and hoped.
But now it was time to leave.

Manpo Revisited

OCTOBER 9, 1951 to AUGUST 12, 1952

we left the camp at Ando-ree, as we left most camps, suddenly. The visiting major crossed the river shortly after break-fast on the morning of October 9 and gathered us together. We were being transferred to a new place, he told us, where we would be well cared for; and from there we would soon go on to an even better place, or perhaps hear very good news. Naturally this speech evoked great excitement all round.

A truck was waiting on the road in front of the barracks, and word was given to clamber on. But we were too many. Eleven of us were still waiting to get on when the driver said he could take no more, and the truck moved off without us. There would be another truck within a day or two, we were told.

The POWs had word that they were to move out, too. Rumour had it that our group was going only as far as Manpo, but the POWs would go further down the river. And that is what happened. A few days after we reached Manpo, they passed down the river in boats, and we heard much later that they had been handed over to the Chinese and were being well cared for.

That night, the POWs celebrated. They broke into several store-rooms, and stole potatoes by the bagful and hundreds of cobs of corn. Fat into the night corn and potatoes were roasted at every available fire in the camp, and more potatoes were secretly boiled in the kitchen. A number of us civilians sat in a room in the hospital and exchanged reminiscences with friends among GIs. Again and again, potatoes arrived in the crowded room for distribution. It was a gay party.

Next morning it was the guards' turn. They searched rooms, rounded up culprits, stormed and abused. One quartermaster was

13

Manpo Revisited

OCTOBER 9, 1951 TO AUGUST 12, 1952

WE LEFT the camp at Ando-ree, as we left most camps, suddenly. The visiting major crossed the river shortly after breakfast on the morning of October 9 and gathered us together. We were being transferred to a new place, he told us, where we would be well cared for ; and from there we would soon go on to an even better place, or perhaps hear very good news. Naturally this speech evoked great excitement all round.

A truck was waiting on the road in front of the barracks, and word was given to clamber on. But we were too many. Eleven of us were still waiting to get on when the driver said he could take no more, and the truck moved off without us. There would be another truck within a day or two, we were told.

The POWs had word that they were to move out, too. Rumour had it that our group was going only as far as Manpo, but the POWs would go further down the river. And that is what happened. A few days after we reached Manpo, they passed down the river in boats, and we heard much later that they had been handed over to the Chinese and were being well cared for.

That night, the POWs celebrated. They broke into several storerooms, and stole potatoes by the bagful and hundreds of cobs of corn. Far into the night corn and potatoes were roasted at every available fire in the camp, and more potatoes were secretly boiled in the kitchen. A number of us civilians sat in a room in the hospital and exchanged reminiscences with friends among GIs. Again and again, potatoes arrived in the crowded room for distribution. It was a gay party.

Next morning it was the guards' turn. They searched rooms, rounded up culprits, stormed and abused. One quartermaster was

201

very angry because a certain store-room had been entered, but seemed less annoyed over the loss of half the contents of the room than over the destruction of a good padlock that some vandal had battered open.

A truck came for us just before lunch. Guards rushed us into a mess-hut, and *bali*'d us out again after a hasty meal. We boarded the truck and away we went. Several Korean officers were travelling with us, and among them was the notorious Burp-gun Charlie, at whom I cast furtive glances now and again. I wondered what thoughts, if any, were going through his mind as we travelled back over the way of our fateful march of nearly a year before. We certainly had our own thoughts as we pointed out to one another scenes that we remembered and schools where we had spent nights.

We had travelled only a mile or two when we stopped at a house. A small, tastefully-dressed woman came out, carrying a child. We helped her on to the truck and found a seat for her on some packs. She settled down demurely with her baby in her arms, after thanking us most graciously. She was extraordinarily beautiful, not merely for her finely formed features, but even more for the sweetness and graciousness of her expression. "Madonna-like" was the word she brought to my mind and, as I found later, to the minds of others also. She was, as we subsequently discovered, the wife of Burp-gun Charlie.

We were travelling in a new Russian truck, and we could have made the hundred-odd miles to Manpo that day, even with the long delays we had at several towns. But towards evening we came to a village where the driver seemed to have friends, and he used a puncture as an excuse to remain there overnight.

We left the truck next day just before we came to Manpo, shouldered our packs, and walked towards town. The star-crested monument, now scarred by bullets and shrapnel, was still standing, and from it we took our bearings. The railway station would be over there on the left, the buildings of new Manpo directly ahead. We walked on, looking round. Apparently our memories of the place were not accurate, we decided. The town must have been farther from the monument than we thought.

We looked harder. Slowly the startling truth broke on us. New Manpo had disappeared. Here and there a tottering wall told that

a town had stood on these fields where crops now grew. We looked
down towards the river. Old Manpo seemed to remain. But closer
inspection later revealed that most of the buildings were only shells.

We went on down the road into the street where, between the
few houses still left standing, crude shacks had been erected. Then
we turned left into the wide valley where the railway ran off in a
wide loop. This valley branched into several lesser ones, and entering
one of these we came to a mud-walled shack that seemed to be an
office. Armed guards stood about, and emaciated prisoners carried
baskets of earth out of a tunnel, emptied them and disappeared. A
dark, fierce-looking major with a scar on his face came out of the
office, and began a loud argument with a lieutenant.

The outlook was not cheery. This was obviously a penitentiary,
the major was the commandant, and we had come to stay. Our
guards beckoned us to follow them, and we came to a series of buildings that were little better than large dugouts. They were built on
a terrace cut into the side of the valley. As we stood waiting on
the terrace in front of a building, Bishop Cooper came down to
meet us. " I think we have struck bedrock this time," he greeted
us. He told us our group was housed in a dugout just up the valley.
It rained the day they travelled down, and they got wet in the
truck : it rained the night they had arrived, and they got wet in their
dugout.

It was a depressing place. The dugout in which we lived was cold
and damp, and the food was poor, consisting usually of *su-su* and
watery soup. But our new living conditions did not depress us as
much as did the state of those around us.

There were about five hundred Korean prisoners in the place.
Their quarters and food were poor. But worse and more difficult
to describe than bad conditions of living was a thing one sensed rather
than saw. It was the merciless grinding down of men, the dehuman-
izing process that went on, the attempt to turn human beings into
sheep. On the move the prisoners walked in pairs, holding hands.
As soon as they stopped they had to squat down. The guards
lectured the men ceaselessly, individually and in groups ; lectured
them for their misdeeds, lectured them on the benefits of living
under a Communistic régime, and on the attitude of mind they
should have towards authority. Many of the men were political

prisoners, some of whom were serving sentences of fifteen years for being reactionaries.

Among the memories I have of that place there is not a single one that brings me pleasure. Depressing, dispiriting scenes come back to me, all too numerous : the conditions at the hospital, the daily funerals, the state of the latrines, the way the *pan-jangs* (section leaders) bullied fellow-prisoners, the trial of an escaped prisoner. . . .

In the hut next to ours there were about forty prisoners from South Korea who seemed to receive better treatment than the local offenders. There were three or four women in the group and some old men. Some of the missionaries in our group recognized one of the old men as a prominent pastor and one of the women as a zealous church worker from Seoul. These people had not always been treated as they were now. We gathered from furtive conversations that their number had originally been eighty.

We stayed in the place ten days, but it seemed much longer. The authorities were actually embarrassed by our presence among the prisoners and anxious to get us out. But no suitable building had been available for our use when we arrived. In an adjacent valley were several sheds which the Chinese army had left behind, and we moved into one of these when regular prisoners had made necessary alterations and repairs.

*   *   *

We were not impressed with our new home. This fifty by fifteen feet building was nearly all roof. On walls three feet high a very steep roof had been built. At one end, separated from the living-room by a thin wooden partition, was a kitchen with a sunken floor. A corridor ran down the centre of the living-room, with a low parapet on either side. These parapets were *ondols*, heated by the kitchen fires. Men and women were put in there together ; the men occupying one side, the women the other.

Fortunately November was a mild month. Even so, we suffered from the cold, for the building was chilly and draughty and many of us had only summer clothes. Some had managed to retain quilted clothes up till the time we left Ando ; but the guards took them then, saying we would get new and better clothes where we were going. However, it was December before bundles of well-used and none-too-clean quilted clothes came for us. About the same time, we

carried from the prison great rough mats of rice straw, which had
been plaited by the prisoners. With these we lined the living-room.
It was a vast improvement, but even then the room could hardly be
described as cosy.

A huge stove made from a petrol drum was brought and set up.
We carried bags of coal-dust from the prison each day. The story
of that stove and its management would be a long and mournful
tale. Ilian Kijikoff was given the position of fireman. Day after day
he wet the coal-dust and shovelled it into the firebox, and then sat
on the parapet before the stove, poking, poking, until all the dust
had fallen through the grate. Coal-dust filled the air and crept into
the mats on the walls. It settled on beds and clothes and blackened
the faces of sleepers. In the gloomy, windowless room, lit by one
feeble electric light, the effect was softened. But to meet a fellow-
internee in the sunlight, especially as the winter advanced and washing was a luxury that could seldom be achieved, was to meet a man
from the coal-pits.

His trying task frayed the edges of Kijikoff's never-too-certain
temper. We hadn't been *bali*'d for a long time. But when we
wished to pass between Kijikoff and his stove, we were urged to do
so *bali*. One day he wished to put coal in the stove, but the door
would not stay open. He gave it three chances before he changed
from words to action. From that day on, the door always wore a
battered look. But in fairness to our fireman it must be said that no
one envied him his job, and there were not too many who thought
they could do better.

I may as well confess that we were very dirty those first two
winters. We were probably dirtier the first winter ; but I think
in the second we were more dirt-conscious, because the problems of
ill health and hunger were not so pressing. After the freeze set in
we couldn't wash outside. Nor was it easy to get a wash indoors,
for we had only one leaking wash-bowl for the whole community.
We hadn't received soap since July, and warm water was seldom
available. In a disused building in a nearby valley there was a
Japanese-style bath, which we were permitted to use a couple of
times in early winter. But the building was soon dismantled.

In one of the buildings below ours some petrol drums were stored.
One evening in late winter, while a certain lady kept guard, two

shadowy figures entered the building by a way that the architect had not envisaged. Presently one was panting up the hill with a drum on his back, while the other stayed to make some repairs to the roof of the building. Next day there followed some banging and clattering on the hillside above the house, and still later a half drum mysteriously made its appearance over a fireplace under the shelter of a bank near a spring. It was used furtively for a few days, until the drum was blackened and looked as if it might have been in use for some time. Meanwhile guards had asked no questions, so from then on we used it openly, and once or twice a week the members of the camp could take a warm bath and wash clothes.

It is an unwritten law among internees that no one steals from a fellow-internee, but the authorities are always regarded as the enemy, and fair game. If our pilfering had been limited at other camps, it was only because of limited opportunities. Here at "second Manpo," as we called this, our second camp at Manpo, we really blossomed out.

One of the two men who had inspected the place before we moved in told Larry Zellers and me where the workmen kept their nails. The nails disappeared when we arrived. So, too, did a wrecking bar that the prisoners had overlooked. Commissioner Lord borrowed a saw from the prison, and forgot to return it. We all seemed to have taking ways, and there came a time when guards in charge of wrecking parties used to borrow tools from our group. Larry and I acquired a crowbar of which we were justly proud. Our feelings were deeply hurt when a sergeant in charge of tools carried it off because it looked like one he had lost. The wrecking parties dismantled buildings around us and carried off the lumber. But not all of it. Father Booth seemed to enjoy life more than usual when a building was being wrecked.

Commissioner Lord's speciality was " padding," by which we meant adding to the rations given us by the guard. For a couple of weeks, for reasons undisclosed, our ration of grain was cut to four hundred grams each a day ; that meant light meals unless there was padding. The guard, who didn't live with us any more, locked the door of the store-room and went off after giving out rations. But he didn't know that Larry had arranged the door so that, with manipulation, it opened on the hinged side also. Naturally we had to help ourselves in such a way that the guard wouldn't grow suspicious, and as Commissioner Lord was our quartermaster, he did the calculating.

If life within the house was a little rugged, outside we had few complaints, for we were free to wander unescorted about the hills. When we moved from the penitentiary one unarmed guard looked after us. He came each day to give out rations, check numbers, escort us to the penitentiary for rations if necessary, hear complaints and give us fatherly advice.

The interviewers followed us from Ando-ree, and the Korean and Blondie remained on in Manpo for some months, summoning one of us to the town for an interview every few days. They discussed religion, politics, and social economy, and tried to get us to write our thoughts on various subjects. We never really found out their aims. Blondie wasn't a bad fellow actually, and often gave some reliable news. Larry Zellers returned from an interview some time before the end of the year with a lot of information about the Kaesong Conference which we found quite exciting. Several times in the following few months our hopes were raised.

Christmas came once more, and 1951 passed into history. Early in the new year the families left us and went to rooms in farm-houses down the valley, where we could go to visit them. Those of us who were on visiting terms with the Salahudtin family were given meals that were real feasts.

The women of our group took over the kitchen, and thereby distinguished themselves. Sister Bernadette, the Carmelite lay Sister, walked into her domain again. She had worked on her parents' farm in France before entering the Carmel at Aire-sur-Adour. She came to Seoul in 1938 with other Sisters from that convent and was given charge of the kitchen. Korean kitchens were no mystery to her, and she could perform wonders with very little equipment and material. Sister Bernadette never raised her voice or became involved in an argument ; but she did what she wanted and got what she wanted, as annoyed guards sometimes discovered—and fellow-internees sometimes discovered, too. Nevertheless we all realized that her efforts were directed solely towards making things pleasant for others, with never a thought for herself. I am sure all members of the camp will remember her with gratitude.

*   *   *

When teams for cooking were finally sorted out I found myself fireman for Miss Dyer and Frau Gliese. I have told Nell Dyer's story already. Charlotte Gliese—"Lotte" to all the camp—was born in Berlin, and when quite young she married a Korean business-man there. The war came, and at the end of it Frau Gliese could give an "insider's" impression of the bombing of Berlin. She had lost four successive homes, and once, with her son in her arms, she fled at night down a whole street that was brighter and hotter than a summer's day with the blaze from burning buildings.

Peace came, but not for her. A few days after the Russians entered East Berlin, she and her Korean husband were sent at two hours' notice on the long journey across Siberia to Korea. But her husband was now as much a stranger there as she was, and life was not easy. She accepted the post of Professor of German in Seoul University. When the Reds came to Seoul her husband disappeared. M. Perruche invited her to take refuge at the French consulate, and from there she was arrested.

Frau Gliese camouflages a very serious nature under a gay and carefree air, and her merry laughter hides many a heartache that her none-too-easy life has brought her. Her unfailingly high morale, her cheery and optimistic conversation, and the struggle she has waged to keep herself neat and clean even under the most adverse conditions, have been stimulating to those about her.

* * *

One day not long before Easter, when I was working at the back of the kitchen, a well-built, pleasant-looking lieutenant, in shabby uniform and battered boots, approached me and courteously in-quired :

"Could you tell me, please, where the comrades are ?"

Prisoners used a building below us as a workshop, and I thought he must be looking for their guards, so I pointed the place out to him.

"No," he said, "I mean the foreign comrades."

It was Lieutenant Ree, newly arrived to take charge of us and our affairs. And take charge of us he did. From that time we were orphaned from the prison, and Lieutenant Ree became our father. He liked us to call him " Sun-saing-nim "—" Honourable Teacher." He was impetuous, he had a hasty temper, he was very sure that he

knew everything and that our affairs needed a great deal of supervision. But in spite of these faults we liked him, and we benefited
by his coming. He fought battles with the prison authorities, got
clothes and better rations for us, took parties to the river for picnics :
and he did all that only by exerting himself on our behalf. For a
Korean, he was amazingly energetic—in Larry Zellers's phrase, an
"eager beaver." He didn't seem to look for his own share of what
he obtained for us, and he didn't eat any better than we did, if as well.

Being young, inexperienced and overconfident, he made many
mistakes. There were the forty sacks of bread that went mouldy,
the decrepit bull that he bought, the house he didn't build. I shall
let him off with a mention of the last item.

The spring rains came, our roof leaked badly, and we told him it
needed a new layer of straw. He came one morning and announced :

"We're going to build a new house. We'll pull this one down,
get additional material from the prison, and build a fine house
for you."

We weren't enthusiastic. We told him we wanted a new house,
but, knowing quite a lot about North Korea from sad experience,
we wanted to keep the old house till the new one was ready. He
seemed piqued.

"Are you not willing to co-operate with me ? "

"We're not," we told him.

"Well, I'm not *asking* you now to build a new house for your-
selves. I'm *telling* you. I'm in charge here, and what I say goes.
Get tools and follow me."

We got spades and straggled down the road after him. Just before
we came to the house in which the Salahudtins lived, he led us to a
vacant space at the foot of a hill, surrounded by fields.

"Clear this of growth," he commanded, "and level it." We set
to work without a will.

The granny who was matriarch of the nearby house and farm came
out and demanded to know what we thought we were doing. We
referred her to the management. She went in search of Lieutenant
Ree, and presently he came to say that we had better stop while he
went to the prison to make some inquiries. He returned later to say
that the People's Committee thought it better to wait. Seemingly
even the Communists couldn't tame Granny. He called a meeting

then, and in a lengthy discourse told us that in view of opposition from Granny and the prison and ourselves, he wouldn't insist on the house being built ; but if we got flooded out of our present home, or froze to death next winter, we should remember that we had no one to blame but ourselves.

Many other incidents of our sojourn at " second Manpo " come jostling through my memory, clamouring to be recorded. Most of them must go untold ; but this one I cannot resist jotting down. One morning a server assembled a row of bowls on a board and carried them to the kitchen to be filled with soup. All went well, until suddenly the flow of soup was stemmed, and the cook was noticed gazing into the next bowl with the look of one who sees visions. Just so must Alice in Wonderland have gazed at the disembodied grin of the Cheshire cat, for in the bowl was the smile of Father Christmas. He had forgotten to remove his dentures from their overnight resting-place.

As a final reminiscence from " second Manpo " days, I mention the two occasions when we understood fire-fighting. Once, when someone was carrying fire to the bath, the wind blew a spark onto the roof of a shed behind the kitchen. A shout of alarm was raised, and Larry Zellers and I dashed out with vessels of water just in time to save the main roof from catching. Monsignor Quinlan, sprinting out to throw himself into the breach, must have wondered whether it was a fire or a flood he was summoned to fight. His exit out the back door brought him to one side of the shed just as Larry aimed a bucket of water at the roof from the other side and overshot the mark. The Monsignor stopped the lot.

The second alarm came one evening when someone noticed that the farmhouse where our lieutenant lived was on fire. We went full speed to the rescue, and Louis Dans led a contingent onto the roof, where long poles were used to make a gap in the thatch just in front of the advancing flames. Danny's plan enabled us to bring the fire under control. Larry Zellers fell off the roof that night and sprained his ankle. I remember that he was still using an improvised crutch when the next exciting incident occurred—the announcement that we were to leave Manpo.

It was on August 12 that our Honourable Teacher came to say that all except the Kilins and Salahudtins were to leave next morning.

Another officer was coming to conduct us on our way. He himself would follow later with the two families. We need take nothing with us, for everything would be provided in the fine new camp prepared for us.

There was great jubilation, tempered a little by the memory of so many rosy promises unfulfilled in the past. We hoped for the best, but most of us decided to take all our gear, just in case.

Valley of Hope

ON THE morning of August 13 we took our leave of the Turkish and Russian families, and climbed aboard a truck. It took us back to the main road, then westward down the Yalu, past the old quarantine station which had been our home two years before, on through Kosan and large town of Chosan. The rumour was that we were going to Pyoktong to be handed over to the Chinese.

We had stopped for lunch and were on our way again when we met a jeep loaded with Chinese soldiers, some of whom were officers. They halted us, and talked long with the officer in charge of our group. He seemed to find the conversation worrying, and when we reached the next town, which was Ujang, he halted the party while he did a lot of telephoning. At length he returned to say that there was a hitch, and that we must spend the night here in Ujang.

A large yard and some rooms in nearby houses were found for us. After taking a look at the rooms, Larry Zellers and I decided to spend the night in the open. The weather was mild, and we slept on a pile of logs in the yard. There was still no sign of a move next day, nor the day after either, so Larry and I spent three nights in all on the woodpile. From the second night on, we had the company of others who had found the bug population indoors far too numerous for comfort.

We waited, but there was still no word of resuming our interrupted journey. When there was question of more permanent quarters in the town we were assured by the officer in charge that we would move to a fine foreign house; but it was to five Korean cottages just off the main road and three miles out of the town that we finally moved.

Seven months later, as I write these lines, we are still waiting. It was here, in these cottages outside Ujang, that I began writing this account, towards the end of 1952.

14

Valley of Hope

AUGUST 13, 1952 TO APRIL, 1953

ON THE morning of August 13 we took our leave of the Turkish and Russian families, and climbed aboard a truck. It took us back to the main road, then westward down the Yalu, past the old quarantine station which had been our home two years before, on through Kosan and large town of Chosan. The rumour was that we were going to Pyoktong to be handed over to the Chinese.

We had stopped for lunch and were on our way again when we met a jeep loaded with Chinese soldiers, some of whom were officers. They halted us, and talked long with the officer in charge of our group. He seemed to find the conversation worrying, and when we reached the next town, which was Ujang, he halted the party while he did a lot of telephoning. At length he returned to say that there was a hitch, and that we must spend the night here in Ujang.

A large yard and some rooms in nearby houses were found for us. After taking a look at the rooms, Larry Zellers and I decided to spend the night in the open. The weather was mild, and we slept on a pile of logs in the yard. There was still no sign of a move next day, nor the day after either, so Larry and I spent three nights in all on the woodpile. From the second night on, we had the company of others who had found the bug population indoors far too numerous for comfort.

We waited, but there was still no word of resuming our interrupted journey. When there was question of more permanent quarters in the town we were assured by the officer in charge that we would move to a fine foreign house ; but it was to five Korean cottages just off the main road and three miles out of the town that we finally moved.

Seven months later, as I write these lines, we are still waiting. It was here, in these cottages outside Ujang, that I began writing this account, towards the end of 1952.

213

Yet the story that we were being brought to Pyoktong to be handed over to the Chinese was probably well-founded. It seems that the Chinese had agreed to take over a party of forty prisoners, and that the Koreans had omitted the detail that these were civilians, and included women, old people and children. We were actually on the way when, as we ourselves had witnessed, the Chinese came upon us, to the discomfiture of the officer in charge. Seemingly the Chinese refused to accept responsibility for us, but finally agreed to supply rations and medical care. The Koreans were to provide accommodation and guards.

The accommodation I have already mentioned. The guard went along with the accommodation, and was there to welcome us to our new camp. The chief custodian was a little, short-necked captain, known to us as "Three Star." He was free in his promises when we arrived but, after a preliminary display of benevolence and industry, he retired to his own quarters, where he spent most of the winter, trying to warm himself over a charcoal pot.

In October he emerged to tell us something about the forthcoming presidential elections in the United States. He expressed the earnest hope that at last the People were going to have a voice in an election. We could not gather the identity of the People's candidate from Three Star's speech. Commissioner Lord, in the interests of fluent translation, settled for "Halibut" as Three Star's man. But the election passed, and he issued no joyous announcement. It took us a month to find out that Wall Street had once again been up to tricks, and that out of the hat had come a Bad Man called Eisenhower.

*   *   *

In our new camp we were now facing yet another winter, our third, in internment, and we were resolved to profit as fully as possible from our previous experiences. Perhaps the department in which our foresight has been most successfully applied is that of fuel.

Koreans cut their supply of winter firewood in the late summer and early autumn, and carry it home before the severe cold sets in. At "second Manpo" it had already been late October when we moved to our own quarters, and the prisoners had by then cleared all the firewood from the nearby hills. For that reason, wood-getting was quite difficult there, and we could only keep up with the demand; we never got ahead. When Larry Zellers and I were assigned duties

at the house in the new year, Monsignor Quinlan remained almost
the only one cutting, though many hauled. Day after day the Monsignor was out for hours on steep hillsides, with snow up to his knees.
There are some more pleasant ways of spending days in winter. We
resolved this would not happen here at Ujang, and we spent every
available minute on the hillsides up to the beginning of December.
It is well to be off these steep and rugged hills in the great cold. As
a result of our exertions and our foresight we cut and stored an
adequate supply of firewood before the severe weather came on.

If our supply of firewood has much improved, our food supply
has improved no less. Here at Ujang there has been an abundance
of food : there is even variety. Millet is now but a memory. We
have white rice in plenty and enough flour to provide bread once a
day. And as long as the very cold weather lasted the Chinese kept
us supplied with pork. There has been work at last for the miniature
can-opener I had often thought of throwing away.

Standards of comfort are very relative. We feel here at Ujang
that we have come a long way from " second Manpo " days. There
had been a time when Lieutenant Ree remarked to Monsignor
Quinlan :

" *Pan-jang*, we must get a couple of suckling pigs, and you could
fatten them on kitchen waste."

" Brother," the Monsignor told him, " any pigs dependent on the
scraps from our kitchen are going to have a thin time. There isn't
enough thrown out to feed a sparrow."

But here at Ujang even stray dogs have been able to pick up a
living around the camp. Larry Zellers says he was watching a dog
loping away from the camp one morning, when the stentorian voice
of Commissioner Lord announced, " Brea-a-a-a-kfast ! " The dog,
Larry avers, stopped dead in its tracks, then spun around and headed
back for the houses at full tilt.

We have been better clothed, too, in Ujang. The Chinese Army
has given us a summer and a winter suit of the dark-blue cloth it issues
to all prisoners. The summer suits are light, but the winter suits
are padded, and with them we were given padded caps, gloves, and
boots. Each of us has received, too, a new blanket and quilt ; so we
sleep now with a comfort unknown in previous camps.

Smokers get a regular monthly ration of tobacco. We have been

given things that we had abandoned hope of seeing in captivity :
toilet soap, large sheets of writing-paper, pencils, even notebooks,
ink and nibs—gifts that brought back the thrill of a childhood
Christmas.

It is only in matters of community equipment that we are still
in difficulties, and this affects chiefly the sorely-tried women who do
our cooking. Even the primitive contrivances we left behind at
"second Manpo" would now be prized. Among them I recall a
ladle and a colander of Western origin. They were made from the
tail of a bomb that Mother Eugénie found on a hillside. Here at
Ujang we have similarly made some odds and ends from a fuel tank
jettisoned by a plane.

*   *   *

It was well that we were warmer, better fed, and better clothed,
for that winter of 1952–3 was a very long and cold one. By early
December the irrigation ditch near the houses was completely frozen,
and not long after that you could cross the river dry-shod. For a
couple of months, despite the heated floor, two walls of our room
were white with frost. It was the severest of the three winters we have
spent in captivity, though it has been much the easiest to bear, thanks
to our improved conditions.

During this winter we lost another of our number. Poor Kijikoff
had begun to go downhill even before we left "second Manpo" in
August. When we came here he seemed to get weaker and weaker,
and the Chinese doctors who came shook their heads over him. He
died on December 17, and we buried him on a hillside across the
road from our houses.

In early March our guards and the officials in Ujang town all
wore black armbands for a few days, but they refused to disclose the
reason. Some school-children confided to us that they had been
warned not to tell us that Stalin was dead.

*   *   *

On the morning of March 21 Three Star called Commissioner
Lord to his office and made a number of inquiries about him and
Bishop Cooper. According to Three Star, the resulting information
had to be sent to Pyongyang, the Northern capital. Perhaps there
were some letters for them there.

After lunch they were both summoned, and a Korean doctor

prepared a report on them for identification purposes. He measured their fingers and toes and hair, and went on solemnly with a lot more foolishness. Three Star was by now admitting that these proceedings might be the prelude to good news.

Monsignor Quinlan went as usual that day to lop pine branches for firewood and returned to grind beans. After supper he set off for a distant spring to bring a bucket of drinking water. On his way back he was called into Three Star's office and made identify himself. Then he was told he would be leaving the camp in half an hour with Commissioner Lord and Bishop Cooper.

They packed up, and some high-ranking officers called for them in a truck. We waved them out of sight. They were going, so they had been told, to Pyongyang. There was a great deal of speculation in camp next day, some sadness over the departed members, and even a few tears.

Five days later an official in civilian clothes arrived in a jeep and immediately interviewed the French group. He seemed concerned about the French who had died, and had statements about their deaths drawn up. That evening a truck arrived, and we bade farewell to the French.

The official stayed on and interviewed all other members of the camp. On March 30 Frau Gliese was called for a special interview. She was asked what were her connections with France, the French group and the French consulate. To these inquiries she could only reply that she had known the French consul and had been arrested from the French consulate while sheltering there. That night, after she had retired, she was summoned to the office and told to be ready to leave in the jeep in ten minutes.

Life was now thoroughly unsettled. We were for ever waiting for more news and more vehicles. A Chinese official came to interview us, but professed to know nothing about those who had gone.

Meanwhile Three Star was replaced. Early on Monday morning, April 20, the "Two Star" in charge came into our rooms with a list of the names of the Americans. They were to pack up, he said, and be ready to move to a new house. I laughed at him and told him they were going to Pyongyang. But he strongly denied it. Three hours later a truck carried off the Americans. With them went the last of my close friends in camp and half of my soul.

Postscript

A WEEK after the Americans left camp a guard showed us a copy of a Pyongyang newspaper carrying a picture of the French group decked out in new clothes. The caption said that these foreigners were leaving North Korea to return to their own country. It was wonderful news. Then we heard the astounding rumour, soon afterwards verified, that those who had left our camp had returned home by way of the Soviet Union. That news was not so wonderful. The others in camp were very depressed. They could not see any hope of their being repatriated through Russia. They hoped that I had been left to be released at Panmunjom and that they, too, could go that way to freedom.

For me, time began to drag again, and I waited on from day to day. The folk left in camp with me were kind, but I was lonely.

On May 6 we were listening to a lecture from a visiting Chinese colonel, who had much to tell us of the latest military successes of the Chinese Volunteers. During the course of his lecture a policeman arrived from Ujang, and I was called to the office to face the usual barrage of questions. Late that night Two Star sent for me. He repeated all the familiar questions, and I repeated all the answers. This time he paid particular attention to my name. More than once he asked me what it was, and then wanted to know was I *sure* that was it. Had I ever used any other, he inquired? Finally he packed up his papers and went off into the night.

He returned at dawn to say that he had been in touch with Pyongyang by telephone, and that they were looking for a person answering to my description in every detail except my troublesome name. There the matter rested.

On Sunday, May 17, we went to the town to carry rations to the camp. Sagid and Two Star dropped far behind the rest of us, and when they returned to camp Sagid sought me out to say that Two Star had been called into the police station and told that there was a message from Pyongyang. "Crosbie," it seemed, was the right name after all, and I was to be taken there at once.

Next day, in the company of a guard from camp, I boarded a

passing truck and travelled to Sinwiju. We passed anti-aircraft batteries manned by European soldiers. I noticed they had an encampment near Sinwiju—or what was left of Sinwiju. We spent the night at a police station near the destroyed town. Next day my guard returned to camp, and another police-officer escorted me to Pyongyang. That, too, had suffered terrible destruction, and so had the towns and villages between it and Sinwiju.

I was quartered in military barracks in the hills near Pyongyang, where I was treated well and given new clothes. During the journey from the camp and later in the barracks, the officials, even army officers and policemen, were friendly ; and in more than one place I was offered cigarettes and shown courtesy by officials who did not know that I was about to be released. This kindness and courtesy that I met in ruined cities was quite a tonic. I had always thought these admirable traits peculiarly Korean, but had found little trace of either among the police and soldiers of our various camps. There is not much that is lovable in Communism, but there is often a great deal that is lovable in the individuals that are degraded by it.

There is much I could say about the colonel who was in charge of me at Pyongyang. He was a fanatical Communist, but he was a sincere and, I think, a good man. Yes, the North Koreans did atrocious things. I have told some of them. But only the North Koreans ?

The colonel told me this story, and I believe he was telling the truth. When he went back to his native district after the retreat of the U.N. armies that followed their earlier advance, he found six hundred bodies, all relatives of Communists, sealed up in an air-raid shelter. One of the corpses was that of his own mother.

In those days I talked with several officers. When they asked my objections to Communism, I usually kept to one point : the system wouldn't give the political and religious freedom to which a human being is entitled. They would then protest that this freedom is given by a Communist régime. This is what I found most interesting. When we got down to first principles and began to discuss what we meant by freedom, they would almost invariably admit that my idea of freedom and theirs were quite different. A Communist régime, they argued, could not hope to achieve its object if it allowed individuals the freedom I deemed so necessary.